EXPLORING DALLAS
WITH CHILDREN

EXPLORING DALLAS

WITH CHILDREN

A Guide for Family Activities

FOURTH EDITION

KAY McCASLAND THREADGILL

Taylor Trade Publishing
Lanham • New York • Boulder • Toronto • Plymouth, UK

Published by Taylor Trade Publishing
An imprint of The Rowman & Littlefield Publishing Group, Inc.
4501 Forbes Boulevard, Suite 200, Lanham, Maryland 20706
http://www.rlpgtrade.com

Estover Road, Plymouth PL6 7PY, United Kingdom

Distributed by National Book Network

British Library Cataloguing in Publication Information Available

Library of Congress Cataloging-in-Publication Data

Threadgill, Kay McCasland.
    Exploring Dallas with children : a guide for family activities / Kay
McCasland Threadgill. — 4th ed.
        p. cm.
    Includes index.
    ISBN 978-1-58979-432-0 (pbk. : alk. paper) — ISBN 978-1-58979-
433-7 (electronic)
        1. Family recreation—Texas—Dallas—Guidebooks. 2. Family
recreation—Texas—Dallas Region—Guidebooks. 3. Dallas (Tex.)—
Guidebooks. 4. Dallas Region (Tex.)—Guidebooks. I. Title.
    F394.D213T48 2010
    976.4'2812—dc22
                                                                            2009024368

♾™ The paper used in this publication meets the minimum
requirements of American National Standard for Information
Sciences—Permanence of Paper for Printed Library Materials,
ANSI/NISO Z39.48-1992.

Printed in the United States of America

To my parents, John and Icie McCasland, for
sixty years of encouragement and love

CONTENTS

INTRODUCTION

Part of our Texas heritage is the spirit of adventure handed down from courageous, pioneer ancestors. The spirit of the West still urges both native Texans and those who have understandably adopted Texas as home to search out exciting and mind-expanding adventures around Dallas and the Lone Star State.

Usually, the major drawback is finding the time to plan ahead and to decide what a family, with a wide range of ages and interests, would find entertaining. That is where this guide will be invaluable, not only to those who live in and around Dallas but to visitors, youth organizations, and child-care institutions as well. The bulk of the legwork (literally) is done. Not only are vital statistics, like addresses and prices, listed, but special hints about things to try, notice, or bring are mentioned to make your visit as comfortable and worthwhile as possible.

I am thrilled to be able to publish this fourth edition. In five years, some favorite hangouts have closed their doors, but many new and exciting ones have opened to inform and amuse. Rewriting the guide has enabled me to rekindle friendships made while writing the first and to meet many new, enthusiastic people as well.

In the original 1993 edition, my family, with children ages five to thirteen, faithful friends, and Girl Scout Troop 956 were invaluable explorers in the quest to unearth and investigate a wide variety of places, some that entertain and excite, some that enlighten, and some that do an exceptional job of both. Having grown up with and in Dallas, I was astonished by what has been available for years that I had not known existed, such as a charming two-story Victorian farmhouse from the early 1900s and a large exhibit of mounted African animals housed by a Brookshire's warehouse. Also, many landmark places offer opportunities of which many natives are unaware. Did you know that the Museum of Nature and Science hosts birthday parties or that a family may have a picnic at the Heard Museum and adopt a raptor? (What's a raptor?)

Dallas continues to grow and change. Because of changing needs and economy, attractions usually stipulate that all prices and hours are subject to change without notice. Some even go out of business without notice. Thus, it's always better to call before an outing to confirm information vital to your enjoyment of the trip. Also, many of the prices listed do not include tax.

Many of the museums and wildlife centers offer memberships, which not only keep members in close touch with programs but also supply financial support, which is vital to their existence. If your family is interested in science or nature or art or history, inquire about a family membership. Volunteer support is also essential to enable them to offer the range of educational programs and to schedule exhibits that make every visit fascinating.

We have had some wonderful times together compiling data for this guidebook. Few trips were disappointing. One unfailing, remarkable quality was the warm Texas hospitality offered wherever we toured. Everyone wanted us to have a great time. And we did.

1. Places to Go

Family entertainment at its Texas best is described in detail in this chapter. Turn off the television and the lights and head out for exciting adventures that may not be far from your own neighborhood but may offer literally acres of fun! Some attractions you seek may be listed in **Chapter 2: Tidbits: More Good Things to Do** because they are smaller or attract a more specialized interest group. Remember, it is smart to **call ahead** because things can change overnight.

AFRICAN AMERICAN MUSEUM

Fair Park: 3536 Grand, P.O. Box 15057, Dallas 75315-0157 (214) 565-9026 Website: www.aamdallas.org

In 1993 the 38,000-square-foot African American Museum opened its new building in Fair Park. The museum is dedicated to research and acquisition of visual art forms and historical documents that relate to the life and culture of the African American community, as well as to an outreach program to enable all to understand the African American experience through exhibits, classes, day camps, and workshops. The building houses both permanent and traveling exhibits.

Architect Arthur Rogers designed a building with a rotunda capped by a 60-foot dome. Four galleries, which represent Africa's quadrants, radiate outward from the central rotunda. The floor tiles are terra cotta, the ceilings are exposed yellow pine, and the effect is light and airy.

On the first floor is a cafe and bookstore, and a balcony is on the second floor. Classrooms, a library, and an amphitheater are in the basement. The museum is designated by the State of Texas as the official repository for African American culture, so it houses important historical documents and collections.

- Call Artreach-Dallas for information about group tours: (214) 219-2049.
- Restrooms and water fountains are available.
- The museum is handicapped accessible.
- Gift shop.

Hours: Closed Monday; Tuesday to Friday, 12 PM to 5 PM; Saturday, 10 PM to 5 PM; Sunday, 1 PM to 5 PM. Closed major holidays.

Admission: Free, except for groups of 10 or more.

Directions: Take the Grand Ave. entrance (Gate 5) from Robert B. Cullum Blvd. in Fair Park. Parking is free except during the Texas State Fair and special events.

AUDUBON NATURE CENTERS

Trinity River Audubon Center

6500 South Loop 12, Dallas 75217 (214) 398-TRAC Website: www.trinityriveraudubon.org

The Trinity River Audubon Center, opened in 2008, is the gateway to the Great Trinity Forest, a 6,000-acre site that hosts the largest urban bottomland hardwood forest in the United States as well as grasslands and wetlands. The 120-acre center was once an illegal dump site that was reclaimed by the city of Dallas and the Audubon Society and transformed into a $14 million "green" education center with hands-on exhibits, more than four miles of hiking trails through natural habitats, a Children's Discovery Garden, birding site with more than 100 species, conservation center, and living outdoor laboratory.

Inside the center, visitors may watch a brief colorful video about the conservation area while sitting on benches made of recycled cardboard. Hands-on exhibits include one that allows you to see how a river is formed and another that shows you the layout of the Trinity River floodplain. Cut-out viewing areas allow visitors of all sizes to see nature outside the center, and birds and their songs can be selected along exterior walls. A glass wall is angled to reflect the ground so birds won't fly into it. Another section of the center has classrooms.

Children's programs, such as Birds of Play and nature clubs, and Saturday family programs are offered in addition to adult programs and academic programs for students from elementary school through college.

Trails of various lengths are available. The shortest takes about 15 minutes round-trip and goes to an overlook of a beautiful bend in the Trinity River. Several pretty ponds are along the trails and provide habitats for birds and water for local forest creatures.

- On the third Thursday of each month, admission is free and the center is open until 9 PM. See its event calendar for special evening programs.
- For information about nature clubs and education-related questions, call (214) 309-5814. Visitors may also register at the front desk.
- The smooth boardwalks are made of recycled plastic milk jugs. They run out and the remainder of the trails is crushed granite. **Very sturdy** wheelchairs and strollers could navigate them. A baby sling

or backpack carrier would be best for very young children. Tennis shoes are recommended. No flip-flops.

- Parking is in front of the center and is free.
- Water fountains and restrooms are available indoors and outdoors.
- A gift shop also has snacks and drinks. Tables and chairs are located inside and outside.
- A brochure called "Common Birds of Trinity River Audubon Center" lists common area birds in checklist form. Visitors may wish to bring binoculars and a pen.
- Memberships are available, and donations are appreciated. Group rates and special tours may be arranged.

Hours: Monday to Wednesday, Friday to Saturday, 9 AM to 4 PM; Thursday, 9 AM to 9 PM; Sunday, 10 AM to 5 PM.

Admission: Adults, $6; seniors (60+), $4; ages 3–12, $3; under 3, free. Third Thursday of each month, free.

Directions: From downtown Dallas, take I-45 south; exit Loop 12 east (2.8 miles). Entrance is on the right side of the road. It's about 10 minutes from downtown.

Dogwood Canyon Audubon Center
7171 Mountain Creek Parkway, Dallas 75249 Website: www.audubondallas.org

Audubon Dallas and the City of Cedar Hill in partnership are developing a $7.4 million project that includes a 6,000-square-foot education and visitors center as well as a conservation site covering 270 acres. The Dogwood Canyon Center is located in Cedar Ridge Preserve on FM 1382, and should open in spring 2009. Currently the Audubon Dallas, Dallas County, and City of Dallas parks operate 10 trails labeled easy to difficult, 0.2 miles to 1.2 miles. A Cedar Ridge Preserve brochure provides a checklist for birds, flowers, reptiles, mammals, and insects that live in the area. The sanctuary is a nesting place for two endangered birds, the golden-cheeked warbler and the black-capped vireo.

- Recommendations to visitors: wear sturdy shoes (no flip-flops); stay on the trails.
- No specimen collection is allowed without permission from Audubon Dallas.
- Guided tours with a naturalist may be arranged.
- Memberships are available.
- Little Bluestem Trail and the Butterfly Garden are ADA trails. The education center is handicapped accessible.
- Restrooms and water fountains are in the education center.

- Look online for hours and admission fees. At the time of publication, this had not been decided.

BACHMAN LAKE

3500 W. Northwest Hwy., Dallas 75220 (214) 670-6374, (214) 671-1385

A popular oasis amid the noises of Love Field Airport and business traffic, the 205-acre Bachman Lake offers a wide variety of entertainment, most of which is good for the body and spirit.

On a 3.08-mile bike/hike trail along the lake, joggers, skaters, and bicyclists pursue fitness and fun. The **Dallas Rowing Club** has a boathouse on the south side of Bachman Lake at 2827 Shorecrest (www.dallasrowingclub.org). Occasionally, visitors see the rowing club out on the lake. They may be seen in the evening on weekdays and in the morning on weekends. Motorboats and swimming are not allowed.

On days when the park is not too crowded, it's a great place to picnic and feed the birds. At Northwest Hwy. and Lakefield is a covered, lighted pavilion that can hold about four picnic tables; this site and three other sites are available for rent. Call Dallas Athletic Events and Reservations at (214) 670-8740. One grill for cooking is on the north side, and another is on the south side of the lake.

For 10 years, the **Bachman Lake Recreation Center**, located at 2750 Bachman Drive, has offered special programs for those with special mental and physical needs. Serving ages 6 to elderly, it is therapeutically color coordinated and has rails along the walls. Call (214) 670-6266 for a brochure.

- Always lock your car and do not leave valuables in it.
- Restaurants are nearby on Northwest Hwy.
- The trail is handicapped accessible.
- Playgrounds are located by the pavilion and the recreation center.
- The two portable restrooms are at the Northwest Hwy. and the Shorecrest entrance. A water fountain is by the pavilion. Accompany your children to the restroom.
- Parking is free. On weekends, you may want to park at the concession and recreation center parking area.

Hours: Open 5 AM to midnight, but staying after dark is not advisable.
Admission: Free.
Directions: Take the W. Northwest Hwy. (Loop 12) exit off Central (US 75) or off North Dallas Tollway and go west. The lake is on the south side. Or from I-35E, exit Northwest Hwy. and go east.

CEDAR RIDGE PRESERVE

7171 Mountain Creek Parkway, Dallas 75249 (972) 709-7784
Websites: www.audubondallas.org; www.dallasparks.org/parks/trails

Just 30 minutes south of downtown Dallas, the Cedar Ridge Preserve encompasses 633 acres of environmentally rich land on the White Rock Escarpment. In April 2003, **Audubon Dallas** took over management of the preserve, formerly the Dallas Nature Center. The organization is very busy with habitat restoration and development of educational programs. Please check the website for new events and information.

Families enjoy hiking on 10 marked trails that range from easy to difficult through prairie and woodlands where native animals and birds live in a protected environment.

Visitors may spot native plants, such as yucca, sunflowers, and orchids. In spring the butterfly garden comes alive with brilliant flowers to attract the butterflies, and the orchards are in bloom.

In 2009 the Audubon Society will open **Dogwood Canyon Audubon Center**, which is located on FM 1382. The 6,000-square-foot C. E. Doolin Education and Visitors Center is surrounded by 270 acres of wildlife habitat for some endangered species and a variety of plant life.

- A picnic area is available.
- To hike, wear sturdy shoes, take water, and watch your footing.
- The easy .25-mile Little Bluestem Trail is wheelchair accessible.
- Parking is free.

Hours: Grounds open Tuesday to Sunday. From November 1 to March 31, hours are 6:30 AM to 6 PM. From April 1 to October 31, hours are 6:30 AM to 8:30 PM. Gates are locked at sundown.

Admission: Free. Donations are appreciated.

Directions: Go south on I-35 to Hwy. 67 South (sign says Cleburne); take I-20 West (sign says Fort Worth); exit Mountain Creek Parkway and go south (under the highway). Drive two miles to the center's gate on the right.

CELEBRATION STATION

4040 Towne Crossing Blvd., Mesquite 75150 (972) 279-7888
Website: www.celebrationstation.com

Indoors in the 16,000-square-foot facility is a restaurant downstairs offering great pizza, hot dogs, and more. On the first level are games that give tickets that may be redeemed for prizes, and on the second level are more challenging video games.

Go-carts, bumper boats, batting cages, a few kiddie carnival rides, laser tag, paintball, rock wall, and two miniature golf courses are offered for more fun outdoors in the six-acre park. Height and age requirements are enforced for some activities.

- Group rates (15 or more) are available. Birthday parties (minimum of six) are welcome. Call for reservations. Lock-ins and special holiday events are popular.
- Miniature golf courses are handicapped accessible.
- Restrooms and water fountains are available.
- Parking is free.

Hours: Open daily, weather permitting. Hours change seasonally. Some activities have different hours from others.

Admission: No entrance admission fee. Purchase tokens for games. Various packages are available, depending on what you want to do. All-day unlimited play passes are offered.

Directions: Going east on I-30 toward Mesquite, take the Gus Thomasson Rd. exit. Pass Gus Thomasson, stay on the service road to Towne Crossing, and turn right. From I-635, exit at Town East Blvd. and go west. Turn right on Towne Crossing.

DALLAS ARBORETUM AND BOTANICAL GARDENS

8617 Garland Rd., Dallas 75218 (214) 515-6500 Website: www.dallasarboretum.org

Even before you arrive at the entrance, you will see some of the gorgeous, lush gardens of the 66-acre Dallas Arboretum from the road—but that is only a glimpse of the acres of beauty to come. Located on the eastern shore of White Rock Lake, the arboretum provides education in horticulture, a haven for wildlife, vibrant flower displays, and numerous special events for families. Children love not only the trees and flowers, but also the winding paths and fountains. Here, they really have room to stretch and enjoy the outdoors. In 1996 the $1.4 million **Women's Council Garden**, which is behind the Degolyer House, was opened to the public. The 2.5-acre garden incorporates water as a symbol of strength and unity. Don't miss the frog sculpture, an interactive fountain in which four bronze frogs shoot 20-foot streams of water. Other new gardens include the **Boswell Family Garden** called *El Inesperado* (the unexpected), which is next to the **McCasland Family Sunken Garden**.

Favorite times to visit include Dallas Blooms Spring in March and April and Dallas Blooms Autumn in October. The **Jonsson Color Garden** features more than 2,000 varieties of azaleas, while over 30 varieties of ferns grow in the **Palmer Fern Dell**. More than 200,000 flowers bloom during this festival, and children's activities are scheduled on weekends.

The $20 million **Trammel Crow Visitor Education Center**, built with native limestone, opened in 2003. It provides indoor classrooms, an exhibit hall, gift shop, gazebo, orientation theater, and an outdoor dining terrace that provides year-round dining.

- Tours of the **DeGolyer's Spanish Colonial Revival Mansion**, now a museum, include the oilman's study and other rooms filled with interesting art and furniture. Tours leave every 30 minutes.
- Garden-hunt sheets are available daily and change seasonally.
- Picnics are encouraged, and food service is offered year round in the dining terrace and increased during special events.
- Christmas at the arboretum in December includes a holiday market and many festive decorations and activities, such as a Christmas tea.
- Children's Nature Club events are usually held in May and June for ages 4–12. Classes last two to three hours. Classes are offered for pre-K through sixth grade all year long.
- In June through August are family focus summer events, with special activities for kids during each event.
- Currently, the arboretum is raising money to develop the seven-acre Rory Meyer's Children's Adventure Garden.
- Restrooms and water fountains are provided.
- Parking is $5. The fee may be higher during special events.

Hours: Open daily, year round. 9 AM to 5 PM. Evening hours are often extended for summer musical programs on Thursday. The gardens are closed Thanksgiving Day, Christmas Day, and New Year's Day.

Admission: Adults, $8; seniors (65+), $7; ages 3–12, $5; members and children under 2, free. Memberships are available.

Directions: Located on the north side of Garland Rd. at Whittier, just west of the intersection of Garland Rd. and Buckner Blvd. Signs direct visitors to the parking area.

DALLAS ARTS DISTRICT

Dallas Arts District Alliance (214) 953-1977 Website: www.artsdistrict.org

Dallas Center for Performing Arts 2403 Flora Street (214) 954-9925 Website: www.dallasperformingarts.org

The new and exciting Dallas Arts District includes a 19-block area covering 68.4 acres on the northeast side of downtown Dallas. Pearl St. passes through the middle.

The newest additions to the district, most opening in fall 2009, are part of the Dallas Center for the Performing Arts: Annette Strauss Artist Square, Margot and Bill Winspear Opera House, Performance Park, Dee and Charles Wyly Theatre, and City Performance Hall. Most of the buildings are bounded by Woodall Rodgers Fwy., Ross Ave., Pearl St., and Routh St. The area is also home to the Dallas Museum of Art, the Nasher Sculpture Center, the Meyerson Symphony Center, and the Crow Collection of Asian Art.

The 2,200-seat Margaret McDermott Performance Hall is inside the **Winspear Opera House**, as is the smaller Nancy Harmon Education and Recital Hall. The Dallas Opera (formerly at Fair Park Music Hall), the Texas Ballet Theater, traveling Broadway productions, and many other performance groups will light up the stages each season.

A restaurant and cafe will be available. The Grand Portico shades three acres of Performance Park so visitors may relax outdoors without the direct heat of the Texas sun.

The 12-level **Wyly Theater** will host drama, music, and dance performances. Potter Rose Performance Hall seats 600 and includes space for the Dallas Theater Center (moving from the Oak Lawn Kalita Humphreys Theater), Anita N. Martinez Ballet Folklorico, and Dallas Black Dance Theatre, as well as numerous other organizations.

The 750-seat **City Performance Hall** will be home to smaller arts organizations. Groundbreaking is set for 2009–2010.

Named to honor a former Dallas mayor, **Annette Strauss Artist Square** along with **Performance Park** will be outdoor performance venues that can accommodate audiences up to 5,000 as they watch concerts, theatrical performances, festivals, and dance events. Located between the Winspear Opera House and the Meyerson Symphony Center will be a permanent band shell for outdoor performances.

Connecting all the performance venues is a 10-acre urban park, the **Elaine D. and Charles A. Sammons Park**. This new civic destination will be admired for its gardens, reflecting pools, trees, and grassy areas alongside walkways.

- A free guided **Arts District Stroll** is offered the first Saturday of every month at 10:30 AM or by appointment for a nominal charge. It begins at the Crow Collection of Asian Art at 2010 Flora St. Call (214) 953-1977.
- A monthly **Arts District Calendar** is offered in print and online at www.artsdistrict.org.
- One parking garage, the Arts District Garage at Ross and Leonard. A surface lot already exists by the Meyerson Symphony Center. Another belowground garage will open with the Performing Arts Center. Elevators will usher visitors to Performance Park.
- Nearby are the West End Historic District's museums and restaurants and Victory Park's American Airlines Center and more restaurants.

- A 7-Eleven convenience store is located inside the One Arts Plaza building on Routh St.
- The Cathedral Shrine of the Virgin of Guadalupe and DISD's Booker T. Washington High School of the Performing and Visual Arts are also in the Arts District.

DALLAS CHILDREN'S AQUARIUM AT FAIR PARK

1462 First Ave. and Martin L. King Blvd. at Fair Park, Dallas 75210 (214) 670-8443 (Mailing Address: P.O. Box 150113, Dallas 75315-0113) Website: www.dallaszoo.com

The Dallas Children's Aquarium building, which dates from the 1936 Texas Centennial at Fair Park, closed for remodeling in fall 2008. It's expected to reopen in the spring of 2010, housing bright fish, exotic coral, tidal touch pools, and special programs with multisensory experiences. Announcements about its progress will be on the website. Parking is free except during the state fair.

Directions: From the Robert B. Cullum Blvd. side of Fair Park, enter at the Martin L. King Blvd. gate and park. The aquarium is just past the Texas Discovery Gardens to the left, very close to the Texas Star Ferris Wheel. See directions to Fair Park.

DALLAS FIREFIGHTER'S MUSEUM: OLD TIGE

3801 Parry Ave., Dallas 75226 (214) 821-1500 Website: www.dallasfirerescue.com/museum.htm

Located in the 1907 Old No. 5 Hook and Ladder Co. Station, the Dallas Firefighter's Museum houses a collection of wonderful retired fire trucks. *Old Tige*, named after then-mayor W. L. Cabell, is an 1884 horse-drawn steam pumper.

Recapture the early days of firefighting in the alarm office complete with clanging bell and in the old firehouse setting with its wood-burning stove. Visitors see the progress in the last 100 years in firefighting equipment through the collection of photos, fire tools, helmets, suits, and extinguishers. Sometimes, you can hear today's Dallas Fire Department radio as dispatchers conduct business. A favorite of most children is the fire engine, which they can climb on, as well as the collection of toy fire trucks. Pieces of wooden water main unearthed from the Farmer's Market area, which date from around the 1880s, are on display.

The museum is dedicated to firemen who fell in action, a tribute to their courage and devotion to duty.

- Tours are available with reservations.
- There is no food or drink in the museum, but the Old Mill Inn just across Parry in Fair Park is open for lunch Tuesday to Sunday.

- Only the lower floor is handicapped accessible.
- Restrooms and water fountains are provided.
- Parking is available in front or on the side street. During the Texas State Fair, park at the Fair Grounds and walk across Parry.
- Gift shop.

Hours: Wednesday to Saturday, 9 AM to 4 PM. Closed major holidays.
Admission: Ages 4–16, $2; ages 17–64, $4; ages under 3 and over 64, free. Groups of 20+ receive a discount.
Directions: Located on the northwest corner of Parry at Commerce. If on I-30 going west, take the Fair Park /First Ave. exit and circle under the bridge to Exposition. Take it to Parry and turn left. If on I-30 going east, take the Fair Park Second Ave. exit to Parry. Turn left and go three blocks.

DALLAS HERITAGE VILLAGE

1515 South Harwood St., Dallas 75215 (214) 421-5141 Tickets: (214) 428-5448. Website: www.dallasheritagevillage.org

One of Dallas's historical and architectural treasures is Dallas Heritage Village at Old City Park, 13 acres on which rest 36 restored 19th-century homes, buildings, and preserved arts.

A tour will take visitors by the 1904 Worth Hotel, 1901 Blum Bros. General Store, and 1847 Miller Log House. Children will love the Miller's Log Playhouse. Notice that the Gano cabin dog-trot house has an open breezeway with rooms on each side to allow for circulation. "Living history," in which costumed townspeople go about daily life, occurs in the 1860s Living Farmstead, the 1901 Blum household, the Pottery, and the Clementine Freight and Delivery Service with its two live donkeys.

With younger children, very interesting days to visit are the special event days, such as the annual Candlelight in mid-December.

- There is handicapped accessibility to the grounds but not to all of the buildings.
- Printed tour programs are available at the Ticket Office. At 1:30 PM are docent-guided tours of Millermore and Sullivan. To arrange private tours, call (214) 413-3674. Information about tours and field trips as well as a "virtual tour" is on the website.
- Dallas Heritage Village offers birthday party packages, summer camps and classes, Scout workshops, field trips, and special events for families.
- The Museum Store is located in the Ticket Office.
- Drinks and snacks are available in the Ticket Office. Picnic tables are located in Nancy's Garden, just past the Blum household.

- Cameras are welcome, but no flash photography is allowed inside buildings.
- Restrooms are located near the Worth Hotel and the Pilot Grove Church. There are water fountains.
- Parking is free.

Hours: Grounds are open Tuesday to Saturday, 10 AM to 4 PM; Sunday, 12 PM to 4 PM.

Admission: Adults, $7; seniors, $5; and ages 4–12, $4. To ask about group discounts, call (214) 413-3675.

Directions: From the west on I-30, exit at 46B Ervay. Turn left at St. Paul and left again at Gano. From the east, exit 46A Downtown Central. At Harwood, turn right. The first right is Gano. Parking is past City Park School.

DALLAS HOLOCAUST MUSEUM/CENTER FOR EDUCATION AND TOLERANCE

211 North Record St., Ste. 100, Dallas 75202 (214) 741-7500 ext. 105 Website: www.dallasholocaustmuseum.org

Dedicated as a tribute to the memory of the six million who died during the Holocaust and as a hope that such an atrocity will never occur again, the Dallas Holocaust Museum/Center for Education and Tolerance was conceived by a group called Holocaust Survivors who wished to tell their stories and help others understand the impact of the Holocaust on themselves and on world history.

The tour, covering 1933–1945, is divided into seven main areas with titles such as "One Day in the Holocaust: 4/19/43," "Warsaw," "Bermuda Conference," and "Dallas/Fort Worth: 4/19/43." Visitors first see a wall collage of representative pictures of war crimes that are explained by the audio-guide. In front of them are 13 pillars of various heights, one for each year from 1933 to 1945, which indicate the number of Jews killed by the Nazis that year. In the next area is an actual boxcar that was used to transport the Jews to death camps. A film played on a screen on the boxcar tells the story of the brave rescue of 231 Jews by three men with only one pistol among them. Artifacts, personal items, Torah scrolls, and pictures of this black period in history are showcased in each section of the tour. Visitors may be chilled by the front pages of 1943 newspapers from Dallas and Fort Worth, which chronicled what editors thought the public wanted to read about the war—omitting the daily slaughter of the Jews of Europe. Near the end of the tour is a monument to the lost families surrounded by pillars naming the concentration camps. Next, in a small theater, is a powerful film of Nazi survivors telling of their ordeals and hoping we will remember.

- Museum personnel recommend that only children fifth grade (age 12) and up should tour. Some knowledge of the Holocaust prior to the tour is advisable.
- A new museum located across from the nearby Sixth Floor Museum is slated to open in 2011.
- Group tours are available by appointment; self-guided tours daily.
- Educational materials are available for teachers.
- Handicapped access: Just past the main museum entrance is another door that has a lift for wheelchairs that will take visitors up to museum level. A restroom with handicapped access and water fountains are available.
- There is no food in the museum, but the West End Historic District has several restaurants around Market Street.
- Nearby is the Sixth Floor Museum, the Old Red Museum, and Dallas World Aquarium.

Hours: Monday to Friday, 10 AM to 5 PM; Saturday to Sunday, 11 AM to 5 PM. Closed on Jewish and most national holidays.

Admission: Adults, $6; children, seniors, active military, and groups of 15 or more, $4. Admission includes a self-paced bilingual audio-guide. Memberships are available.

Directions: To see the museum in its temporary home, ride the DART rail line, exit at the West End Station, go one block west, and turn right on Record St.

From the Dallas North Tollway, exit Commerce and go east to Market St. Turn left onto Market, left on Ross, and left on Record. Parking lots (on the right/west side) that charge a fee are located between Market and Pacific. Walk across the DART Rail Line tracks.

Going south on US-75, merge onto TX-366 W/Woodall Rodgers Fwy. via Exit 1A toward I-35E S/Waco. Keep left at the fork, and take the exit toward Field St. Continue on Broom St. Take a slight left toward McKinney Ave. and a slight right at McKinney Ave. Turn left at N. Record. The museum is on the right. The museum is in an office building and faces Record. Near the main museum door is another door that has a lift for handicapped access.

DALLAS MUSEUM OF ART

1717 North Harwood, Dallas 75201 (214) 922-1200 Website: www.dallasmuseumofart.org

The DMA is known internationally for both special exhibitions and permanent collections. One fascinating collection on long-term loan from Boston is "Eternal Egypt: Objects of the Afterlife," which includes both funerary objects and pieces from the daily life of ancient Nubia.

Other major collections include post–World War II contemporary and African, Asian, and Oceanic art objects; American and European paintings, sculptures, and decorative arts; and the Wendy and Emery Reves Collection, in which they re-created six rooms of their Mediterranean villa featuring prized impressionist paintings.

The 140,000-square-foot Hamon Building includes larger exhibition areas, the Museum of the Americas, the Atrium Café, and performance space for jazz and classical music.

In 2008, the DMA opened the **Center for Creative Connections** for young and old alike. Looking and touching are encouraged in the exhibitions, which range from paintings to sculpture to special demonstrations. Museum officials hope the center will help visitors "see art in a new way."

Another favorite area for children, especially those who need to stretch, is the outdoor sculpture garden with its cascading wall fountains and sculptures in a maze-like layout. Children cannot climb on the sculptures, but they can take their lunch out there to enjoy the garden. The nearby Trammel Crow Collection of Asian Art is encircled with outdoor sculptures, and the Nasher Sculpture Center is across the street.

- An information desk, which has maps and information about current exhibits, is at the entrance. Check online for family activities.
- The museum shop invites youngsters to select art-related books, puzzles, calendars, games, and toys.
- Free public tours meet at the information desk. School tours are free but require three weeks' notice. Call (214) 922-1331.
- The DMA has the non-circulating Mayer library and teacher resource room. Call for details about use.
- Special events include Jazz Under the Stars and Late Nights. Activities geared toward youngsters are Kids Club, Studio Creations, BooksmART, Collection Connections, and Family Films.
- Go van Gogh program offers free one-hour art programs for school classrooms. Call (214) 922-1230.
- For fine dining, the second-floor **Seventeen Seventeen** restaurant prepares lunch Tuesday to Friday from 11 AM to 2 PM. Call (214) 880-9018. The casual **Atrium Café** is open Tuesday, Wednesday, and Friday, from 11 AM to 2:30 PM, Thursday evening including live jazz, and Saturday and Sunday from 11 AM to 2 PM. Call (214) 922-1835. The **Sculpture Garden Kiosk** offers sandwiches, snacks, and beverages Tuesday to Sunday from 11 AM to 3 PM.
- The museum is handicapped accessible.
- There are restrooms and water fountains.

- Underground parking is available from Harwood or St. Paul. A fee is charged for parking. The trolley route brings you to St. Paul and Ross, right by the museum.

Hours: Tuesday, Wednesday, and Friday to Sunday, 11 AM to 5 PM; Thursday, 11 AM to 9 PM. Closed Mondays, New Year's Day, Thanksgiving, and Christmas Day.

Admission: Adults, $10; seniors 65 and older, $7; children under 12, free except for special exhibitions. Also, free on Thursday from 5 PM to 9 PM and the first Tuesday of each month. Memberships are available. Tickets in advance: call (214) 922-1803 or look online. Discounted combination tickets are available for the DMA and Nasher. Higher ticket prices may apply to special exhibitions.

Directions: Located downtown in the **Arts District** on Harwood between Woodall Rodgers Fwy. and Ross Ave. From US 75, exit Woodall Rodgers (toward I-35 and Pearl St.). Take the St. Paul exit. Coming from the west, exit Field St. in the right-hand lane.

THE DALLAS WORLD AQUARIUM AND ORINOCO RAINFOREST

1801 North Griffin, Dallas 75202 (214) 720-2224 Website: www.dwazoo.com

Something fishy has been going on downtown since 1992. Located at Hord and North Griffin in the West End Historic District, the Dallas World Aquarium surrounds visitors with more than 85,000 gallons of saltwater, including a 22,000-gallon tank with a walk-through tunnel and ten 2,000-gallon tanks with beautiful displays of aquatic life from all over the world. Each tank represents a different area, such as the Red Sea exhibit, and the corals and other plants are also from that region. It doesn't take long for visitors to discover the lively black-footed penguins that were used in a Batman movie.

Self-guided tours are available with a brochure that explains each tank and provides a list of feeding times.

Orinoco: Secrets of the River is modeled after a Venezuelan rain forest. Visitors usually enter at the treetops and see various exotic birds, monkeys, and sloths; then continue over a bamboo-planked path spiraling down past river otters, anacondas, Orinoco crocodiles, piranhas, and Antillean manatees. A waterfall inspired by the Venezuelan Orinoco River Basin adds to the tropical atmosphere. An elevator also goes to each level.

The newest addition is the **Mundo Maya** exhibit which features a 40-foot walk-through tunnel exhibiting sharks and rays. As the path ascends, visitors see rabbits, snakes, beaded lizards, Jabiru storks, flamingos, and other Mayan creatures.

- The restaurants eighteen-O-one and Café Maya are open daily from 11:30 AM to 2:30 PM; the Jungle Café snack bar is open from 11 AM to 4 PM.
- The gift shop offers nature-related gifts as well as educational and fun items.
- The aquarium offers educational group rates for field trips Monday through Friday. Please call (214) 720-2224 and ask for the education department for more details.
- There are scheduled feedings and talks. The first one is at 10:30 AM and the last at 4 PM.
- Restaurants are located in the West End within easy walking distance.
- Also nearby are the Sixth Floor Museum and Dallas Holocaust Museum.
- Visitors may park on surface lots across the street for a fee.

Hours: Aquarium is open daily, 10 AM to 5 PM. Closed Thanksgiving and Christmas.

Admission: Adults, $16.95; children ages 3–12, $9.95; and seniors, $13.95. Additional tax. Call or check the website for current rates.

Directions: From Central (US 75), exit onto Woodall Rodgers (Spur 366). Take the Field exit and turn left. Stay in the right-hand lane, which will curve to Griffin. The first right is Hord. You can see the fish sculptures on top of the building. The DART rail line stops at the West End, about two to three blocks from the Aquarium.

DALLAS ZOO

650 South R. L. Thornton (I-35E), Dallas 75203 (214) 670-5656
Website: www.dallaszoo.com

Since 1888, the Dallas Zoo has been fascinating families with its collection of exotic and endangered species. In 1997 a 67-foot giraffe sculpture, the largest sculpture in Texas, was installed at the Marsalis entrance to welcome visitors. The zoo covers 95 acres and was the first zoo to open in Texas.

A family favorite at the zoo is the **Wilds of Africa** exhibit, in which zoo visitors travel through six habitats on a one-mile monorail ride with a narrator. More than 86 species of mammals and birds roam freely in this 25-acre exhibit. It is open from September 15 to December 1 and March 1 to June 15. One adult is required for every seven children. This safari continues as visitors then walk along a wooded quarter-mile nature trail. Of further interest is the two-acre Jake L. Hamon **Gorilla Conservation Research Center,** where gorillas may be viewed without their realizing that they are being observed. A rain forest is simulated, and everything in it is edible.

The Dallas Zoo is a breeding facility for both Sumatran and Indochinese tigers. The ExxonMobil **Endangered Tiger Habitat** allows guests to come face-to-face with tigers through glass viewing areas and to find out how to help save these big cats from extinction.

The **Lacerte Family Children's Zoo** offers educational, interactive exhibits for toddlers to pre-teens and features The Farm, with touchable animals, pony rides, and activities; The Underzone, with naked mole-rats, mongooses, and other underground creatures; and The Nature Exchange, where children can trade objects from nature at a hands-on store.

- The zoo sponsors special events, such as Family Safari Days, Summer Fun Weekend, and Boo at the Zoo. Check the website or call for the dates of special events.
- **Zoo Ranger™** may be rented to enhance a visit to the zoo. It is a lightweight device with sound and a four-inch LCD touch screen. A signal is triggered when passing featured exhibits for "a closer look," and visitors can see and hear information about the animals in that habitat. The zoo maps it provides will help visitors navigate through exhibits and locate cafes and restrooms.
- **Preschool at the Dallas Zoo** educates and entertains 3- and 4-year-olds from September to May through nature and conservation topics. Saturday and summer classes are also offered.
- A popular volunteer program for ages 11 and 12 is **Junior Zookeeper**; applications need to be requested in November for summer jobs. Ages 13 and older may apply in early March to be **Conservation Guides**, and **Junior Camp Counselors** apply in February.
- The zoo has an Adopt-an-Animal program.
- The Jungle Shop located in the Entry Plaza offers a variety of souvenirs, books, and toys related to birds, reptiles, and mammals.
- The Ndebele Café, Prime Meridian Food Court, and Children's Zoo Snack Shop offer meals and snacks. Picnic tables are provided.
- The paved pathways are accessible to wheelchairs, but the area is hilly. Parts of the zoo are hard to negotiate. Strollers, wagons, and wheelchairs may be rented inside the main gate. Call (214) 943-2771, ext. 302, for more information.
- Teacher workshops, Scout programs, and field trips are offered.
- Restrooms, benches, and water fountains are available.
- Parking is $5.

Hours: Daily, 9 AM to 5 PM; 9 AM to 4 PM in winter. Closed Christmas Day. Monorail rides run from 10 AM to 4:30 PM, September 1 to December 1 and March 1 to June 15, weather permitting.

Admission: Ages 12–64, $8.75; ages 3–11, $5.75; and seniors 65+, $5; ages 2 and under, free. Monorail rate: ages 3 and over, $2.50. Endangered Species Carousel rides, $2 for ages 3 and up; seasonally, pony rides (kids under 80 pounds), $2. Group rates and memberships are available. On Mondays and Tuesdays, a same-day DART pass discounts zoo admission prices.

Directions: Three miles south of downtown off I-35 South. Take the Marsalis exit, go north on the service road, and turn right at the base of the giant giraffe statue into the zoo parking lot. A separate entrance for DART riders is available on Clarendon Drive, just across the street from the DART light rail Dallas Zoo station.

FAIR PARK

1300 Robert B. Cullum Blvd., Dallas 75226 (214) 565-9931; State Fair, (214) 670-8400: Fair Park (Mailing address: P.O. Box 15009, Dallas 75315) Website: www.fairpark.org

Fair Park, location of the outstanding **State Fair of Texas**, has been close to the hearts of native Dallasites and those who visit from around the state since R. L. Thornton Sr. persisted in the selection of Dallas as the site of the Texas Centennial in 1936. The largest historical landmark in Texas, this 277-acre park is well known for its major museums, **Music Hall**, **Cotton Bowl** stadium, and **Superpages.com** concerts, which are active year round.

Fair Park at its finest should be visited during the state fair, which lasts for three weeks beginning at the end of September (www.bigtex.com or 214-565-9931). During that time young children pet furry animals in the Barnyard, giggle at puppets in the Midway Puppet Show, and try Midway rides designed especially for them. The 212-foot Texas Star Ferris Wheel and 78-year-old carousel are yearly favorites. Museums prepare fascinating exhibits for the fair, and the Texas-Oklahoma football classic is a thrill for all fans. Families look over prime livestock brought from area farms and ranches and attend rodeos in the Coliseum, watch amazing free-flight bird shows in the Band Shell, select the car of their dreams in the Automobile Building, puzzle over exotic displays of wares in the International Bazaar, and admire prize-winning crafts in the Creative Arts Building.

Those who love the night lights of the fair stay for the Starlight Parade and the "Illumination Sensation," when lights, fireworks, and familiar tunes create dazzling special effects nightly on the Esplanade.

Many families will confess that, although the shows and exhibits alone are worth the trip and putting up with the crowds, the real draw is the tantalizing aroma and anticipation of foods such as corn dogs and greasy fries followed by giant cinnamon rolls, cotton candy, and ice cream. Indoors at the Tower Building and outside at Cotton Bowl Plaza and other locations are foods for every palate. The blend of these aromas, the tumultuous sounds of the Midway, and the welcoming voice of a 52-foot-tall cowboy named **Big Tex** invite everyone to relax and have a wonderful time.

Families are advised to arrive early enough to park in well-lighted areas inside the fair grounds and to walk in groups. Do not wear expensive jewelry. Police are highly visible on raised stands, on horses, and in small vehicles. Their headquarters are southeast of the Cotton Bowl. At the entrances, there are usually identification tags that children can wear as necklaces. Their name should not be written where a stranger could easily read it and call to them. Families should agree on a meeting place in case they are separated, or contact a police officer.

- The *Dallas Morning News* reports special events daily during the fair, and the fair provides a map and guide to activities upon entering the gates.
- Talented family members might enjoy entering one of the arts and crafts or food contests in September. Winners are displayed during the fair.
- Children especially love climbing on the orange serpentine sculpture along the lagoon. Picnics in this area are fun. There may be some ducks to feed.
- Museums at Fair Park are listed individually. They include the Museum of Nature and Science with its Omni-Max Theater and Planetarium Building, Dallas Children's Aquarium (closed, but re-opening in 2010), Texas Discovery Gardens, Museum of the American Railroad, Hall of State, D.A.R. Building, African American Museum, and the Women's Museum. Some museums are closed on Monday.
- The **Fair Park Passport** offers a 40 percent discount admission to eight museums. Call (214) 428-5555 or check online.
- Most of Fair Park is handicapped accessible. Midway rides during the fair will vary.
- Restrooms are not plentiful, but there are some in the major exhibition buildings, outside the Cotton Bowl steps, near the Magnolia Lounge, and in the livestock area. All the major museums have restrooms, and most have water fountains. Outdoor water fountains are turned off during the winter.
- The **Old Mill Inn** is a restaurant located near the Magnolia Lounge and the Music Hall. It is open for lunch Tuesday to Saturday from 11 AM to 2:30 PM and is generally open during the state fair from 10:30 AM to 8 PM. A kids' menu is available. Call (214) 426-4600.
- Flea markets are scheduled as well as special events such as football games, ethnic celebrations, and craft fairs.

- Superpages.com and Dallas Summer Musicals provide wonderful summer and fall entertainment. Special concerts featuring popular artists are held during the fair at the Chevrolet Main Stage.
- Another museum kids love is the Firefighters Museum, located across Parry from Fair Park.
- Parking for about 10,000 vehicles is available on the grounds. A substantial parking fee is charged during the fair. Call DART, (214) 979-1111, for information about State Fair Flyers bus service, the DART rail line, and ticket combinations.

Hours: The grounds are open daily. The museums are listed under individual headings in this text. Their days and hours of operation vary.

Admission: Some of the museums are free, and some have a fee. State fair admission is approximately $14 for adults; ages 3 and over, $10 (2008 rates). Discount coupons are usually available at Kroger. Special days offer lower fair admission if specified items, such as canned food, are brought to the gate. Tickets and coupons may be purchased online at www.bigtex.com.

Directions: Fair Park is two miles east of downtown. From Central Expressway (US 75), exit Fitzhugh or Haskell. From I-30W, exit Barry or Carroll and head southwest. From I-45 North, exit MLK Blvd. and proceed northeast. Scyene Rd. going west becomes Robert B. Cullum Blvd. and leads to Fair Park. Or take Abrams Rd. south, which changes name to Columbia; turn left on Carroll, and then right on Parry, which goes around the park.

FRONTIERS OF FLIGHT MUSEUM

Frontiers of Flight Museum at Love Field Airport, 6911 Lemmon Ave., Dallas 75209 (214) 350-3600 Website: www.flightmuseum.com

The Frontiers of Flight Museum moved into a spacious new two-story building in 2004. The facility provides a 20,000-square-foot **Education Experience Center** with interactive display exhibits for three age groups, preschool through high school. A collection of rare aviation artifacts will guide you from Early Concepts of Flight through The Jet Era to Aviation Opportunities. The *SR-71 Blackbird* spyplane simulator is in the Education Experience Center.

Eras in aviation history are illustrated through mounted newspaper and magazine articles; personal items such as uniforms of famous aviators and the fur parka belonging to Rear Admiral Richard Byrd; and items used during flights of various airships, such as remnants of the *Hindenburg*.

Visitors will see models of the *Kitty Hawk Flyer*, the Red Baron's favorite triplane, and large replicas of modern passenger planes and space shuttles. Aviation enthusiasts can look over full-size aircraft and 20 major aviation history galleries, ending with the *Apollo 7* command module. Be sure to look up at the airplanes hanging from the ceiling, and peruse exhibits on the second floor.

- The Friends of the Museum and museum personnel present special Focus Nights programs, such as bringing aircraft used in the Persian Gulf and the Confederate Air Force to Dallas, as well as authors and specialists in fascinating aspects of the aviation field.
- Group tours are available with reservations (tours@flightmuseum .com).
- Scouts work on aviation badges at the museum.
- Children who can read and have some knowledge of major figures in aviation would benefit most from the tour. Children under 8 must be accompanied by an adult.
- The cafe offers fountain drinks and vending machines.
- A gift shop carries books, videos, and toys related to aviation, as well as freeze-dried food for astronauts.
- The museum offers Summer Flight School for pre-K through eighth grade, as well as special events for families on Saturdays.
- Birthday party reservations may be made.
- Two computer-ready classrooms may be used to enhance the visit of school groups.
- The museum is handicapped accessible.
- Restrooms and water fountains are available.
- Parking is free.

Hours: Monday to Saturday, 10 AM to 5 PM; Sunday, 1 PM to 5 PM. Closed some holidays.

Admission: Call or look online for new prices. Memberships are available. Children under 12 must be accompanied by an adult.

Directions: The museum is located at Love Field Airport on Lemmon at University.

HALL OF STATE

Fair Park: 3939 Grand Ave., Dallas 75226 (214) 421-4500 (Mailing address: P.O. Box 150038, Dallas 75315) Website: www.hallofstate .com; www.dallashistory.org

Operated by the Dallas Historical Society, the Art Deco–style Hall of State at the end of the Esplanade in Fair Park is the home of both permanent and temporary exhibits that reflect the history of Dallas and Texas. As part of the 1936 Centennial, the Hall of State was built of Texas limestone in a T-shape for $1,200,000. A statue of a Tejas warrior occupies the niche above the entrance, and the blue background represents the state flower, the bluebonnet. The symbols in the bronze grills on the entry doors—cotton bolls, spurs, and oil wells—are representative of Texas agriculture and industry. The statue out front is of R. L. Thornton, who was largely responsible for bringing the Centennial to Fair Park, in honor of his 41 years of service to Dallas.

Just inside is the Hall of Heroes, where stand bronze statues of heroes of the Republic of Texas, such as Sam Houston and William B. Travis. The four-story Great Hall to the back has an Aztec motif in its hand-stenciled ceiling. A gold-leafed medallion with a five-pointed star and six figures around it represents the rulers over Texas. The large murals on each side tell the story of Texas history and industry. The shafts of light indicate changes in time. Notice native wildlife in mosaics on the floor.

The other four exhibit rooms, two on each side of the Hall of Heroes, represent East, West, North, and South Texas through murals, figurines, frescos, photographs, and mosaics. In the north and south rooms is a permanent history exhibit on Texas.

- The "Hall of State: Tour Guide" brochure is a helpful guide available at the museum.
- The Dallas Historical Society's website (www.dallashistory.org) includes a teacher resource page with PDF files that include a Hall of State tour and tales about early Dallas and Texas history, as well as activity pages for grades K–8.
- Guided tours for groups are available with reservations. A small fee may be charged.
- The G. B. Dealey Library is housed in the West Texas Room.
- In a display case are some books for sale about Dallas and Texas.
- There is no food or drink in the museum.
- Handicapped access is available.
- Restrooms and water fountains are on the lower floor. A water fountain is on the upper level.
- Parking is free on Washington Ave. except during the state fair. The Hall of State is near the Museum of the American Railroad.

Hours: Monday to Saturday, 9 AM to 5 PM; Sunday, 1 PM to 5 PM. Closed Christmas Day and New Year's Day.

Admission: Free. Memberships are available.

Directions: From Parry Ave., go east on Washington in Fair Park past the railroad museum. It's the large building across from the parking lot at Grand and Nimitz inside Fair Park.

HAWAIIAN FALLS ADVENTURE PARK

4550 N. Garland Ave., Garland 75040 (972) 546-3046
Second location: 4400 Paige, The Colony 75056
Third location: 409 Heritage Parkway South, Mansfield 76063
Website: www.hawaiianfalls.com

Aloha, Hawaiian Falls Adventure Park invites swimmers to challenge the 62-foot-high Waikiki Wipeout and shoot the loop on the Hawaiian Half-pipe. When you need a break, relax on the Kona Kooler lazy river, floating along carefree in your tube. Music in the background keeps things lively.

Smaller children never seem to tire of the Keiki Cove, where they can climb, splash, and explore. This jungle-themed kiddie park has interactive water guns and sprinklers.

At the Garland location, grab some lunch and relax on this island of family fun in **W. Cecil Winters Regional Park.**

- Concessions for food and drinks are available. Cannot bring in coolers, food, alcohol, or beverages. Exceptions include things necessary for infants and special needs.
- A public picnic area is located outside the main gate. Visitors can leave and re-enter with a hand stamp.
- Concerts and movies are scheduled during the summer and are included in park admission.
- Group ticket prices are available and birthday parties may be scheduled.
- Season passes may be purchased.
- Restrooms and water fountains are in the park.
- The park is handicapped accessible for many activities.

Hours: Open seasonally. Monday to Saturday, 10:30 AM to 7 PM; Sunday, 12 PM to 7 PM. The three parks may have different hours.

Admission: Adults, $16.99; children under 48 inches and seniors (60+), $9.99; ages 2 and younger, free.

Directions: From LBJ Fwy. (I-635), exit Garland Ave. going east. The Garland park is at the intersection of Spring Creek Way and N. Garland Ave.

HEARD NATURAL SCIENCE MUSEUM AND WILDLIFE SANCTUARY

1 Nature Place, McKinney 75069 (972) 562-5566 Website: www-heardmuseum.org

The 289-acre wooded wildlife sanctuary, the legacy of Miss Bessie Heard, is dedicated to preserving and encouraging native wildlife and vegetation as well as to educating the community to appreciate and conserve nature. Around 100,000 visitors wander each year along the nature trails, spotting rabbits, raccoons, and hawks as well as favorite wildflowers and native trees. Self-guided and guided trails are available. Groups, such as Scouts or bird watchers, may take special guided tours. The Hoot Owl Trail, the basic half-mile trail, takes about 30 minutes to cover. Outings in canoes and night hikes are sometimes offered.

In addition to the looping, beautiful trails is the 16,250-square-foot museum, which has added another 8,000 square feet for classrooms. On the upper floor are exhibit halls, and live-animal displays are on the lower floor.

Each year more than 6,000 students, grades two through junior high, take part in the education program, which includes subjects such as animal families with related arts and crafts. A nature photography contest is also held each year for community entries.

- Consider bringing binoculars or a camera.
- Ask about current special events and exhibits.
- The Heard museum offers birthday parties and numerous education programs.
- Volunteer opportunities are available for ages 14 and up.
- The Nature Store offers a variety of nature-oriented gifts.
- A small picnic area is available. A soft drink machine is on the outside balcony.
- A paved trail and the museum building are handicapped accessible.
- Restrooms and water fountains are in the museum.
- Parking is free.

Hours: Open Monday to Saturday, 9 AM to 5 PM with last departure for self-guided trails at 4 PM; Sunday, 1 PM to 5 PM with last departure for self-guided trails at 4 PM. Contact the museum to reserve a guided trail. Closed New Year's Day, Thanksgiving, and Christmas Day.

Admission: Adults, $8; ages 3–12 and seniors, $5; memberships are available.

Directions: From US 75 (Central), take Exit 38 (Hwy. 5) north and stay in right lane. Proceed 1 mile, turn south on Hwy. 5 and go another .7 mile. Turn left on FM 1378. Drive east on FM 1378 1 mile to the museum, which is located on the north side. It's located southeast of McKinney about 25 miles from downtown Dallas.

HERITAGE FARMSTEAD

1900 West 15th St., Plano 75075 (972) 881-0140 Website: www.heritagefarmstead.org

Heritage Farmstead includes a two-story Victorian blackland prairie farm home and 12 outbuildings. One step onto its wrap-around porch, and visitors are transported back in time to 1891, when it was located on a 360-acre working farm owned by Hunter Farrell and his wife, Mary Alice.

A short film in the Orientation Center explains what farm life was like at the turn of the 20th century and through the advent of the tractor and what farm families did to survive. As the tour goes into the main house, the rooms, such as the two parlors, music room, sewing room, farm office, and kitchen with a wood-burning stove, come alive. Check under the beds for chamber pots and in the children's bedrooms for period toys. On the first floor, look for the framed hair wreath.

Some items in the rooms are changed four times per year to reflect the way it would have looked during a particular season or holiday. Adult visitors will likely find items they remember from their grandparents' houses, a way of life that would be lost to the younger generation if not for the efforts of preservationists.

Other favorite buildings are the curing shed, corn crib, broodhouse for chickens, and livestock area with its mule, sheep, and pigs. Look under a shelter for a horse-drawn carriage, Model T truck, and Fordson tractor. Throughout the growing season, various vegetables and herbs are planted. The pole barn has picnic tables and a small stage that may be rented for outdoor meetings, such as wedding receptions. Children also find interesting the cistern, windmill, and storm cellar. A reproduction one-room school allows visitors to sit at the connected desks, write on slates, and imagine sharing the small building with eight grades and one teacher. There is also a small auxiliary farmhouse on site, dating to the 1880s, that is used for educational programs. This structure, too, may be rented.

Opened as a museum in 1986, the four-acre museum is accredited by American Associates and listed on the National Register of Historic Places. Tour guides dressed in period costumes explain life as it once was on a Collin County farm.

- Special events include the Lantern Light Tour. Usually only the house's lower floor is toured on event days. Call for more special events or check the website.
- Self-guided tours of the grounds are available Tuesday to Friday from 9 AM to 3 PM and weekends from 1 PM to 5 PM. Going on a dry day is recommended. Self-guided tours with children can be enhanced by borrowing seek-and-find scavenger hunt clues at the museum entrance. See guided tour schedule below.
- Handicapped access to the lower floor. Pictures of the upstairs are by the first-floor telephone. Pathways and most outbuildings are accessible.

- Group tours of 10 or more are asked to preregister at least six weeks ahead. Spanish-speaking docents may be available.
- There is no concession.
- The Country Store has farm-related children's books, stuffed toy animals, dolls, and other toys as well as gifts with historical emphasis and items made on the farm by crafters.
- Restrooms are located in the altered hen houses, and a water fountain is nearby.
- Parking is free.

Hours: Open year round Tuesday to Sunday from 10 AM to 4:30 PM. Closed Monday and major holidays.

Admission: Under 4, free; ages 5–17 and senior citizens, $3.50; adults 18 and over, $5. Fee includes guided tour. Memberships are available.

Directions: Take the 15th St. (544) exit off Central (US 75) and go west. Turn south on Pitman, which is between Alma and Custer. Look for signs and two-story house on the left.

LAS COLINAS/WILLIAMS SQUARE

204 Mandalay Canal, Irving 75039 (972) 869-1232, (972) 556-0625

Las Colinas is a carefully planned 12,000-acre development of attractive office buildings, homes, recreational businesses, and retail stores. Boy Scouts of America, Kimberly-Clark, Exxon, and others have their world headquarters there.

If you enter the Las Colinas Urban Center on O'Connor Rd. from the south, be sure that just before driving under Hwy. 114 (Carpenter Fwy.) everyone looks to the right for the beautiful **flower clock** with the words "Las Colinas" spelled out in shrubs.

On the west side of O'Connor just past Las Colinas Blvd. is a parking garage and then the West Tower of Williams Square. Between the West and East towers is a plaza larger than two football fields, on which nine larger-than-life Spanish horses called the **Mustangs of Las Colinas** appear to be galloping across a stream. Fountains under the horses' hooves give the look of splashing water. Families can climb steps along the water and cross it on granite stepping stones. In the lobby of the West Tower is the **Mustang Sculpture Exhibit**, which explains, through photographs, models, and a slide presentation, the process used to sculpt and install the horses. African wildlife sculptures by mustang sculptor Robert Glen are also on display. The exhibit is open Wednesday to Saturday. Call (972) 869-9047.

Near the Urban Center on the east side of Hwy. 114 at Rochelle Rd. is the **Marble Cow Sculpture**, which includes five large marble cows atop Bluebonnet Hill. A sidewalk goes up the hill, and kids love running from cow to cow. Benches are under the trees. It is across the street from the Texas Commerce Tower.

- North of Las Colinas Urban Center on O'Connor Rd. is the **Las Colinas Equestrian Center**.
- A bike trail runs through Las Colinas.
- Sometimes special events, such as fireworks, are held in Las Colinas.
- Williams Square is handicapped accessible. The canal is accessible through an elevator in the East Tower parking garage on Las Colinas Blvd.

Admission: Mustang exhibit, free.
Directions: Located in Irving, the Urban Center is at O'Connor Rd. and Hwy. 114.

MESQUITE CHAMPIONSHIP RODEO

1818 Rodeo Drive, Mesquite 75149 (972) 285-8777 Website: www.mesquiterodeo.com

Don your Levis and Ropers and recapture the thrilling days of the Wild West with its daring cowboys and powerful livestock at the Mesquite Championship Rodeo. Families can experience the true flavor of Texas beginning with a hickory-smoked barbecue buffet at the 300-seat **Bull's-Eye Pavilion**.

Pony rides ($4) and the Kiddie Korral barnyard ($4) entertain young buckeroos awaiting the exciting prelude to rodeo events, the majestic Grand Entry. During the rodeo, kids can sign up for a chance to participate in the Mutton Bustin' event for kids ages 4+ and under 55 pounds. After donning a protective helmet and vest, they ride on the back of a sheep up to 6 seconds and are "judged" for the length of time they hold on and the "bucking" of their sheep. To sign up, go to the east side of the arena by the pony rides between 6:30 PM and 7:30 PM. At 7:45 PM, a random drawing is held to select eight children to participate. Also for the young'uns is the Calf Scramble for ages 8 and under.

Eyes widen and pulses race as the crowds watch calf ropers, steer wrestlers, and bronc and bull riders brush with danger and conquer it with courage and skill. Lovely barrel racers, crazy clowns, covered-wagon races, and country music add to the entertainment.

The $8 million air-conditioned Mesquite Arena has grandstand and reserved box seating as well as 70 luxury Champion Suites. Call for the date of the Mesquite Rodeo Parade, which kicks off the rodeo season usually in early April.

- A gift shop and emporium are on the rodeo grounds.
- Concessions sell food and beverages.
- Section D-1 is a non-alcoholic section only.
- Cameras may be used.
- The arena is handicapped accessible.
- Restrooms and water fountains are available.
- Parking is $5. Arrive around 7 PM to miss heavy traffic. There is sometimes a long line exiting from I-635.

Hours: April to September, Friday and Saturday nights, 8 PM to 10 PM. The gates open at 6:30 PM.

Admission: Reserved grandstand tickets: adults, $12; ages 3–12 and seniors 59+, $7. Reserved box seats range from $14 to $30. Group rates available for 20 and up. Bull's-Eye Barbecue: adults, $11; ages 12 and under, $7. Tickets may be ordered at the arena, online, or by calling (972) 285-8777.

Directions: Exit Military Pkwy. off I-635 (LBJ Fwy.) in Mesquite. Arena visible from freeway on west side.

THE MUSEUM OF NATURE AND SCIENCE

1318 Second Ave. and 3535 Grand Ave., Dallas 75210 (214) 428-5555 (Mailing address: P.O. Box 151469, Dallas 75315) Website: www.natureandscience.org

An exciting merger has taken place among the Science Place (est. 1946), the Museum of Natural History (est. 1936), and the Children's Museum (est. 1995) to form a new museum called the Museum of Nature and Science. Currently housed in three buildings at Fair Park, plans are in place to move the museum to a 150,000-square-foot building in Victory Park, Woodall Rodgers Fwy. and Field St., by 2013. The current buildings will still play a role in the study and enjoyment of science and nature.

The Art Deco **Nature Building** was built by the Works Progress Administration for the Texas Centennial in 1936. The collections of fossils, live animal room, mounted native birds and animals in more than 50 life-like dioramas, land and freshwater mollusks, and Texas pollinating insects span 1.7 billion years. The most awe-inspiring pieces are the 32-foot Heath Mosasaur found at Lake Ray Hubbard in Rockwall and the 20,000-year-old, 13-foot-tall skeleton of a Trinity River mammoth.

The **Science Building** encompasses more than 200 permanent, hands-on science-related exhibits as well as new exhibits and galleries. The **Children's Museum**, which was located in Valley View Mall, has been incorporated into the Science Building. It consists of five galleries where children can explore the world they live in through areas such as

Little Urban Farm, Water Room, and Explore Your Town, House, and Backyard.

The TI Founders **IMAX** Theatre with its 79-foot domed screen is also housed in the Science Building. Visitors will see the "floating staircases" rising up from a design of the solar system in the black terrazzo flooring. Show titles, times, and tickets are available online. An elevator makes it handicapped accessible.

The cosmos is explored in the **Planetarium Building**, which is located next to the Science Building. Check the MNS website for the calendar of events and shows or call (214) 428-5555.

Very popular with children is the **Science School** at the MNS, which provides a dual-language program of English and Spanish. Science- and nature-based hands-on programs for preschool through kindergarten may be two-, three-, or five-day weeks. Extended day programs are also offered. Some scholarships are available. More information is available on the website, or call (214) 428-5555, ext. 1381.

- Birthday parties, overnight stays, Scout workshops, camps, lectures, family activities, holiday events, lectures, special traveling exhibits, and festivals are some of the attractions at the Museum of Nature and Science.
- Gift shops offer books, toys, games, costumes, and other science and nature-related items.
- In the Science Building, a cafe offers light fare from soups to sandwiches and a variety of snacks. Hours: weekdays, 10 AM to 3 PM; Saturday, 10 AM to 5 PM; Sunday, 12 PM to 5 PM. Picnic tables are usually located behind the museum by the lagoon, but visitors should bring a blanket just in case the tables have been moved.
- Handicapped access is available.
- Restrooms and water fountains are provided.
- Parking is free except during the State Fair of Texas.
- Nearby are Texas Discovery Gardens and the African American Museum.

Hours: Monday to Saturday, 10 AM to 5 PM; Sunday, 12 PM to 5 PM. Closed New Year's Day, Cotton Bowl Day, Thanksgiving Day, and Christmas Day. The museum closes at 3 PM on Christmas Eve and New Year's Eve.

Admission: EXHIBITS only: adults, $8.75; ages 3–11, $5.50; ages 12–18, students 18+ with ID, and seniors, $7.75. IMAX only: adults, $7; all others, $6. PLANETARIUM only: $4. Combination tickets are available.

Directions: Enter Fair Park through the Grand Ave. gate off Robert B. Cullum Blvd. Parking is available by the museum buildings.

MUSEUM OF THE AMERICAN RAILROAD

Fair Park: 1105 Washington St., Dallas 75210 (214) 428-0101
(Mailing address: P.O. Box 153259, Dallas 75315-3259) Website:
dallasrailwaymuseum.com

One of Dallas's oldest train depots, built around 1905, stands at the
Museum of the American Railroad alongside an outdoor exhibit of passenger cars, freight trains, and engines that operated from 1896 to 1999.
The world's largest steam locomotive, named Big Boy, cabooses, and a
1920s passenger train including sleeping cars is part of this tribute to the
glory days of the railroad. Children will come to understand how the engines and cars evolved and catch some of their old spirit.

The depot was renovated to house the gift shop as well as other memorabilia of the days when it was a vital part of railroad life. It's the entrance to the museum, except during the state fair, when visitors enter at
the east end. An extensive booklet is available for sale as well as a souvenir guide. The tour begins at the east end and goes the length of the
trains and then back up again. Visitors climb steps to peek in some of the
trains, and some of the passenger cars may be boarded.

Look for *Doodlebug*, the 1931 Santa Fe Railroad self-propelled railcar
that made the rounds between Carlsbad and Clovis, New Mexico. The
GG1 electric locomotive #4903 that pulled the 1968 funeral train of
Senator Robert Kennedy rests in the museum. In all, 28 vintage trains are
on display.

At the publishing date of this guidebook, the museum is seeking another home to accommodate its growth, perhaps near Frisco's heritage
museum at Main and John Elliott Drive—so please check before you visit.

- Browse in the gift shop for railroad-related items, including toys.
- There is a soft drink machine outside the depot. Have lunch Tuesday to Saturday at the Old Mill Inn located near the Music Hall in
  the Fair Park grounds, or bring a picnic lunch. Birthday parties may
  be held here.
- Guided tours for groups may be arranged with reservations. Tours
  for children are $2.50 per child. Adults are $2.50, and one adult is
  free with a group of 15 people. To schedule a tour, call the museum
  or Artreach-Dallas at (214) 219-2049.
- The museum is somewhat handicapped accessible. The path between the trains is sometimes rocky, and stairs lead up to all the
  doors. Go on a dry day, and wear comfortable shoes.
- Restrooms are available in the nearby Hall of State. A water fountain is in the depot as well as soft drink machines.
- Parking is free except during the state fair. A parking lot is at the
  east end of the train yard.

Hours: Wednesday to Sunday, 10 AM to 5 PM. Call before going in bad weather. Closed major holidays. Hours change during the Texas State Fair.

Admission: Adults, $5; ages 12 and under, $2.50.

Directions: See directions to Fair Park. The train museum is on the north side of Fair Park on Washington east of Parry Ave. Enter at Gate 3.

NASHER SCULPTURE CENTER

2001 Flora St., Dallas 75201 (214) 242-5100 Website: www.nashersculpturecenter.org

An "oasis in the city," the $70 million Nasher Sculpture Center is the only spot in the world completely dedicated to the display and advancement of sculpture. The $400 million masterworks collection of the late Ray Nasher and his wife Patsy covers 2.4 acres. Its focus is on the history of modern sculpture and the pieces range from Auguste Rodin to Richard Serra. A 55,000-square-foot building, designed by Italian architect Renzo Piano, houses sculpture galleries, a cafe, and a store. Larger pieces are installed in the outdoor garden, where 175 trees shade the sculptures, fountains, terraced theater, and three granite walkways. At the far end of this "roofless" museum is the Turrell skyspace *Tending*, a 26-foot black granite cube that seats 25 people who can look at the sky through a 10 × 10-foot opening. The play of light is most spectacular at dawn and twilight. The museum rotates the works in its collection.

- Across the street is the **Dallas Museum of Art**, and the two museums collaborate on some special exhibits and events. The DMA also has an outdoor sculpture garden.
- Special events may include **Target First Saturday**. On the first Saturday of the month, special family activities are planned, and admission is free from 10 AM to 2 PM. Check the website for more family-centered programs.
- The center offers an art education curriculum. School and other group tours may be arranged by calling (214) 242-5170.
- Inside the museum building are restrooms, water fountains, and a cafe. A kids' meal may be offered on family event days.
- No flash photography, tripods, or video cameras are allowed.
- The museum is handicapped accessible.
- Parking: Ace and Star lots are between Flora and Woodall Rodgers. A fee is charged. The DMA garage has entrances on St. Paul and Harwood.

Hours: Daily, 10 AM to 6 PM; hours may change for special evening events. Closed major holidays.

Admission: Adults, $10; seniors (65+), $7; students, $5. The price includes the audio tour. Check to see if admission is free on the first Saturday of the month from 10 AM to 2 PM.

Directions: From North Central Expwy. (US 75S), merge onto Woodall Rodgers (TX 366W) via exit 1A toward I-35E S/Waco (0.70 mi.). Take the St. Paul exit. Turn left onto Woodall Rodgers service road and turn right onto N. Harwood.

OLD RED MUSEUM OF DALLAS COUNTY HISTORY AND CULTURE

100 South Houston St., Dallas 75202 (214) 745-1100 Website: www.oldred.org

Renovation of the red sandstone 1892 "Old Red" courthouse provided a venue for the preservation of the history and culture of Dallas County. The Romanesque revival–style four-story building next to Dealey Plaza offers a **Dallas Convention Center Visitors Bureau**, which has brochures on area attractions and a small gift shop on the first floor, a historical museum on the second floor, restrooms and offices on the third floor, a great hall and courtroom on the fourth floor, and a clock tower on the roof. The large lighted **Pegasus**, the iconic winged symbol of Dallas that was originally built for the 1939 World's Fair Magnolia Petroleum Exhibit, greets incomers on the first floor (photo op) as does a museum store and a guest services counter where visitors may purchase tickets, buy drinks and snacks, sign up for programs, and meet for tours.

The history and culture of Dallas County is portrayed in four galleries on the second floor: "Early Years: Prehistory to 1893," "Trading Center: 1874 to 1917," "Big D: 1918 to 1945," and "World Crossroads: 1946 to 2002." Interesting topics, such as entertainment, sports, religion, outlaws, war, civil rights, clothing, oil, education, and pioneering ventures, are covered through vintage films, oral history, rare photographs, memorabilia, and more than 40 touch-screen kiosks for further oral explanation. The 1,500-square-foot **Children's Learning Center** is a very hands-on, entertaining place for youngsters to discover their "roots." Fun comes in the forms of "Try It On Clothes Closet," "Discovery Cart Games," "Big Cotton," "A Dallas Child's Life," and more.

Children will enjoy the museum more if they can read fairly well. A visit might include at least two adults, one to stay with young children in the Learning Center while the other walks through the exhibits, and then they could switch.

Check the website or call for special exhibits, films, and family activities.

- A guided 30-minute Building Restoration Tour is offered Monday to Saturday at 2 PM. It's included in the ticket price. Young children would probably not enjoy this. For a fee, group tours may be arranged by calling (214) 757-1949.

- Drinks and snacks are available on the first floor.
- Next to the museum is the JFK Memorial Plaza. Nearby in the West End Historic District are the Sixth Floor Museum, Holocaust Museum, Dallas World Aquarium, House of Blues, and numerous restaurants.
- Educational programs and history labs are offered for teachers and students.
- The museum is handicapped accessible.
- Restrooms and water fountains are available.

Hours: Daily, 9 AM to 5 PM. Closed major holidays.

Admission: General, $8; seniors 65+, $6; children under 16, $5.

Directions: From the north on US 75 (Central), follow the signs for I-35, exit onto the ramp to the right (Woodall Rodgers, exit 1A); take Field St. exit on the right; turn left at light; follow the signs to Griffin. Drive down Griffin to Main, and turn right onto Main; drive down Main to Houston. Old Red is located just before Houston St. on the left. See the website for directions from I-35, Dallas North Tollway, I-45, and I-30.

Parking: $2 with ticket validated by the museum in county garage directly under Old Red. The entrance is on Commerce St. or Elm St. Some metered parking is available (carefully monitored for expiration by meter attendants).

OWENS SPRING CREEK FARM

1401 East Lookout Drive, Richardson 75082 (972) 235-0192 Website: www.owensinc.com/owens_scfarm.htm

Rolling green hills and white buildings complete the home of Owens Country Sausage at Spring Creek Farm. The Owens Museum located near the entrance takes visitors 100 years back in time in the Butcher Shop, Country Store, Country Kitchen, and Farmer's Workshop.

Outside the museum are farm animals and the Antique Wagon Showroom. What children remember most about the farm are the stables that house the Owens Gentle Giant, one magnificent blonde Belgian draft horse that weighs about 2,300 pounds. The stable also has an eight-horse pony hitch with matched miniature horses that pull a variety of miniature wagons.

Just inside the gates is a two-story farmhouse dated about 1887 and called **Miss Belle's Place** after the spinster schoolteacher who held classes in her home. Tours of the home may be arranged through the Junior League of Richardson; call (972) 644-5979.

- Guided tours are available with reservations. Call (972) 235-0192.
- There is no food or drink at Owens, but at the intersection of Plano Rd. and Campbell are Purdy's and the Feed Bag for burgers.
- Handicapped access is available.
- Restrooms and water fountains are provided.
- Parking is free.

Hours: Open daily, 9 AM to 4 PM; closed 12 PM to 1 PM for lunch. Tours are given on the hour from 9 AM to 4 PM with reservations. Closed major holidays.

Admission: General admission Monday to Friday, $5; Saturday and Sunday, $3; daily, children under 2, free. Admission includes a hayride, feed for the animals, a tour of the museum, and all the fun the farm has to offer.

Directions: Exit Campbell Rd. east from US 75 and go north on Plano Rd. Or take Plano Rd. north from I-635. The farm is on the right.

PALACE OF WAX, RIPLEY'S BELIEVE IT OR NOT! AND ENCHANTED MIRROR MAZE

601 Palace Parkway, Grand Prairie 75050 (972) 263-2391 Website: www.palaceofwax.com

Three very unique attractions located together just seven minutes east of Six Flags are Louis Toussaud's Palace of Wax, Ripley's Believe It or Not! and the Enchanted Mirror Maze. The building that houses these museums is modeled after King George IV's Royal Pavilion at Brighton. More than 175 lifelike figures of the famous and infamous have eyes that seem to follow visitors as they go from one vignette to the next. Those remembered in wax vary from Jesus Christ to U.S. presidents to Hollywood's stars and starlets to Sleeping Beauty and her prince. Walk through Behind the Scenes to a working wax studio and costume shop to see how these amazing wax figures are created.

Bring a camera to capture the collection of incredible oddities in Ripley's Believe It or Not! museum. Major theme galleries invite visitors to experience tornadoes and earthquakes and walk across coals of fire. On display is an enormous collection of curiosities that Robert Ripley collected on his tour of 198 countries. Visitors marvel at his strange treasures, such as a Leaning Tower of Pisa made of matchsticks, "The Lord's Prayer" handwritten on a single piece of rice, and a mask formed from human skin. Many hands-on exhibits challenge guests to Believe It or Not!

With one admission price, visitors may spend the day trying to navigate through the Enchanted Mirror Maze. Ripley promises that it's "never the same experience twice."

- The Haunted House at the Palace of Wax is a favorite Halloween event. Families might call for more information before taking young children.
- Birthday parties, lock-ins, and group rates are offered.
- Facilities include a gift shop, snack bar, and game area.
- On the website a **4-Kids Fun Page** includes puzzles and painting.
- A study guide is offered to teachers and youth group leaders.
- The museums are handicapped accessible.
- Restrooms and water fountains are available.
- Parking is free.

Hours: Open daily year round, except Thanksgiving, Christmas, and New Year's Day. Memorial Day to Labor Day: 10 AM to 9 PM. Remainder of year: Monday to Friday, 10 AM to 5 PM; Saturday and Sunday, 10 AM to 6 PM. Ticket office closes one hour before listed closing time.

Admission: Adult: 3-way combo, $27.99; combo, $21.99; single museum, $16.99. Children, ages 4–12: 3-way combo, $17.99; combo, $12.99; single, $8.99. Senior or military: 3-way combo, $25.99; combo, $19.99; and single, $14.99. Coupons and tickets are available online.

Directions: From I-30, exit north at Belt Line Rd. The museums can be seen from the highway.

RANGER BALLPARK IN ARLINGTON

1000 Ballpark Way, Arlington 76011. Tickets (972) RANGERS; executive offices (817) 273-5222. Website: www.texasrangers.com

"Take me out to the ballgame" became an even more frequent request in April 1994 when the Ballpark in Arlington opened as the new home of the Texas Rangers. Costing $189.4 million to build, the stadium complex consists of sunset red granite and red brick exterior, eight towers, five seating levels, three concourses, and a Home Run Porch. The asymmetrical playing field is natural grass. Entrances are provided at each of the four corners.

The two sections of the main concourse provide many food and beverage concessions as well as the following seating options: field boxes, terrace boxes, left-field reserved, and bleacher seating. The upper concourse/upper deck seating offers upper boxes, upper reserved, and grandstand reserved. The other levels are suites and club seating. **Rawlings Grille**, (817) 469-8900, is located on the upper suite level behind the Home Run Porch.

As you walk around the exterior of the stadium, notice the 35 cast-stone steer heads and 21 Lone Stars, as well as 10 murals of Texas scenes located between the upper and lower arches that surround the stadium.

Fans may only bring in paper and plastic containers (no cans or glass bottles) and coolers measuring 16" × 16" or smaller that will fit underneath the seats. No alcoholic beverages may be brought in. No flash photography is allowed, but cameras and handheld video cameras are acceptable. Tailgate parties are allowed as long as they do not take over more parking spaces. Fans may also picnic in **Vandergriff Plaza**, a park area behind the center-field fence.

In addition to Ranger games, the complex provides the **Dr Pepper Youth Park** baseball facility for ages 12 and under organized youth groups, birthday parties, tournaments, summer camps and clinics, rental, and other occasions.

The **Legends of the Game Baseball Museum** features baseball memorabilia and exhibits from the National Baseball Hall of Fame in Cooperstown, New Jersey. In the third floor **Learning Center**, interactive exhibits for school-age fans include the Science of Baseball, Baseball History Tunnel, Baseball Geography and Math, and Baseball Communications. Special programs, such as summer day camps, sleepovers, story time, and special day activities, are scheduled throughout the year. Call (817) 273-5600 for information, hours, and admission fees. Try museum.texasrangers.com for more information.

If you need help, the Fan Assistance Center is located behind home plate on the main concourse.

- **Tours** of the Ballpark may be arranged by calling (817) 273-5099. Combination tickets for the tour and the museum may be purchased. Contact tours@texas rangers.com.
- A Wiffle Ballpark, two tee-ball cages, Speed Pitch, Ring-a-Coke, and picnic tables are some of the attractions at the **Coca-Cola Sports Park** in Center Field's Vandergriff Plaza. Games are one to two tokens. The park opens two hours before game time.
- The Lower Level Picnic Area is behind Sections 39 and 40. Upper level picnic areas are across the Upper Concourse.
- Fans 13 and under are invited to join the **Dr Pepper Jr. Rangers**. Call (817) 436-5934.
- Arrange a birthday party by calling (972) RANGERS.
- To be included on the Birthday and Anniversary Parade on the video board, call (817) 273-5137. Advanced purchase is required.
- Areas of the stadium are handicapped accessible. Call (817) 273-5222 for more information.
- Water fountains and restrooms are provided. Diaper-changing areas are in both men's and women's restrooms.
- ATMs are located on all three levels.
- Section 335 is designated as a non-alcohol section. Smoking is prohibited in restrooms and all seating areas.

- **The Texas Rangers Grand Slam Shop** is on ground level behind center field. Call (817) 273-5222.
- Parking is cash only. Season Parking Pass holders park in a designated area. Everyone else parks in General Parking. The lots open three hours before the game.
- Almost everything can be purchased in advance online.

Hours: For evening games, the gates open three hours early, and for afternoon games, two hours early. This is subject to change. On non-game days, ticket office hours are Monday to Friday, 9 AM to 6 PM, and Saturday, 10 AM to 4 PM. Night game hours are Monday to Saturday, 9 AM to 9 PM, and Sunday, 12 PM to 9 PM.

Admission: Tickets may be purchased online, at the ticket office, or by phone at (972) RANGERS and may be charged on Visa, MasterCard, or American Express. Tickets may also be purchased at Dillards. Ticket prices depend on selection of seating. There are some discounts for ages 13 and under.

Directions: RBIA is located at 1000 Ballpark Way, just south of I-30. Check online at www.texasrangers.com/parking or call (972) PARKING for the best route to the ballpark.

SANDY LAKE AMUSEMENT PARK

I-35E North at Sandy Lake Rd. (Exit 444), Carrollton 75006 (972) 242-7449 (Mailing address: P.O. Box 810536, Dallas 75381) Website: www.sandylake.com

A favorite swimming hole of Dallasites for more than 30 years, Sandy Lake continues to delight families with its large pool designed for all ages. Lifeguards watch the pool area closely.

A hilly miniature golf course, paddleboats, and 19 amusement rides add to the fun. Screened in along the lake area in the Bird Barnyard are peacocks, ducks, geese, guineas, and turkeys to watch.

During April and May, local school bands, orchestras, and choirs compete there.

- Tickets are bought for the attractions, and discount books are available.
- Birthday party packages, which may include a meal, are offered. For group rates for birthday parties, company picnics, and youth groups, e-mail vickie@sandylake.com.
- Paddleboat riders must meet height requirements or ride with an adult. Small children wear life jackets.
- Shetland pony rides are offered for children on Saturdays, Sundays, and holidays.
- Four concessions with pizza, hot dogs, and snacks are convenient. Families may bring only home-prepared food with no glass bottles

for picnics. Picnic tables are provided, but groups of 15 or more need a reservation and there is a fee.

- Most areas are handicapped accessible, but the miniature golf course is too hilly.
- Restrooms and water fountains are available.
- Parking is free.

Hours: April to September. Hours and days vary from month to month.

Admission: General admission at the gate is ages 4 and up, $2; 3 and under, free. Swimming, $4; paddleboats and miniature golf, $2; and amusement rides, $1.50 to $2.50.

Directions: Take I-35E north and exit at Sandy Lake Rd. (Exit 444) in Carrollton. Go west a short distance to the park on the right. Also, visitors could take Bush tollway to Sandy Lake Rd. and go east to the park entrance.

SIX FLAGS HURRICANE HARBOR

1800 East Lamar, Arlington 76006 (817) 265-3356 (Mailing address: P.O. Box 90191, Arlington 76004) Website: www.sixflags.com/hurricaneharbortexas

Aptly named, the 47-acre Hurricane Harbor water park offers around 24 exhilarating ways to cool off during the hot Texas summertime. Whether taking a leisurely inner-tube cruise around Arlington's Lazy River ride or dropping into a free fall from 76 nautical feet of Der Stuka, family members will find nonstop entertainment during their day at Hurricane Harbor. Young and old are drawn to Captain Hook's Lagoon, which has five stories of fun on net ladders and slides. Next, they may want to try Suntan Lagoon, an activity pool with geysers, fountains, and waterfalls surrounded by a deck.

The more adventuresome try the Bubba Tub, in which four ride a rubber tub from a six-story height. The white-water rafting of Colorado is replicated in the inner-tube ride on the Ragin' Rapids of a man-made river with slides and waterfalls to add to the experience. Rides like Hydra Maniac and the Black Hole live up to their names in thrilling speed and splashing finales. New in 2008, Mega Wedgie is a waterslide that is four stories high and 83 feet wide, sending visitors sliding down at speeds of up to 23 mph.

- Lifeguards are professionally trained and are very visible. Some rides have height requirements or caution those with heart problems or those who are pregnant.
- Park maps are available online and at the park entrance.

- Soft rafts and tubes for the wave pool are available for rent or sale, but you will probably want to bring your own.
- Adults must accompany young children, who must use approved flotation devices. Watch children very carefully in the pools, especially on crowded days.
- Picnic tables are available outside the park, where visitors may bring their own food and non-alcoholic drinks. No glass containers are allowed. Concessions provide drinks and fast food, such as hamburgers, pizza, chicken fingers, and salads.
- Across the highway is Six Flags Over Texas amusement park.
- There are coin-operated lockers for valuables, shower facilities, an arcade, gift shop, sand volleyball courts, and lounge chairs.
- There is handicapped access to the pool areas. No strollers or wheelchairs are for rent.
- Restrooms and water fountains are provided.
- Parking is $15.

Hours: Open from mid-May through mid-September. Hours vary. Call or check online for specific days and times. Summer hours are usually Fridays and Saturdays from 10:30 AM to 8 or 9 PM, Sundays through Thursdays from 10:30 AM to 7 or 8 PM.

Admission: A 2008 one-day pass to the Arlington park: adults, $24.99; seniors (55+) and kids under 48 inches tall, $19.99; ages 2 and under, free. Discount rate sometimes given for evening admission. Season passes are available.

Directions: The Arlington park is just off I-30, directly across from Six Flags Over Texas. Exit the Hwy. 360 service road. The park is on the north side.

SIX FLAGS OVER TEXAS

2201 Road to Six Flags, Arlington 76010 Metro (817) 640-8900 (Mailing address: P.O. Box 90191, Arlington 76004) Website: www.sixflags.com/overtexas

As children see the bright, waving flags and dancing fountains of Six Flags Over Texas, their excitement in anticipation of the thrills to come overflows. For over 30 years, this 205-acre family theme park has entertained all ages with a variety of rides, shows, and special events.

Young children are drawn to the antique Silver Star Carousel, Looney Tunes Land, and the Good Time Theater where Bugs Bunny and pals entertain. Older children brave the roller coasters, which range from the tamer Mini Mine Train to the 14-story wooden roller coaster called The Texas Giant. Towering 325 feet into the air, the *Superman* Tower of Power fits riders into a launch vehicle, sends them up "faster than a speeding bullet," pauses, and then sends them hurtling down. For those who need a cool-down, a liberal drenching is promised by the Roaring Rapids and the Log Ride. Tony Hawk's Big Spin spinning coaster was unveiled in 2008, with moves much like those of skateboarder Tony Hawk.

Everyone loves the shootouts between Six Flags cowboys, the shows at the Crazy Horse Saloon and Southern Palace, as well as special concerts at the 10,000-seat Music Mill Amphitheater. The lush landscaping, cheerful employees, and cleanliness are always appreciated. Emporiums with T-shirts and other souvenirs are plentiful.

- Some rides have height and age requirements. On the website is a list of all rides that gives these requirements as well as "thrill ratings" and locations.
- Discount coupons and information about special events are often available in Friday newspapers or other promotions. Special prices are sometimes offered for purchasing evening tickets or bringing designated soft drink cans.
- Special events include September's Heritage Craft Fair, Halloween Fright Nights, and Holiday in the Park in December and January.
- There are diaper stations and Lost Parents headquarters in Looney Toon Land. Stroller rental is located after the Entry Plaza on the left.
- Admission to the park includes all rides and shows, except some special concerts in the amphitheater. Food, arcade games, and souvenirs are not included in the fee but may be needed in the budget. ATMs are located in the park.
- The Flash Pass allows visitors to reserve their ride time, which shortens wait time. A one-person pass begins at about $32.
- At Guest Relations, you may get a copy of the *Guide to Family Fun*. A *Tips* page is on the website.
- Indoor restaurants serve fried chicken, Mexican dishes, burgers, and pizza as well as other fast foods at food stands with picnic-type outdoor seating. No outside food, beverages, or coolers are allowed inside the park, with the exception of special dietary requirements. A shaded family picnic area with tables is located in the parking lot between rows 25 and 30. Get your hand stamped at the gate for re-entry.
- There is handicapped access to the park. Rides vary. A guide to ride accessibility is available at the gate, as well as wheelchair rental.
- Restrooms and water fountains are available throughout the park and are noted on the park map. Lockers are provided near the entrance.
- Parking is about $15. Preferred and valet parking are available. Trams transport visitors from the remote parking to the entrance and back. A park map is distributed at the entrance to the parking lot.

Hours: Open weekends in spring and fall; daily in summer. There are special schedules for events, such as Fright Fest and Holiday in the Park. For specific hours and information, call Metro at (817) 640-8900. In summer, hours are usually daily 10 AM to10 PM.

Admission: 2008 one-day pass: Adults, $49.99; children under 48 inches and seniors (55+), $29.99; ages 2 and under, free. Two-day passes and individual and family season passes are available. Discount rates offered for groups of 10 or more and for AAA members. Call (817) 640-8900, ext. 4100, for group information.

Directions: Located between Dallas and Fort Worth off I-30 on the south side. Exit at Hwy. 360 in Arlington. The orange Observation Tower can be seen for miles.

THE SIXTH FLOOR MUSEUM AT DEALEY PLAZA

411 Elm St., Dallas 75202 (214) 747-6660, (888) 485-4854 Website: www.jfk.org

The Sixth Floor Exhibit: John F. Kennedy and the Memory of a Nation is a permanent collection of historical information regarding the assassination of President John F. Kennedy on November 22, 1963. Located on the sixth floor of the former Texas School Book Depository, photographs, 40 minutes of documentary film, and significant artifacts are presented to help visitors understand the events leading to and following this tragic event. Museum personnel believe all materials are appropriate for viewing by families.

Tours are self-guided and an audio tour is available; about 75 minutes should be allowed to cover the exhibit adequately. Also, the museum recommends a walking tour around Dealey Plaza. As visitors leave the Sixth Floor, they are invited to write their own memories of the assassination in books that will always be part of historic record. No photography is allowed.

- The Visitor Center has a small bookstore. You may write or call for a free brochure.
- Parts of Oliver Stone's movie *JFK* was filmed in the area.
- The museum offers special events, such as "CSI for Families," along with special seventh-floor exhibits and programs throughout the year.
- On Market between Commerce and Main is the **John F. Kennedy Memorial Plaza**.
- Restaurants are located in the nearby West End Historic District and Victory Park.
- The handicapped accessible entrance is on the northwest corner of the building nearest Pacific.
- There are restrooms and water fountains.

- Paid parking is available to the north of the Visitor Center. Ample parking is next to the Visitor Center on the west side of the building. Visitors can ride the DART train, get off at the West End station, and walk about a block west. Visitors may also ride the Trinity Railway Express, get off at Union Station, and walk three blocks north. The museum offers admission discounts to both DART and TRE passengers.

Hours: Open Monday, 12 PM to 6 PM; Tuesdays to Sundays, 10 AM to 6 PM (last ticket sold one hour prior to closing). Closed Thanksgiving Day and Christmas Day.

Admission: Adults, $13.50; children ages 6–18 and seniors 65+, $12.50; free for children 5 and under (unless they want an audio tour, $3.50); The audio tour is included in admission. There is an audio tour for ages 6–12 as well as adult audio tours in seven languages. Group rates are available.

Directions: The Visitor Center faces Dealey Plaza on Houston St. between Elm and Pacific in the old Texas School Book Depository Building, which is now called the Dallas County Administration Building.

SURF AND SWIM

440 Oates Rd., Garland 75043 (972) 205-3993, (972) 205-2757
Website: www.surfandswim.org/

Nestled in a shady greenbelt area, this large wave pool is operated by the City of Garland in Audubon Park. Excited whoops go up as the surf is turned on, producing rolling waves that lift and lower inner-tube riders.

Lifeguards carefully monitor the area and can push a button to stop the waves if necessary.

Wally's Cove is a splashground for children 6 years and under. They can play with spray toys, bouncy seats, and water-dropping frog buckets.

Plenty of shaded and unshaded grassy areas are provided for spreading out beach towels. Picnic tables are provided and food may be brought in, but glass bottles and alcoholic beverages are not allowed. Ice chests are checked at the entrance.

- Inner tubes are provided by Surf and Swim. A tube makes the waves more enjoyable. Don't take an inner tube into deep water unless you can swim.
- Very young children should be watched carefully, especially on crowded days, to see that they do not get caught underneath some tubes. The waves will lift them off their feet, and their heads go under water. They might wear life jackets or swim wings.

- **Audubon Park** has a wonderful shaded playground area east of the pool. Passes are honored all day, so swimmers may leave and return on that day.
- Call ahead if the weather has been stormy. The pool is closed if the water is clouded. Even in summer it can be cool there on a cloudy, windy day.
- Rental after closing time is offered for groups. Birthday packages are available.
- The concession sells fast foods and snow cones.
- Handicapped accessible into pool area.
- Restrooms, an open shower, water fountains, and a pay telephone are available.
- Parking is free.

Hours: Open from Splash Day about mid-May on weekends to daily while school is out until Labor Day, 11 AM to 7 PM. Open Friday until 9 PM. Crowd thinnest early morning and late afternoon.

Admission: 48 inches and taller, $6; under 48 inches, $5; 2 years and under, free with paid admission. Rates are lower after 5 PM. Group rates for 25+.

Directions: Take the Oates Exit off LBJ Fwy. (I-635) and go east one mile. The pool is past the baseball fields on the right at Audubon Park.

TEXAS DISCOVERY GARDENS IN FAIR PARK

3601 Martin Luther King Jr. Blvd., Dallas 75210 (214) 428-7476 (Mailing Address: P.O. Box 152537, Dallas 75315) Website: www.texasdiscoverygardens.org

Celebrating its 60th birthday in 2001, the Texas Discovery Gardens in Fair Park continue to share "butterflies, bugs, and botany" with children and adults. This Art Deco building is a National Historic Landmark, built for the 1936 Texas Centennial Exposition. TDG is the first public garden in Texas to be certified organic. The TDG maintains a visitor center and 7.5 acres of 10 themed areas, including a butterfly habitat, native wildlife pond, scent garden, shade garden, and heirloom garden.

At family events offered throughout the year, children and parents share the experience of being amazed and inspired by nature's intricate web of life. Gardening workshops and guided tours provide expert advice on using native and adapted plants to create backyard habitats for butterflies, birds, and other native wildlife.

Texas Discovery Gardens is once more experiencing a metamorphosis. Slated to be completed by summer 2009, the Rosine Smith Sammons Butterfly House and insectarium will encourage visitors to broaden their horizons as they view tropical plants and butterflies. Entering on the second floor at the canopy level and descending on a spiral walkway to the lower level, visitors will stroll among more than 100 species of free-flying tropical butterflies. Through unique underground and underwater windows on the lower level, the secret lives of beetles, earthworms, and aquatic insects will be revealed. The new EarthKeepers Children's Classroom will serve to expand and challenge young minds through hands-on scientific observation. The adventure will continue into the garden, as visitors experience a symphony for the senses in beautiful flora and fauna and water accents as well as in the many classes and activities.

- Areas of the center may be reserved for parties, events, and meetings.
- There is no food service, except during the state fair. The Old Mill Inn, across from the Music Hall, is within walking distance for lunch.
- Handicapped access is available.
- There are restrooms and water fountains.
- Parking is free except during the state fair and Fair Park special events.

Hours: Open Monday to Saturday, 10 AM to 5 PM. Hours vary during the state fair. Closed most holidays.

Admission: Adults, $3; seniors (60+), $2; and ages 3–11, $1.50. Garden members and children under 3 admitted free. **Tuesdays** include **free admission** to the gardens. Call for Butterfly House pricing.

Directions: Enter Fair Park through the Martin L. King Jr. Blvd. entrance off Robert B. Cullum Blvd., Gate 6. Parking is to the right. See directions to Fair Park.

WEST END HISTORIC DISTRICT

West End Association (214) 741-7180 Website: www.dallaswest-end.org

The Dallas West End Historic District is an area downtown loosely bound by Elm, Houston, Lamar, and Woodall Rodgers Fwy., with Market St. slicing through the middle. Historic brick buildings, such as the former cracker factory where my father worked as a boy, now house restaurants, museums, clubs, and a small number of retail stores. Visitors and locals alike stroll the brick streets and absorb both the Old World and modern-day atmosphere.

The West End hosts several festivals and special events, such as Hoop It Up, Taste of Dallas, circus exhibit, and elephant walk. Call for a calendar of events, check the website, or watch for newspaper announcements on Fridays.

More than 20 restaurants and entertainment venues include Sonny Bryan's Barbecue, Corner Bakery, Gator's Croc and Roc, Landry's Seafood House, Hoffbrau Steaks, Spaghetti Warehouse, Palm Restaurant, House of Blues, and the Y.O. Ranch Steakhouse. Restaurants open and close often so if you want a particular one, call ahead or look online. Wild Bill's Western Wear is located at 311 N. Market Street.

- The West End is near the Dallas Arts District, Dealey Plaza, Dallas World Aquarium, Dallas Holocaust Museum, the Old Red Museum, American Airlines Center in Victory Park, and the Sixth Floor Museum.
- A visitor center is located in the Old Red Museum.
- Max-A-Million provides horse-drawn carriage rides around the West End and downtown, weather permitting. During Christmas, they offer tours through Highland Park. Call (214) 796-6637 for information.
- The restaurants and museums are handicapped accessible.
- Restrooms and water fountains are available inside restaurants and museums.
- The DART rail line brings visitors to the West End Station at Market St.
- Variety of parking lots with fees; some metered street parking; six-story West End Parking Garage at Munger and Lamar, east of Record St.; better not to travel alone or wear flashy, expensive jewelry after dark.

Directions: From I-35 (Stemmons Fwy.), exit Continental, which changes name to Lamar (at Munger); turn right for the restaurants or turn left for the garage. From US 75 (N. Central Expressway), take Woodall Rodgers (I-35E) to Field St. Veer left under the highway to Lamar, and turn left on Lamar. At Munger, turn left for the parking garage.

WHITE ROCK LAKE

8300 East Lawther Drive Dallas (972) 622-7283 (Mailing address: PMB 281, 381 Casa Linda Plaza, Dallas 75218) Websites: www.whiterocklake.org; www.dallasparks.org; www.dallascityhall.org (to visitors, to park and recreation to white rock)

Built for water supply in 1910, White Rock Lake is now operated as a public park that consists of more than 1,000 acres of lake and 1,000 acres of parkland. Main avenues surrounding White Rock include E.

Northwest Hwy., Buckner Blvd., Mockingbird Lane, Garland Rd., and Lawther Drive. On sunny days, the shaded park is highly populated with sailors, rowers, fishermen, joggers, bicyclists, skaters, and picnickers.

On a 9.33-mile trail around the lake, those jogging, skating, and bicycling get their exercise protected from city traffic. An 8-to-10-station par course is between Emerald Isle and Poppy Drive on the lake's east side. The White Rock Creek Trail continues north through the greenbelt area to Valley View Park. A pretty ride is from Greenville Ave. and Royal Lane to Lawther Drive. A **playground** has been built at Tee Pee Hill as well as six pieces of par course equipment. Close by are bathrooms, a drinking fountain, and cool spray. Enter the park at Williamson and West Lawther.

Boats with motors of 10 horsepower or less as well as sailboats, kayaks, canoes, and paddleboats are welcome on the lake. Sailing clubs sometimes hold regattas that are beautiful to watch. Fishermen line the creek banks and piers, hoping for white crappie, largemouth bass, and catfish. They must have a fishing license and follow length and limit regulations. White Rock provides 12 fishing piers and five boat ramps, two on the east side and three on the west.

At one time, visitors could take Lawther all around the lake, but the crowds were unpopular with residents of the area. Now it is divided into four sections with entrances at Emerald Isle, from Poppy to the Dreyfus Club building off Buckner, by the spillway on Garland, and at Lawther off Mockingbird. Visitors can drive the entire length of the west side.

Shaded picnic areas with nearby playgrounds are plentiful. Covered pavilions and buildings may be rented for large groups. The old **Pump House** at the south end is now a historical site and management office for the Water Department. A sculpture is in front of the building. At Sunset Bay is a life-size bronze statue called *CCC Worker*, which honors Civilian Conservation Corps Company 2986, which helped develop White Rock Lake Park from 1935 to 1942. From Buckner Blvd., go west into the park on Poppy. Turn left on E. Lawther, and go .3 mile to Sunset Bay, near the Park Office and the ducks.

- At Mockingbird Point, 8000 Mockingbird, just west of Buckner Blvd., is a **dog park**. Call (214) 671-8001; websitewww.dallasdogparks.org. Open 5 AM to midnight. Closed Monday. When the ground is wet, call to see if the park is open.
- The **White Rock Boathouse, Inc.**, located in a 1930s boathouse, promotes rowing through rowing events, programs, lessons, and high school programs. It's located at 3240 W. Lawther on the southwest side of the lake by Tee Pee Hill. Website: www.whiterockboathouse.com.

- Perched on the hill on the southeast corner of Mockingbird and Buckner is a small, pretty playground and covered picnic table that overlooks the lake. Another picnic/play park is just a little farther north beside the baseball diamonds on Buckner.
- **Flag Pole Hill**, with its playground, covered pavilion for picnics, and wonderful hill to climb, is also a great place to fly a kite, throw a Frisbee, or listen to special outdoor summer programs by the Dallas Symphony.
- Since swimming has not been allowed for many years, the old 1930s bath house is now the **Bath House Cultural Center**, which is used as a gallery, center for performing arts, and educational center for various workshops. Inside the Bath House is the **White Rock Lake Museum**. Its mission is to present the natural and human history of the lake with an emphasis on the ecology of water. From Buckner Blvd., go west on Northcliff to E. Lawther. Call (214) 670-8751 for a calendar of events.
- For building and pavilion rental as well as tennis court reservations, call the Park Department at (214) 670-8740. For bike trails and maps, call (214) 670-4100.
- South American Monk Parakeets nest by an electric utility switching substation on St. Francis Ave. near Barbaree Blvd.
- **For the Love of the Lake** is an organization of enthusiastic volunteers who are dedicated to the preservation and enhancement of White Rock. They organize Second Saturday lake spruce-ups and other events. Address: PMB 281, 381 Casa Linda Plaza 75218. Lakeline: (972) 622-SAVE Website: www.whiterocklake.org..
- The **Corinthian Sailing Club**, chartered in 1939, promotes sailing and hosts regattas. It offers summer youth sailing classes and an official junior race team. Address: 441 E. Lawther Drive. Call (214) 320-0841. Website: www.cscsailing.org.
- The **Dallas Arboretum** is near the spillway on Garland Rd.
- The Lakewood Service League hosts an annual **Walk, Wag, and Run** fundraiser in October, which includes 5K and 10K races, a dog walk, kids' fair, and more. Volunteers are appreciated.
- Portable restrooms in winter are not handicapped accessible. After April 1, five permanent restrooms are opened that are accessible. Water fountains are located nearby. Eight water fountains are along the trail.
- Free parking. Lock car. Do not leave valuables in sight.

Hours: Daily, 6 AM to midnight. It is not advisable to be there after dark. It is safest to travel with a buddy.
Admission: Free

Directions: Access to the park is on Garland Rd., E. Northwest Hwy., Lawther Drive, and N. Buckner Blvd. Signs direct visitors.

THE WOMEN'S MUSEUM

3800 Parry Ave. (at S. Washington in Fair Park), Dallas 75226
(214) 915-0860 Website: www.thewomensmuseum.org

Once a 1910 coliseum in Fair Park that served as a cattle auction barn by day and a symphony hall by night, the $25 million Women's Museum: An Institute for the Future has blossomed.

Designed by New York architect Wendy Evans Joseph, the three-level museum celebrates the history and contributions of women in America. The Art Deco look was added in 1936 for the Texas Centennial Exposition. A statue of Venus rising from a cactus greets visitors at the front door.

Exhibits inside focus on a variety of topics, such as inspirational quotes, unforgettable women, health and sports, "mothers of invention," art, computers, and the future. A 30-foot-tall electronic quilt publishes 35 still and moving messages concerning the lives of women.

- Ongoing classes, events, and camps get girls involved in areas such as web design, television production, creativity, sports, and fitness. Programs are available for Girl Scouts.
- The Texas Girls State Fair is a three-week event during the state fair to showcase interests of girls ages 10–18.
- Tours are available for groups of 10 or more.
- Soft drink, juice, and snack machines are located in the museum.
- The museum is handicapped accessible. Some wheelchairs on site.
- Restrooms and water fountains are available.
- Parking is free except during the state fair.

Hours: Tuesday–Sunday, 12 PM to 5 PM. Closed Monday and major holidays.

Admission: Adults, $5; students ages 13–18 and seniors, $4; ages 5–12, $3; under 5, free.

Directions: The museum is located at the Washington Ave. entrance to Fair Park across from the Music Hall. From downtown Dallas, take I-30E and exit at 48A Haskell/Peak. Cross over Parry and enter at Gate 2 near the Music Hall. Follow the signs to the Women's Museum parking lot.

2. TIDBITS: MORE GOOD THINGS TO DO

The first chapter only scratched the surface of the many things to see and do in and around Big D. The listings in this chapter may be a little smaller or appeal to a certain age or interest group, but they still offer entertaining and educational activities to explore and enjoy. As Dallas grows, sometimes getting off the beaten path is the most rewarding.

For all sorts of information about Dallas parks, entertainment, recycling, pet adoption, and so forth, a great site to visit is www.dallascityhall.com.

MORE AMUSEMENTS

Entertaining activities abound around town, no matter how old one is or what the ever-changing Texas weather is doing. In addition to these listed, many shopping malls also have an arcade, a carousel, a choo choo, or a soft play area to entertain family members who would rather play than shop. Celebration Station is listed in **Chapter 1: Places to Go**. Also, look under **Individual, Family, and Team Sports** for activities such as ice hockey, skateboarding, go-carting, rock climbing, ice skating, bicycling, bowling, swimming, paintball, hiking, and miniature golf.

ADVENTURE LANDING

17717 Coit Rd., Dallas 75252 (between Frankford and Campbell) (972) 248-4966 Website: www.adventurelanding.com

Three 18-hole miniature golf courses allow players to test their swings, after which they may want to visit the large arcade, take a few laps on the speedway in go-carts, hit a few balls at the batting cages, defeat opponents in Laser Tag, make a teddy bear at the Teddy Bear Factory, or relax in the cafe with some pizza. For children ages 4 to 10 who are at least 56 inches tall, the track has junior go-carts. Also, a two-seater allows young children to ride with a licensed adult. Specials are offered daily. The prices of attractions vary, and a child's ticket is offered for ages 3 to 5.

AMAZING JAKES

831 N. Central Expwy. at 15th St., Plano 75075 (972) 509-5253 Website: www.amazingjakes.com

The question at Amazing Jakes is not "What will we do?" but "What will we do first?" in this 90,000-square-foot, two-story indoor entertainment center located on the east side of Collin Creek Mall. Just riding the center's escalator will entertain some, but more fun and food abound here daily. Older kids will probably start with the large arcade, Laser Tag, go-carts, miniature golf, climbing wall, and bumper cars. Younger folks will like the carousel, train, and Star Jets. The whole family may gather at the buffet, which features pizzas, pastas, soups, and a Potato and Salad Bar. An elevator is inside the park. The second-floor entrance may be closed on weekdays. Visitors may enter from the mall or the parking lot. A television/video room is available. Some rides/games have height/weight requirements. A three-hour unlimited pass costs from $11 to $22. Coupons are available online. Birthday packages are available.

INCREDIBLE PIZZA

1330 N. Town East Blvd., Mesquite 75150 (972) 279-2009 Website: www.ipmesquite.com

Fun begins in the pizza buffet line at Incredible Pizza, but you could select pasta, a baked potato, salad, and dessert. A meal and drink are required for entry. The buffet runs from $6 to $10. The fees for mini-golf, bumper cars, go-carts, and mini-bowling range from $2.25 to $5.50. Video games and a tiny kids' play area round out the entertainment.

MAIN EVENT

3941 North Central Expwy., Plano (972) 881-8181

2070 S. Stemmons Pkwy., Lewisville (972) 459-7770

407 W. State Highway 114, Grapevine (817) 416-1111

9375 Dallas Pkwy., Frisco (469) 362-7227

Website: www.maineventusa.net

Fun at Main Event takes the form of bowling, billiards, Laser Tag (48 inches+), arcade games, and a cafe. Some Main Events offer glow-in-the-dark mini-golf. On Monday, Wednesday, and Friday beginning at 7 PM, Main Event has **Laser Jam**: blacklight bowling, fog, lasers, and music. Reservations should be made 24 hours or more ahead. Bumper bowling, birthday parties, and lock-ins are available. Hours are Sunday to Thursday, 11 AM to midnight; Friday, 11 AM to 2 AM; Saturday, 10 AM to 2 AM. Only ages 18 and older may remain Sunday to Thursday after 10 PM and Friday and Saturday after midnight. Check to see if younger children may remain if accompanied by an adult 25 or older. Look at the website for special deals such as Monday Night Madness, which offers several activities from 4 PM to midnight for $20, including a $10 game card. Main Event is usually open on holidays.

PLANET PIZZA

3000 Custer Rd. at West Parker, Unit 310, Plano 75075 (972) 985-7711

Ferrari bumper cars, a swinging pirate ship, tea cup ride, and a large soft play area with tunnels, balls, tubes, and slides are only part of the fun at Planet Pizza, an indoor playpark. A Tot Spot is available for youngsters ages 1 and 2 who may not be ready to mix in Soft Play. Arcade games with a ticket redemption center and a fast-food menu add to the entertainment for children ages 1 to 10. Individual tickets or unlimited rides and soft play hand stamps may be purchased. The unlimited play is about $8 weekdays and $10 weekends. Soft Play is $3.99. Birthday party packages are available for a minimum of six children. Families may register online to win a monthly birthday party giveaway. Look for coupons online, in *Around Town Kids*, and in *North Texas Kids*.

SEGA GAMEWORKS

Grapevine Mills Mall, 3000 Grapevine Mills Pkwy., Ste. 525, Grapevine 76051 (972) 539-6757 Website: www.gameworks.com

Sega Gameworks is a mega-arcade located in Grapevine Mills Mall. Fun takes the shape of a grill with a kids menu, interactive games, simulators, and other attractions.

RONALD'S PLAYPLACE

14770 Preston Rd., Dallas (972) 233-8788

13105 Montfort at LBJ Fwy., Dallas (972) 233-5952

Both of these McDonald's have entertaining indoor playparks with tunnels and slides and toddler areas. The unique McDonald's on Montfort was built to look like a Happy Meal box. McDonald's restaurants abound in the Dallas area.

SPEEDZONE

11130 Malibu Drive (I-35E at Walnut Hill), Dallas 75229 (972) 247-RACE Website: www.speedzone.com

The focus is on race cars of various types at 12-acre Speedzone. In addition to the Grand Prix race cars, which are primarily for licensed adults who are at least 5' tall, the two-seat Sidewinder cars are for drivers who are at least 4'-10" tall and passengers who are at least 3'-6" tall. Speedzone also has two miniature golf courses, a restaurant, an Electric Alley game room (which has 100 simulator and skill redemption games), and a Fireball looping roller coaster. Check online for special deals and coupons.

WHIRLYBALL

3641 W. Northwest Hwy. at Webb Chapel, Dallas 75220 (214) 350-0117 or (214) 350-0129 Website: www.whirlyballdallas.com

Whirlyball is a unique team game that combines jai-alai, basketball, and hockey. Team members ride in bumper cars while they try to score points using a scoop. Facilities include a concession, small video arcade, pool table, air hockey, skee ball, two courts, and two party rooms. Teams must have a minimum of six players (three on three), and the courts rent for around $150/hour daily for package deals. Players must be age 9 or older.

WHIRLYBALL LASERWHIRLD

3115 W. Parker at Independence, Plano 75075 (972) 398-7900 Website: www.whirlyball.homestead.com

This location has both Whirlyball as listed above (although the two are owned separately) and Laserwhirld, a two-story laser-tag arena where up to 25 people engage in active play for 15 minutes each game. Participants can play solo or in team competition. Birthday parties are welcome. For laser play, players must be 48 inches tall or taller and wear a lightweight vest. One person playing one hour is about $15. An arcade is in the main lobby.

INDOOR BOUNCE ENTERTAINMENT CENTERS

If a child has more energy than Mom can channel, these indoor bounce house amusement centers are just the ticket. The stadium is filled with exciting inflatable structures and, unlike Mom's couch, jumping is encouraged. Socks must be worn. They have open jump time where anyone may play, and other times slated for parties. Some have special slots for teens, family nights, and special needs. It's always good to call ahead and/or look at the website for up-to-date details.

JUMP TOWN

3045 W. 15th St. at Independence, Plano 75075 (972) 867-5867 Website: www.thejumptown.com

BOUNCE U

2532 Summit Ave. near Jupiter, Plano 75074 (972) 422-3399

3050 North Josey Lane #110 at Frankford, Carrollton 75007 (972) 939-5000

Website: www.bounceu.com

BOOMERANGS PARTY AND PLAY
6205 Coit Rd. Ste. B near W. Spring Creek Pkwy., Plano 75024
(214) 473-9995 Website: www.boomerangspartyandplay.com

NATURE, ECOLOGY, SCIENCE

As the Metroplex grows in population and the natural areas are developed to accommodate new and expanding families and businesses, preservation of those natural areas and their wildlife in preserves and parks has become a priority of both state and local park departments and organizations such as the Texas Conservation Alliance and Sierra Club, as well as families who wish to escape city life to undisturbed settings. Even though "the stars at night / Are big and bright / Deep in the heart of Texas," sometimes city lights obscure all but the brightest stars. If you can't get out of town, local planetariums offer celestial programs day and night. Of further interest to naturalists is the progress in recycling and other conservation efforts in the Dallas area. Some local businesses are specializing in products to encourage and equip families who are interested in science and outdoor activities.

An amazing guide to natural resources is the **Natural History of North Central Texas** website to explore flora, fauna, fossils, frogs, etc.: www.nhnct.org. It's a collection of links, data, and original content to promote appreciation of the natural world in North Central Texas. "Nature Study" allows you to click on the county you're interested in to reach nature preserves, hiking trails, and wildlife in that particular area. Some links include Texas Parks and Wildlife, Butterflies of Texas, DFW Herpetological Society (reptiles), and Texas Freshwater Fisheries Center in Athens.

The **Texas Parks and Wildlife Department** (www.tpwd.state.tx.us) offers a great deal of information for students of nature and the outdoors on their website, www.tpwd.state.tx.us/learning. Its Texas Outdoor Family Workshops will help families learn basic outdoor skills. A calendar is available online. It also explains the Junior Naturalist Program.

About a two-hour drive southwest of Dallas is **Comanche Peak Nuclear Plant**. Area colleges and businesses are offering courses, such as computer science, to help youngsters understand this field. Although some of the Dallas area's science museums and nature centers are listed in **Chapter 1: Places to Go**, the following should be of special interest.

NATURE

BOB JONES NATURE CENTER AND PRESERVE

355 E. Bob Jones Rd., Southlake 76092 (817) 491-6333 Website: www.bjnc.org

Hiking trails, a butterfly garden, nature classes, star parties, bird hikes, and an indoor nature center with small critters are among the many attractions at the Bob Jones Nature Center and Preserve, an 85-acre preserve in Southlake, near Grapevine Lake. The preserve and the adjacent Bob Jones Park were named for a Civil War–era slave and pioneer farmer. Two popular programs are the Second Saturday Club for families with children ages 4 to 12, and the Outdoor Action Kids program, which is an eight-week course for students in the sixth through eighth grades that is given twice yearly to train them in nature activities that will enable them to volunteer at the center. Birthday parties are also welcome here. Visitors do not have to live in Southlake to participate.

CONNEMARA CONSERVANCY

P.O. Box 793808, Dallas 75379 (214) 351-0990 Website: www.connemaraconservancy.org

Located along Rowlett Creek north of Plano in Allen, Connemara Conservancy is a 72-acre nature preserve that in years past featured outdoor sculpture and performances of music and dance. However, at the date of this publication, the preserve is usually closed in order to let the land rest and recuperate.

Members work with landowners and communities to conserve and protect the natural landscapes of North Texas. They also plan periodic events and guided walks at Connemara, such as bird watching and nature journaling, while the preserve is closed to the public on a regular basis. A Family Nature Club has been formed. Events are usually free, but call or reply online to register. No water or restroom facilities are on the premises. Sturdy shoes are recommended.

Directions. From I-75 in Allen, exit Bethany. Go west one mile and turn left (south) on Alma. Take the next left through an open gate. Park to the left. If you see Hedgcoxe and a Tom Thumb, you've gone too far.

DALLAS COUNTY PARK AND OPEN SPACE PROGRAM

411 Elm, Ste. 250, Dallas 75202 (214) 653-6653 Websites: www.dallasparks.org; www.dallascounty.org

Beginning in 1977, Dallas County and various private interests have been working together to acquire natural areas to preserve as public open space parkland. More than 3,000 acres are in the system. The terrains vary from grasslands to wetlands to woods, and they all welcome visitors free of charge. Most are suitable for hiking and informal picnicking. Insect repellent would be handy to have along. Remember to bring water and something to store trash in to leave the area undisturbed. These areas are maintained by the cities in which they are located. For more information, call the city's park department or Dallas County Park and Open Space Administrator at the number above. You might ask for a brochure that outlines all of the preserves.

Cottonwood Creek Preserve is known for its beautiful display of wildflowers in the spring. It includes 220 acres of natural land. Points of interest are noted along the creek trail. It's recommended for nature study, picnicking, and hiking on the two-mile natural surface trail that loops around. To reach this preserve in Wilmer, take I-45 South and turn east on Belt Line. Turn north on Goode and then east to the end of Cottonwood Valley Rd. Call (972) 441-3222.

Elm Fork Preserve is 44 acres of heavily wooded land in northwest Dallas County used for hiking and nature study. Take Sandy Lake Rd. west from I-35 to R. J. McInnish Park and go south through the park entrance to the preserve at the southeast corner of the park. Park at the back by the softball complex in McInnish Park. There are restrooms and a picnic/playground area. A trail has been paved along the river. Call Carrollton Parks and Recreation Dept./Elm Fork Preserve at (972) 466-9813.

Cedar Ridge Preserve covers 604 acres of wilderness in Dallas next to City of Dallas Escarpment Park. It's suitable for study of plant and animal habitats and hiking. The Dogwood Canyon Audubon Center is here. (See **Audubon** in **Chapter 1: Places to Go.**) Drive south on I-35 to Hwy. 67 South (sign says Cleburne) and take I-20 West (sign says Fort Worth). Exit Mountain Creek Pkwy. and go south (under the freeway). Drive two miles to the preserve, formerly the Dallas Nature Center. Restrooms and picnic areas are at the Audubon Dallas buildings; call(214) 653-6653.

Grapevine Springs Park Preserve in Coppell was originally established as a park in 1936, but it was abandoned after a few years and became very overgrown. In 1991, Dallas County acquired the property, so it is again part of the park system and a subject of interest to both archaeologists and historians. In 1843 it was the temporary capital of Texas for about three weeks while Sam Houston tried to sign a treaty with a delegation of Cherokee Indians. The treaty was to be executed at the full moon, but it was a blue moon month with one full moon at the beginning and one at the end of the month. Sam Houston was at the site for one moon and the Indians for the other. They met at another place later.

The 15 acres of this park are said to look like a sunken water garden when it rains, for the WPA built channels in a drainage pattern along the creek. The park has one mile of bark-covered pathway and a natural surface nature trail as well as picnic tables. To reach the park, go north on Denton Tapp Rd. to Bethel Rd. and turn west. Go about one mile to Park St. and turn south. It dead-ends into the preserve. Call Coppell Parks at (972) 462-8495.

Joppa Preserve includes a 142-acre lake along the Trinity River, surrounded by 133 acres of prairie woodland. A footpath is suitable for hiking and nature study. Picnicking near the park entrance and bank fishing are popular. Take Old Central Expressway-Texas 310 south from Loop 12 (Ledbetter Drive) to River Oaks and go east to the preserve. Call the Dallas Parks Department at (214) 670-4100.

McCommas Bluff Preserve covers 111 wooded acres on the Trinity River's east bank. It's also the site of a historical marker called the Navigation of the Upper Trinity concerning the barge commerce and the locks on the Trinity during 1900–1910, as well as the riverway for the *Sally Haynes* steamboat. But the area is just as famous because it contained the spring where notorious characters like the Daltons, Jesse James, and Belle Starr watered their horses. It is being surveyed by archaeologists because it was also the site of the abandoned Trinity City from 1871–1911. Now it has a nature trail and is used for hiking, fishing, nature study, and informal picnicking. From Loop 12 in Dallas, go south on Longbranch (which becomes Riverwood at the dead end) and west to the preserve. Or from Longbranch go west at Fairport to the dead end. Call (214) 653-6653.

Post Oak Preserve features an ADA trail that is 1.7 miles round trip from the parking area to the lake and back. An additional 1.75 miles of interlocking natural surface trails are cleared as well. Here is the last large stand of Post Oak savannah that once stretched through this part of the county. It's located in SE Dallas County on Bowers Rd. just south of the DISD Environmental Education Center in Seagoville. The **Earth Day Celebration** is free and open to the public on a Saturday in mid-April from 9 AM to 4 PM. There's no formal parking lot. Call DISD at (972) 749-6900 for information about Earth Day. Dallas County: (214) 653-6653 Website: www.dallascityhall.com.

Trinity River–Mountain Creek Preserve offers an all-weather parking lot, pavilions, tables, grills, playground, canoe launch, equestrian parking lot, and a two-mile ADA trail that loops through the preserve. This 55-acre preserve is located at 1000 Hunter-Ferrell Rd., south of Bolden St. in western Dallas County. Call Irving Parks at (972) 721-2501.

Windmill Hill Nature Preserve consists of 75 acres in DeSoto. The three-mile hiking trail is shady, with hills and slopes. The bridge that crosses 10-Mile Creek is named for musician Stevie Ray Vaughn. There is a 0.5-mile ADA trail. The preserve is located at the southwest corner of Duncanville and Wintergreen roads in DeSoto. Call (972) 230-9653.

DUCK CREEK GREENBELT

For those who prefer some development in their nature areas, Duck Creek Greenbelt offers three miles of concrete trails that loop along Duck Creek in Garland. In February 1992, a Garland girl found a bison bone that was more than 500 years old beside Duck Creek and donated it to the Museum of Nature and Science. Visitors often enter the area at Audubon Park at 342 Oates Rd., east of I-635, where there are paved parking, picnic tables, and a playground as well as the Surf and Swim wave pool. Call (972) 205-2750.

EARTH DAY

Every year on April 22, many families in Dallas and the surrounding areas celebrate the Earth and dedicate themselves to bettering its condition through efforts such as preservation of natural environments and wildlife, elimination of hazardous products, and recycling. Activities range from planting begonias in the front yard to cleaning a local park to attending a city festival. Watch local newspapers, *dallas child*, and *North Texas Kids* for announcements of activities, or call the U.S. Environmental Protection Agency, Region Six at (214) 665-6444. Another source for events is the TXU Energy website: www.txu.com/earthday.

The Sierra Club or the Texas Committee on Natural Resources may also know of other family-oriented Earth Day events. The Heard Museum, the Museum of Nature and Science, the DISD Environmental Education Center, and the Trinity River Audubon Center plan special events in honor of Earth Day. The state parks also participate with special activities. Call to find out what they have planned at the ones near Dallas.

HOME AND GARDEN SHOW

Begin watching newspapers the last week of February for announcements about the Dallas Home and Garden Show, a favorite event for many years. It's usually held on the first weekend in March at Market Hall. The entrance gardens have colorful spring flowers, and beautiful designer gardens are located inside. Usually the Museum of Nature and Science and the Texas Discovery Gardens have exhibits to educate and inspire young gardeners, and children will also enjoy the exhibits about hobbies and ecology. Kids under 12 enter free, and discount coupons may be available. Parking is free. You may want to bring your camera.

L. B. HOUSTON NATURE AREA

More than 300 acres on the Elm Fork of the Trinity River make up the L. B. Houston Nature Area. It is near the area where gold-seekers crossed the Trinity River in the 1800s to reach California. Trails with names like River Trail, Beaver Trail, and Wilderness Way Trail vary from a 0.5-hour walk to a 2.5-hour walk. Restrooms and picnic facilities are at California Crossing Park north of the preserve. Birding and spotting animal tracks are popular activities here. Wait at least two days after a rain. Enter from Tom Braniff Pkwy. north of Highway 114 near Irving. Call (214) 670-6374 for details.

LEWISVILLE LAKE ENVIRONMENTAL LEARNING AREA

201 East Jones at Kealy, Lewisville (972) 219-7980 (gate house); (972) 219-3930 (education coordinator) Website: www.ias.unt.edu/llela

Located south of the Lewisville Lake dam, Lewisville Lake Environmental Learning Area offers almost 2,000 acres of prairies, wetlands, and forests with the Elm Fork of Trinity River running through it. Open to visitors Friday to Sunday. Activities include primitive camping, three hiking trails, birding, kayaking and canoeing, fishing, and picnicking. The third Saturday of each month is a tour of an 1870s **Pioneer Log Homestead**, and the last Sunday of each month is a tour of a **bison herd**.
Admission: $5; children 5 and under, free.

PLANETARIUMS AND OBSERVATORIES

St. Marks School of Texas Observatory is open to the public occasionally for special programs. A program about the Star of Bethlehem is a Christmas favorite. Call (214) 346-8000 for specific dates. The address is 10600 Preston Rd. Occasionally the Texas Astronomical Society hosts novice observer meetings. Call (972) 758-3849.

The Museum of Nature and Science Planetarium is located in the Planetarium Building at Fair Park. Programs are changed periodically and often coincide with exhibits. On the museum's website home page, look under IMAX and Planetarium Shows for programs, dates, and times. It's a public planetarium for Dallas residents and visitors, and times are extended during the state fair. The building has a snack bar and permanent and changing exhibits. Also, birthday parties may be arranged. Buy tickets online or at the Museum of Nature and Science just west of the planetarium building. The planetarium show alone is $4. Enter Fair Park through the Grand Ave. gate off Robert B. Cullum Blvd. Parking is available in front of the museum. Call (214) 428-5555. Website: www.museumofnatureandscience.org.

University of North Texas Sky Theater often performs family planetarium shows on Saturday at 2 PM and 8 PM. It's located in the Environmental Education, Science, and Technology Building. Formal address: 1704 W. Mulberry, Room 150, Denton. Park in Lot 10 across Ave. C.Admission: Adults, $5; children/students, $3. (940) 369-7655. Website:

www.skytheater.unt.edu. From here, if you go to the evening show on the first Saturday of the month, you might ask the director about looking through the domed telescopes at **Rafes Urban Astronomy Center**. No charge. 3250 Tom Cole Rd., west of Denton Municipal Airport, a couple of miles from UNT.

ROWLETT NATURE TRAIL

Rowlett Nature Trail is a 1.3-mile path following the shore of Lake Ray Hubbard in Rowlett. As you enter the greenbelt, you'll find a parking area, picnic tables under ancient pecan trees, and a fishing pond. It's also great for bird watching as well as hiking and other nature studies. Take I-635 to I-30 East. Exit at Belt Line and go left under the overpass. Turn right on Rowlett Rd. and travel about 5 miles. Turn left on Miller, going about 1 mile to the trail, located on the right side of the street. For further details, call (972) 475-2772.

SIERRA CLUB

The Sierra Club is a national organization that was founded about 100 years ago by naturalist John Muir. The club is dedicated to preserving, studying, and enjoying the environment and plans activities for all ages to achieve these goals. It publishes a catalog and newsletter, *The Compass*, which includes notice of environmental issues and activities by nature centers such as the Heard, as well as a calendar of hiking and canoeing outings. Meetings are held monthly at 7 PM at the Center for Spiritual Living, near the NW corner of Inwood and Spring Valley, west of the Tollway. For information about the local chapter call (214) 369-5543, or consult its website: www.texas.sierraclub.org/dallas/.

TEXAS CONSERVATION ALLIANCE

Austin (512) 327-4119
Tyler (903) 592-0909
Website: www.tconr.org/

This non-profit membership organization (formerly Texas Committee on Natural Resources) works with state and local government agencies to acquire and preserve natural areas. Their task forces present programs to schoolchildren and other groups on a variety of subjects, such as recycling, water and air quality, wildlife, pesticides, forests, and wetlands. Each March the Alliance hosts the **Texas Buckeye Trail**, a walk in the **Great Trinity Forest**, to see Buckeyes in bloom, as well as numerous species of shrubs and flowers. A favorite outing is the annual **Texas Wilderness Pow Wow**, which is usually held on an April weekend and includes activities for all ages.

TEXAS TREES FOUNDATION

2100 Ross Ave., Ste. 975, Dallas 75201 (214) 953-1184 Website: www.texastreesfoundation.org

The Texas Trees Foundation (formerly Dallas Trees and Parks Foundation) is dedicated to preserving, beautifying, and expanding parks and other public natural green spaces in a six-county area around Dallas. Through educational programs, this organization hopes to inspire others to build and protect our "urban forest." Texas Trees recommends a trip downtown to **Pioneer Plaza** for a combination history and green field trip. The foundation dedicated the park, which once was a 4.2-acre parking lot, in 1995. In addition to the bronze sculptures of 40 longhorn steers being driven to market by a black cutter, vaquero, and trail boss, look for a trail map and granite replicas of brands from historic cattle ranches, as well as native plants and trees and a stream. The foundation was also responsible for acquiring the land for the Katy Trail. Through the Trees for Dallas program, qualifying local nonprofit organizations and schools may request a 10- to 20-gallon tree.

TURTLE CREEK GREENBELT

Turtle Creek Greenbelt is also for those who prefer a trail more manicured than natural. Both paved and unpaved paths in Dallas and Park Cities begin at Reverchon Park, 3535 Maple Ave., with two miles of paved trail to Stonebridge. The path breaks as it changes from Dallas to Highland Park. It continues along the creek beside Lakeside and St. John's in a beautiful area in Highland Park.

WHOLE EARTH PROVISION CO.

5400 East Mockingbird Lane, Dallas 75206 (214) 824-7444

Exploring the Whole Earth Provision Co. is the next best thing to being outdoors. Provisions include clothing and shoes designed for outdoor activities and travel tools, such as an excellent selection of guidebooks for outdoor activities in Texas and elsewhere. Technical gear includes sleeping bags, tents, compasses, mess kits, and telescopes. Children love the stuffed wild animals, animal masks, backpacks, bug kits, puzzles, books, and many other nature games and toys.

WILDFLOWERS AND SPRING TRAILS

Spring in Texas is gorgeous as the state flower, the bluebonnet, begins to bloom alongside other hardy favorites. Certain areas along highways are seeded and designated non-mowing areas. Towns such as Ennis (25 miles south of Dallas) often create festivals around the bluebonnet in April and feature trails that are great for photography. Contact the Ennis

Chamber of Commerce at (972) 878-4748; website: www.visitennis.org. Bardwell Lake is near the festival. While you're there, you might visit Texas Motorplex, Ennis Railroad and Cultural Heritage Museum, Czech Museum, and Galaxy Drive-in Theatre.

The Texas Department of Transportation provides recorded information updated weekly in the spring about where to find wildflowers, and it has published a pamphlet called *Wildflowers of Texas;* call 1-800-452-9292. Richardson also hosts an annual wildflower festival, and Palestine has the annual **Dogwood Trails**, which is a popular time to ride the Texas State Railroad. Tyler has the annual **Azaleas and Spring Flower Trail**. See **Chapter 6: Day Trips**.

WOODLAND BASIN NATURE AREA

Located in a marshy area on Rowlett Creek at Lake Ray Hubbard in Garland, Woodland Basin Nature Area has a 1,000-foot boardwalk lined by cattails and sedges that extends out into the lake. This is a popular area for fishing and bird watching, and it is wheelchair accessible. There is paved parking. From I-635, go east on Centerville, and turn east on Miller. Follow Miller about one-half mile to the park at 2323 E. Miller Rd. Call the Garland Park and Recreation Department at (972) 205-2750.

ECOLOGY

RECYCLING AND CONSERVATION

Families and businesses are becoming very involved in recycling efforts in their communities, from sorting materials at home and using natural alternatives instead of hazardous house and garden products to buying recycled paper products for home and office uses.

"Too Good to Throw Away" is the motto of Dallas's recycling program. General categories of items collected are plastic, glass, metal, paper, and cardboard. Residents put recyclables in blue recycling roll carts or in blue plastic bags for pickup. To register for a cart and to find out what materials may be recycled and what may not, go online at www.dallascity hall.com/sanitation or call the city's non-emergency number, 311. Also online is a list of drop-off sites. From website www.dallascityhall.com, look under "Health and Environment" to "Clean Air" and "Clean Water" (www.wheredoesitgo.com and www.savedallaswater.com). Follow those links to environmental sites for kids and events. The Dallas Environmental Education Initiative provides environmental programs for Dallas schoolchildren, kindergarten through fifth grade. Look online for this information.

After Christmas, check online under "Sanitation Services" for places to drop off your Christmas tree so it may be recycled as mulch for park gardens and trails, and to find out where to get free mulch. Many other cities in the Metroplex have similar recycling programs. Contact your city hall.

Another excellent website concerning ecology in Dallas is www.GreenDallas.net. It also has a "Green for Kids" link.

DFW Can Recycling benefits Habitat for Humanity. Call (888) 254-9226 for a convenient site. Call AT&T at (800) 953-4400 for locations to recycle your old phone books.

Each March for many years, the Dallas Water Utilities has sponsored the **Water Conservation Poster Contest** for Dallas students in first through eighth grade. The posters are displayed at City Hall during Drinking Water Week. The water education program of the City of Dallas Water Conservation Division includes a speaker's bureau. Call (214) 670-3155 and select "other conservation events" for more information. Look online at www.savedallaswater.com.

SCIENCE

LUMINANT POWER NUCLEAR POWER PLANT

Visitors Information Center, 6322 FM56 Glen Rose 76043 (254) 897-5554

Located about a two-hour drive southwest of Dallas, the Comanche Peak Nuclear Power Plant generates electricity through the nuclear fission process. The plant has two Westinghouse-built reactors. At the visitors information center, families may watch a video presentation, and look over exhibits and displays that explain the operation of the first nuclear power plant in Texas. See **Chapter 6: Day Trips** for other places of interest around Glen Rose. Call for visitors center hours and group visit reservations. Free admission.

COMPUTER SCIENCE

Since Dallas-area elementary schools and some preschools have incorporated computer literacy into their curriculum, today's children are growing up with computers and see them as useful tools and toys in their daily lives. Dallas libraries and museums allow children to use them to gather information and create artwork. For further instruction in computer science, contact the Continuing Education Department of your local university or community college for courses and summer day camps. St. Mark's School of Texas, Greenhill School, and Hockaday offer summer day camps centering on science and computer science.

COLUMBIA SCIENTIFIC BALLOON FACILITY

From the end of April to the end of August is the best time to see this NASA contractor near Palestine working with scientists from around the world who plan to launch scientific instruments (called payload) attached to high-altitude balloons for scientific experiments. The 45-minute tour may be arranged by calling (903) 729-0271 seven to 10 days in advance. Part of the tour is outdoors. Website: www.csbf.nasa.gov. See **Chapter 6: Day Trips** for other interesting activities near Palestine.

SCIENCE FAIR AND DESTINATION IMAGINATION

Dallas-area schoolchildren participate each February and March in the Science Fair and Destination Imagination, formerly the Invention Convention. Winners are selected at each school to go to regional competition. An excellent way to foster curiosity, problem-solving skills, and an interest in science is to be a participant and, win or lose, visit the fair and the convention at the regional competition level. Check with your local school for dates and locations in March or April.

Many college bookstores carry science supplies. In addition to the gift shop at the Museum of Nature and Science in Fair Park, two area businesses that aid in science-related projects are **Heath Scientific** at 320 Texas St., Cedar Hill, (972) 291-4223, and **Lakeshore Learning Store at** 13846 Dallas Pkwy., Dallas, (972) 934-8866. Helpful websites: www.sciencestuff.com, www.sciencebuddies.org, www.societyforscience.org. Destination Imagination website: idodi.org.

FARMERS MARKETS AND PICK YOUR OWN FOOD

FARMERS MARKETS AND NURSERIES

Stopping by the farmers market can be a wonderful experience each week for your family. First, the markets are outdoors, and you can meet the farmers themselves. You are supporting your local economy and encouraging your family to select fruits and vegetables that are so good for their health. Children learn to compare prices among the vendors, to look for ripeness and quality in the produce, and to discover in which seasons certain fruits and vegetables are harvested. Often, the markets make holidays even more special with truckloads of pumpkins or Christmas trees grown in East Texas. Some markets include beautiful plants, crafts, country music, and sometimes barnyard animals. The Wednesday food section of the *Dallas Morning News* lists local markets and what seasonal produce is in good supply. Call the market for hours. Some are only open spring through fall.

CITY OF DALLAS FARMERS MARKET

1010 S. Pearl, Dallas 75201 Info. recording: (214) 939-2808, (214) 670-5885 Website: www.dallasfarmersmarket.org

Serving Dallas for more than 50 years, the City of Dallas Farmers Market has row after row of beautiful fruits, vegetables, and house and garden plants. They also publish an informative yearly calendar. The Fall Harvest Festival at the end of October is a favorite event. The downtown market is located between Harwood and Central, north of I-30 West. Open daily.

FAIRVIEW FARMS MARKETPLACE

3314 N. Central Expwy. (Exit 30), Plano 75074 (972) 422-2500 Website: www.fairview-farms.com

The marketplace has produce, plants, and flowers in late spring and summer. Call for days and times. Sometimes the management offers wagon rides and other entertainment.

FRISCO FARMERS MARKET

6048 Frisco Square Blvd., Frisco (214) 288-2906 Website: www.friscofarmersmarket.org

Seasonally, Wednesdays and Saturdays. 8 AM to 2 PM or until sold out.

NURSERIES

A relatively free (unless like most people you can't resist buying some plants or seeds) nature excursion is one to a local nursery. Children can learn a great deal about identification and care of flowers, trees, and vegetables from this visit. Nurseries usually carry supplies for birds as well as books on gardening, such as Neil Sperry's *Texas Gardener*. Popular nurseries include Nicholson-Hardie, Calloway's, Northhaven Gardens, and Plants 'N Planters. Southwest Landscape Nursery Company at 2220 Sandy Lake Rd. in Carrollton has 40,000 square feet of greenhouse growing space on 10 acres.

PICK YOUR OWN FOOD AND CHRISTMAS TREES, COMMUNITY-SUPPORTED AGRICULTURE

One of the most rewarding family experiences is to leave early before the Texas sun heats up the air and drive out to a pick your own (PYO) farm to hand-pick fruits and vegetables that could not be any fresher. Not only can children see on what kind of tree, vine, or bush the produce grows, but they have the experience of doing something for themselves and will be more likely to enjoy it served later at a meal.

Blueberries, peaches, and a variety of vegetables are most often offered at the farms. Usually, the farm provides a basket, but it's a good idea to ask about containers, restrooms, and picnic areas as well as hours. Do not wear perfume or hair spray because it attracts insects. A hat or visor, tennis shoes, insect repellent, and sunscreen would be wise. Yearly, the Texas Department of Agriculture compiles a list of PYO farms and roadside sales as well as a list of certified farmers markets. The website www.picktexas.com lists PYO farms and farmers markets and offers a "Kid's Corner," which has fun activities and veggie characters. *The Texas Fresh Produce Guide*, which lists the top 20 fruits and vegetables and when they are available, may be ordered from the TDA at 1720 Regal Row, Ste. 118, Dallas 75235, or call (214) 631-0265. Website: www.gotexan.org.

FRUITS AND VEGETABLES

DALLAS COUNTY

Sunnyvale Pecan Orchard. 137 Rebecca Rd. Sunnyvale 75182 (972) 226-7243.

DENTON COUNTY

Smith's Pumpkin Patch at Katie's Country Market. Ride on a wagon to the field and pick your own pumpkins in October only. Fun for families, schoolchildren, and Scouts. Stock up on homemade jam, breads, and crafts. 736 Rock Hill Rd. Aubrey; call (940) 365-2201.

FANNIN COUNTY

Walker's Blueberry Farm (NW of Bonham), 2933 FM 274/Mulberry Rd., Ravenna 75476 (903) 583-4739.

Jenkins Fruit Farm, 269 CR 1600, Ravenna 75418 (903) 583-2220. Blackberries, plums, peaches.

GRAYSON COUNTY

Bailey's Berry Patch, 905 Crawford Rd. (north of Sadler, off FM 901). Call (903) 564-6228 Website: www.txberry.com. Blackberries and muscadine grapes. Summer weekends, activities for kids.

HENDERSON COUNTY

Blueberry Basket, 12462 FM 2588, LaRue 75770 (903) 677-3448 (near Athens) Blueberries and blackberries; May through July.

KAUFMAN COUNTY

Ham's Orchards, 1939 CR 309, Terrell (972) 524-2028 Website: www.hamorchard.com. Popular farmers market store with fruits, vegetables, and ice cream. PYO blackberries May through July.

SMITH COUNTY

Barron's Blueberries, 16478 CR 431, Lindale 75771 (903) 882-6711 (near Tyler).

Rozell's Peach Orchard, 14278 SH 64 W, Tyler 75704 (903) 592-2074 and (903) 597-0864. Mid-June to late July.

The Berry Farm, 9628 CR 429, Tyler 75704 (888) 584-8054. Blackberries, blueberries, raspberries, and preserves; picnic tables, wheelchair accessible, brochure available.

TARRANT COUNTY

Gnismer Farms, 3010 Bowen Rd., Arlington (817) 469-8704 Website: gnismer.com. Berries, melons, vegetables.

VAN ZANDT COUNTY

Blueberry Hill Farms Inc., 10268 FM 314, Edom (903) 852-6175 Website: www.blueberryhillfarms.com.

Lay Berry Farm, Highway 198, Phalba (214) 208-0967 Website: www.layberryfarm.com. PYO berries and vegetables. Fishing on stocked pond. See directions on website. Sixty-five miles from Dallas. Twelve miles from Canton. Located between Canton and Mabank. Might coincide with a trip to Canton's First Monday Trade Days.

COMMUNITY-SUPPORTED AGRICULTURE

GOOD EARTH ORGANIC FARM

8571 FM 272, Celeste 75423 (903) 496-2070 Website: www.goodearthorganicfarm.com

The family offers organically grown items at an affordable price. A member of the Texas Organic Growers Association, Good Earth produces free-range eggs, pasture-raised lamb, and goat milk. Memberships available. Drop-off service.

AUNT SUE'S BARN

13700 N. County Line Rd. Ponder (214) 546-7416 Website: www.auntsuesbarn.com

Community-supported blackberries, raspberries, peaches, nectarines, and more. Limited number of subscriptions available each season. Members receive first picks and know how their produce was grown.

CHRISTMAS TREE FARMS

Not many holiday activities are as festive as loading up the family and heading out to a Christmas tree farm to find the perfect tree for your house. Many of the farms offer extras, such as wagon rides, picnic areas, nature trails, hot apple cider and coffee, crafts, jars of homemade goodies, Santa, small petting zoos, coloring books, and mazes. Children can learn how the trees grow and how the farmer replants as the trees are cut. The farms usually open for business right after Thanksgiving Day. Some offer tours for schools and other organizations. For more Texas locations and details, go online at www.texaschristmastrees.com.

GRAYSON COUNTY

Elves Christmas Tree Farm, 601 Harvey Lane, Denison (903) 463-7260 Website: www.elveschristmastreefarm.com. Virginia pines, school tours. October: pumpkins and activities for families.

HUNT COUNTY

Kadee Farm, 5054 Highway 69 South, Greenville 75402 (903) 883-3279 Website: www.kadeefarm.com. 7 miles south of Greenville. School tours. Activities for families.

KAUFMAN COUNTY

Wells Family Farm, 11051 CR 2312, Terrell (972) 524-9000 Website: www.wellsfamilyfarm.com. Virginia pines, Leyland cypress, family activities. PYO blackberries in May–season end.

VAN ZANDT COUNTY

Canton Christmas Tree Farm, one mile east of Canton. I-20, Exit 528 at FM 17 (214) 808-6467 Website: www.cantonchristmastreefarm.com. Fraser fir, school tours.

WOOD COUNTY

McNew Star M Plantation, 2914 Highway 276 W, Quinlan (903) 356-2195 Website: www.christmastreemcnew.net. Virginia pines, school tours.

PETS AND WILDLIFE

PETS

Bonding between children and their pets is a very important part of childhood, providing them with a loyal friend and teaching them about kindness and responsibility. A trip to a pet store can be very educational and entertaining whether or not you plan to adopt. A highly recommended place to find a family friend is a local animal adoption center/shelter. Check your city's offices or look up Humane Societies in the yellow pages for numbers and call for hours. Then go by for a visit. Most will arrange tours for groups and also mention opportunities for volunteers. These organizations can give you information about low-cost spay/neutering surgery for pets you already own. The Texas Kennel Club presents an All-Breed Dog Show and Obedience Trials, and the North Texas Cat Club schedules cat shows.

CITY OF DALLAS PET ADOPTION CENTERS

1818 N. Westmoreland, Dallas 75212 adoption (214) 671-0249; missing pet (214) 671-0315; registration (214) 671-0106 Website: www.dallascityhall.org (select "Today I Want to...Adopt a Pet")

The City of Dallas operates a new center where citizens may bring homeless animals, arrange spay/neuter, or adopt a pet. A homeless animal without a collar or tags is kept for 72 hours and then checked for adoptability. If not adoptable, it is euthanized. Adopting a pet may cost about $85. These animals are microchipped, sterilized, and current on vaccines. A helpful website is www.petfinder.com. The **Dallas Coalition of Animal Owners** rescues purebred dogs that are not adopted and tries to find them a home. Call (214) 349-4897 if you are interested in these pets.

THE SOCIETY FOR THE PREVENTION OF CRUELTY TO ANIMALS OF TEXAS (SPCA OF TEXAS)

362 S. Industrial Blvd., Dallas 75207 (214) 742-7722, 1-888-ANI-MALS; McKinney Shelter: (214) 742-7722; Websites: www.spca.org; www.dfwpetnet.org

The SPCA was established in 1938, and volunteers have been active ever since in finding homes for homeless animals, offering low-cost spay/neutering surgery, investigating complaints of cruelty, locating lost pets, gathering stray animals for their safety and the safety of citizens, and scheduling youth programs on pet care and responsibility. On the website is a shopping link and lists of rescue groups and other shelters.

To surrender your pet, you must have a reservation. The SPCA no longer euthanizes animals.

The dogs are divided into rooms according to whether they are large or small, male or female, or puppy or full grown. Cats usually occupy a separate room. The SPCA does almost everything a family vet would do, including spay/neutering, and offers the pets for about $80 to $200. They ask families questions about the animal's new home and length of time the animal will be left alone. Also, they answer your questions about health care, behavior, and feeding. Groups may call to arrange a tour of the facility.

The SPCA holds owner and pet fun runs, parades, and walk-a-thons. This is a fun way to show children the many breeds of pets. Volunteers are needed at these events. If you lose a pet or find a lost one, call or go online at www.dfwpetnet.org.

If your family would like to adopt a pet offsite, the SPCA is also at Northpark Center before Christmas, and PetSmart stores periodically offer adoptable cats and dogs from the SPCA.

OPERATION KINDNESS

3201 Earhart Drive, Carrollton 75006 (972) 418-PAWS Website: www.operationkindness.org

Operation Kindness is a no-kill adoption agency for pets. Call ahead or e-mail to surrender a pet. They only accept pets if room is available. The shelter is closed the last Tuesday of each month. The website provides links to emergency information and lists of other shelters and rescue groups. Each year they sponsor a family and pet festival called Dog Day Afternoon.

DOG AND KITTY CITY

2719 Manor Way, Dallas 75235 (214) 350-7387 Website: www.dognkittycity.org

Located near Love Field Airport, Dog and Kitty City is a no-kill shelter operated by the **Humane Society of Dallas County**. They rescue and care for dogs and cats, which are spayed/neutered before adoption.

EMERGENCY ANIMAL CLINICS

First location: 12101 Greenville Ave., Dallas 75243 (972) 994-9110 (west side of Greenville at Markville, near LBJ Fwy., on the back side of the strip mall, behind the stores)

Second location: 401 W. President Bush Turnpike, Ste. 113, Richardson 75080 (972) 479-9110 (located west of Central/75) Website: www.dallasemergencyanimalclinic.com

The Emergency Animal Clinic is a veterinary clinic offered as a service by more than 50 veterinarians for after-hours pet care. Hours are Monday–Thursday, 6 PM to 8AM, and 6 PM Friday to 8 AM Monday; 24 hours on holidays. The fee here may be more than the usual fee for veterinary services during the day. Maps are online.

Additional Clinics:

North Texas Emergency Clinic, 1712 W. Frankford Rd., Ste. 108, Carrollton (972) 323-1310 Website: www.ntepc.com.

The E-Clinic, 3337 N. Fitzhugh Ave. (west of Central/75) Dallas (214) 520-8388 Website: www.eclinic.org.

FRITZ PARK PETTING FARM

312 E. Vilbig, Irving 75060 (972) 721-2501

Offered by the Irving Parks and Recreation Department only in June and July, the Fritz Park Petting Farm has cows, horses, goats, sheep, chickens, pigs, and more that graze and nap among admiring children. The farm also has an incubator where children can watch chicks hatch right out of the eggs. A birthday room may be reserved by Irving residents for parties. Tours are available and volunteers are appreciated at the farm, which is open Tuesday to Saturday from 10 AM to 6 PM and Sunday from 2 PM to 8 PM, if the weather permits. Free admission.

PETPARKS FOR DOGS

Dallas has two off-leash parks designed for dogs and more in the planning stages. Hours are 5 AM to midnight, and they are closed when wet, even if the day is sunny. Call the recorded info line at (214) 670-4100. **Bark Park Central** is located under the Central/75 overpass at the corner of Good Latimer Expwy. and Commerce St. downtown. It's closed on Mondays for maintenance. **Mockingbird Point Dog Park** is at White Rock Lake, 8000 Mockingbird, near Buckner Blvd. It's closed on the second and fourth Monday of every month. Two other off-leash area dog parks are 2222 W. Warrior Trail, Grand Prairie, and Jack Carter Park, 2199 Spring Creek Pkwy., Plano.

WILDLIFE

Texas has abundant wildlife in spite of development, and environmentalists are working diligently to protect it as well as exotic wildlife imported from other lands. In addition to **Dallas Zoo, the Dallas World Aquarium, the Museum of Nature and Science, Dallas Aquarium,** two **Audubon** centers, **White Rock Lake,** and the **Heard Museum** (discussed in **Chapter 1: Places to Go**), wildlife may be studied at some other museums, zoos, and wildlife preserves and parks near Dallas. See

Chapter 6: **Day Trips** for wildlife areas in Fort Worth, Tyler, Denison, Waco, and Glen Rose. Good places to see local wildlife are in the open space preserves listed earlier in this chapter, as well as sites in chapter 4 under **Lakes, State Parks, and Recreation Areas.** The purchase of a Texas Parks and Wildlife Conservation Pass allows you access to many places that are closed to the general public and offers a variety of field trips. A helpful site is www.tpwd.state.tx.us.

CANYON OF THE EAGLES LODGE AND NATURE PARK, VANISHING TEXAS RIVER CRUISE

16942 RR 2341, Burnet 78611 (800) 474-8374, (512) 334-2070
Websites: www.canyonoftheeagles.com; www.vtrc.com

Migrating bald eagles, black-capped vireos, and golden-cheeked warblers stop to winter in the wooded area around Lake Buchanan in the Hill Country. At the Canyon of the Eagles Lodge, visitors can reserve a spot on the **Vanishing Texas River Cruise**. The 70-foot, 200-passenger cruise boat is launched November–March, daily except Tuesday, in search of the bald eagle. The 2½-hour trip goes through scenic wilderness areas up the Colorado River Canyon. In case of bad weather, the boat has an all-weather deck. The tour leaves from the Canyon of the Eagles Park Store. You may want to bring binoculars, a movie camera, sturdy shoes, and a camera with a telephoto lens. A small concession is aboard the boat. Wildflower cruises are offered in April and May. A raptor rehabilitation organization releases healed raptors on Freedom Flight cruises. Check the website for other cruises and services.

Near Burnet, the **Canyon of the Eagles Lodge and Nature Park** is on 940 wooded acres along Lake Buchanan. Forty-four lodge rooms, 20 cottages, and RV and camping facilities are available for guests. Attractions include a preserved wildlife habitat, 14 miles of nature trails, a fishing pier, a five-mile lakeside beach, the Eagle Eye Observatory (which has two telescopes and an "Observing Salon"), Bedrock Grill Restaurant, and the park store, which rents kayaks, canoes, and small sailboats. For more family fun, contact www.lakebuchananadventures.com for wilderness and waterfall guided paddle trips up the Colorado River Valley.

At **Fairfield Lake State Park**, the park ranger can show visitors where to look for bald eagles that migrate there in the winter. Call (903) 389-4514.

INTERNATIONAL EXOTIC ANIMAL SANCTUARY

This big-cat sanctuary cares for lions, tigers, cougars, jaguars, bobcats, leopards, and sometimes bears. It's located west of DFW Airport off Hwy. 114. Take the Bridgeport exit at Boyd. Reservations for ages 7 and older may be made for regularly scheduled tours at 11 AM and 3 PM on Saturday and Sunday. Call (940) 433-5091 for this and weekday tours.

The tour takes about one hour, and guests walk 0.6 miles on a gravel path. Website: www.bigcat.org.

Another sanctuary is **In-Sync Exotics Wildlife Rescue and Education Center**, located in Wylie near Lake Lavon dam. Call (972) 442-6888. Website: www.insyncexotics.com.

WILDSCAPES

Texas Parks and Wildlife offers suggestions for creating a landscape in your yard that will attract wildlife. Patterned after the National Wildlife Federation's Backyard Wildlife Habitat program, the Texas Wildscapes information packet includes lists of native plants, brochures on butterfly and hummingbird gardening, information on feeders and nest boxes, and an application. Send in the completed application after implementing your habitat design, and TP&W will send you an achievement certificate and a sign designating the site. Address inquiries to Texas Wildscapes, 4200 Smith School Road, Austin 78744. You can also read details and get registration materials online at www.tpwd.state.tx.us/nature/wildscapes/.

Demonstration sites in the area include Cedar Hill State Park on Joe Pool Lake and White Rock Lake. For information about the sites, call the Urban Fish and Wildlife program leader at (972) 293-3841.

ANIMAL EDUTAINMENT: CRITTERMAN

Denton (940) 365-9741 Website: www.critterman.com, www.animal.ed.com

Safari guides will bring to your location part of their collection of more than 60 non-releasable, rescued animals that act as "ambassadors" for their species. The collection includes tarantulas, snakes, a beaver, a grey wolf, a hedgehog, an alligator, an owl, and more. This traveling safari costs about $250 and up and is very popular for birthday parties, day care, and school groups.

HISTORY AND POLITICS

Historical organizations in the area are preserving history in museums, homes, farmsteads, and more so that future generations may see and appreciate the artifacts of the developing state of Texas. The **Texas Historical Commission** is promoting "heritage tourism," in which Texas is divided into 10 scenic driving trails. North Texas is in the **Texas Lakes Region**, and the map in their brochure features 30 cities and attractions from the 31-county area. The Commission has developed suggested itineraries, such as the Dinosaur Trail, the North Texas Horse Country Tour, and the

Dallas–Fort Worth Area Arts Tour. The brochure may be downloaded, or visitors can call (817) 573-1114 or look online at www.texaslakestrail.com. **Aviation museums** may be found in this chapter under **Transportation**.

HISTORIC ARLINGTON

ARLINGTON HISTORICAL SOCIETY

1616 West Abram, Arlington 76013 (817) 460-4001 Website: www.arlingtonhistoricalsociety.org

The Fielder House Museum and the M. T. Johnson Plantation Cemetery and Historic Park are operated by the Arlington Historical Society, which is dedicated to preserving the historic landmarks of Arlington and educating the public about their heritage. In early December the museum usually hosts a tree lighting, which includes carriage rides, bake sale, Santa, and home tour.

Built as a private residence in 1914, the **Fielder House Museum** has served since 1978 as a place where the history of Arlington comes to life through exhibits. The upstairs rooms are furnished to represent an early barber shop and a bedroom and nursery. A general store is downstairs. The basement houses a collection of irons and other tools of daily life, a root cellar, and a steam engine train handcrafted to 1/12 scale. Call or look online for hours, tours, and special events. Children who are about 8 or older would probably enjoy the museum the most. The museum is located at 1616 W. Abram at Fielder.

The **M. T. Johnson Plantation Cemetery**, which has Texas state historical markers, is located at 621 Arkansas Lane in Arlington, northeast corner of Arkansas and Matlock. Contact the historical society before going because the gate is usually locked. The gravestones date from about 1831.

At **Knapp Heritage Park** visitors, by appointment, may tour a 1910 North Side School that is furnished with school desks, the Joplin-Melear cabin, and the P.A. Watson cabin, which is a dog-trot house with a furnished kitchen on one side and bedroom on the other. The Front Street Festival is a popular event that includes living history demonstrations, artisans, food, and live entertainment. While in Arlington, visitors may want to drive by the **Stallions at Lincoln Square** sculpture located at Highway 157 and I-30 in North Arlington.

HISTORIC CARROLLTON

A. W. PERRY HOMESTEAD MUSEUM AND BARN

1509 North Perry, Carrollton 75006 (972) 446-6380 Website: www.cityofcarrollton.com

Traveling in a covered wagon from Illinois to Texas in 1844, the Perrys were some of Carrollton's earliest settlers. This 10-room home built in 1909 is furnished with antiques and interesting memorabilia to remind us of the way we were and to share this history with children. Children will like the old farm tools in the barn. The Homestead is open Wednesday through Saturday, 10 AM to 12 PM and 1 PM to 5 PM; tours and birthday parties are available. An Old-Fashioned Christmas is a popular festival. Admission is free, but donations are accepted.

OLD DOWNTOWN CARROLLTON SQUARE

The Old Downtown Square in Carrollton is bordered by Broadway and Main streets and centered around a gazebo, which serves as a focal point for festivities during special events and on holidays such as the Carrollton Christmas Parade and the October Country Fair. Just a little north of the square at Main and Carroll is a historical marker.

HISTORIC CEDAR HILL

PENN FARM AT CEDAR HILL STATE PARK

1570 FM 1382, Cedar Hill 75104 (972) 291-3900 Website: www.tpwd.state.tx.us/park/cedarhil/

Overlooking Mountain Creek Valley in southwest Dallas County, **Penn Farmstead** is located in Cedar Hill State Park by Joe Pool Lake. In 1854 John Anderson Penn settled here, and his descendants owned the family stock farm for more than a century. The original farm was about 1,100 acres and some of the original structures, built of local oak and eastern red cedar, still survive. Both reconstructed and historic buildings from the mid-1800s through the mid-1900s serve as an educational resource and setting for demonstrations, special events, and displays. Self-guided tours are available daily. Groups should make reservations for guided tours.

HISTORIC DALLAS

Dallas's founder **John Neely Bryan** (1810–1877) was a Tennessee lawyer and adventurer who heard about the Three Forks area of the Trinity River and decided to see what was there. Around 1841, he staked a claim on a bluff overlooking the Trinity and went about the business of negotiating with the local Indians, farming, and planning a town that he named Dallas. A replica of his cabin is located at Dallas County Historical Plaza in front of the Old Red Courthouse Museum.

In addition to **Dallas Heritage Village, Hall of State, Museum of the American Railroad, African American Museum, Dallas Firefighter's**

Museum, Dallas Holocaust Museum, Frontiers of Flight Museum, Old Red Museum, Sixth Floor Museum, Fair Park, and West End Historic District mentioned in Chapter 1: Places to Go, Dallas has many other landmarks worth visiting that are still very active.

The websites of these historical societies are very informative about Dallas history and offer links to other nearby points of interest. The Dallas County Heritage Society is located at Dallas Heritage Village, (214) 421-5141, and the Dallas Historical Society (www.dallashistory.org) is located in the Hall of State at Fair Park, (214) 421-4500. The Historical Society offers tours of the Dallas area, often led by historians. The Dallas County Historical Commission (www.dallaschc.org) is located in the Old Red Museum, (214) 653-7601. A good website provided by the University of North Texas is the "Portal to Texas History": www.texashistory.unt.edu.

Preservation Dallas, located at 2922 Swiss Ave., offers walking tours of the Wilson Historic District and information on historic sites and neighborhoods as well as related books and periodicals. Call (214) 821-3290. Website: www.preservationdallas.org.

DALLAS CITY HALL

1500 Marilla (Ervay and Young), Dallas 75201 (214) 670-3011
Website: www.dallascityhall.org

The four-acre plaza surrounding City Hall with its imaginative sculpture by Henry Moore will first catch the interest of youngsters. The plaza is the setting of festivals during the year and the site of the city Christmas tree and its annual lighting ceremony. Architect I.M. Pei designed the 10-level cantilevered building, which opened in 1978. Inside, there is a good view of the levels from the seventh floor, and there are usually art exhibits. Tours may be arranged by calling your local councilman or (214) 939-2701. The Dallas Police and Fire Communication Center is located here. While you are in the neighborhood, visit the historic Pioneer Park Cemetery about a block west at Griffin and Young, where many early Dallasites are buried. Dallas Convention Center is also nearby on Griffin. See Tours of the Working World (just below) for more details about City Hall.

Outdoors, between the cemetery and Convention Center, are the 70 bronze longhorn steers and watchful bronze cowboys erected to commemorate the cattle drives of the Old West.

DALLAS COUNTY HISTORICAL PLAZA

The Dallas County Historical Plaza is a memorial to Dallas history. Located in the center of Elm, Houston, Commerce, and Market streets, the plaza is home for a representation of the John Neely Bryan log cabin, built before 1850. A historical marker explains the contribution of the log cabin pioneers of Dallas County. On the southwest side, the **Old Red Museum of Dallas County History and Culture**, a sandstone Romanesque Revival structure completed in 1891, offers individual and guided tours of its collection of memorabilia related to Dallas history. The **John F. Kennedy Memorial**, a white cenotaph, is in front of Dallas's current courthouse. **Dealey Plaza**, located one block west, was the actual site of the assassination.

DEALEY PLAZA

Bordered by Houston, Elm, and Commerce, Dealey Plaza is dedicated to George B. Dealey, who founded the *Dallas Morning News*, but its location near the Texas School Book Depository, now the Dallas County Administration Building, has also made it the site of a memorial plaque to John F. Kennedy. The **Sixth Floor Museum** (see **Chapter 1: Places to Go**) is located in the Dallas County Administration Building.

DAUGHTERS OF THE AMERICAN REVOLUTION HOUSE

Open to the public during the State Fair of Texas, the Daughters of the American Revolution Continental DAR House is a colonial white house located at the north end of Fair Park. The Jane Douglas Chapter houses a library of 3,500 genealogical books and bulletins as well as 19th-century memorabilia, such as furniture, dishes, campaign buttons, and tools used in everyday life. The displays change each year. It is free to the public and handicapped accessible by the side door. It's located in Marine Corps Square in front of the Women's Museum. Call (214) 670-8400 for more information.

INTERNATIONAL MUSEUM OF CULTURES

7500 W. Camp Wisdom Rd., Dallas 75236 (972) 708-7406 Website: www.internationalmuseumofcultures.org

Opened in 1981 on the International Linguistics Center campus in southwest Dallas, the International Museum of Cultures has several permanent exhibits, including displays of contemporary cultures of Ecuador; Papua, New Guinea; and Amazonian Peru. The museum focuses on the indigenous peoples of existing communities in remote locations of the world, as well as our own communities. There are some hands-on exhibits and an International Expressions gift shop, and tours are available. It is handicapped accessible, and there are picnic tables outside the dining hall.

From I-20, take the Cedar Ridge Rd. exit and go .5 mile south to Camp Wisdom Rd. Turn right and go 1 mile west to the ILC entrance, and then turn west to the museum parking area. The museum is near Joe

Pool Lake and Cedar Ridge Preserve. Tours may be arranged for groups of 10 or more.

Admission: $3 for students/seniors; $4 for adults.

Hours: Monday to Friday, 10 AM to 4 PM; closed Saturday and Sunday.

JUANITA J. CRAFT CIVIL RIGHTS HOUSE

2618 Warren Ave., Dallas (214) 670-8637 for tours

Dallas Office of Cultural Affairs: (214) 670-3687

Website: www.nps.gov/history. Search: Juanita J. Craft

A leader in the Dallas Civil Rights Movement beginning in the 1930s, Juanita Craft became the first black woman to vote in a Dallas County primary in 1944, when Texas black residents were first allowed to participate in the Democratic primary. She helped organize more than 100 NAACP chapters in Texas and became a leader in the desegregation of the University of Texas Law School, the University of North Texas, and the state fair. Ms. Craft served as a Democratic precinct chairwoman for 23 years, and she became the second black woman elected to the Dallas City Council in 1975 at 73 years old. She died in 1985 at age 83. Her home is in Wheatley Place Historic District. A recreation center and post office are named for her.

Black Dallas Remembered was very influential in preserving the house as a Dallas Historic Landmark and the civil rights ideals for which Juanita Craft stood. Call (214) 670-8637. Website: www.dallasblack.com.

PEGASUS PLAZA

The theme of this beautiful plaza, located at Akard and Main, is based on the Greek myth of the flying horse Pegasus. This symbol is particularly meaningful to Dallasites because of Mobil Oil Company's flying red horse that has resided on top of downtown's Magnolia Building for more than 60 years. The fountain is fed by a natural underground well. Trees, walkways, and boulders carved with symbols of the nine Muses provide a pleasant refuge from city traffic.

SWISS AVENUE AND WILSON HISTORIC DISTRICTS

"Butcher Pen Road" was the original name of Swiss Avenue, which connected Jacob Nussbaumer's farm to the city of Dallas. He changed the street's name to Swiss Avenue to honor his Swiss relatives and friends who settled nearby. In their glory days, the mansions along Swiss Avenue were owned by wealthy Dallas merchants and physicians, but now they are mainly used as offices for Dallas organizations. The neoclassical house at 5303 Swiss, built in 1905, is the oldest along the area between Fitzhugh and LaVista, which has been designated as a historic district. Children can see the differences in architecture from their own homes to those of the early 1900s. Some of these homes are usually on tour at Christmas or Mother's Day. At **Central Square** on Swiss Avenue just west of Hall near Baylor Hospital is a unique preschool playground with swings, slide, and little structures to climb in and on. Azaleas bloom here in the spring, and there are picnic tables and a Victorian gazebo. While on Swiss Avenue, you may also want to visit **Dallas Contemporary**, an art gallery at 2801 Swiss, (214) 821-2522.

Frederick Wilson married a niece of the Nussbaumers and built Queen Anne–style houses on the block to rent or sell. His family home, built in 1899, was at the corner of Swiss and Oak, and it was kept in the Wilson family until 1977. The Meadows Foundation renovated a block of these historic homes and offers rent-free office space to nonprofit community agencies. Free 45-minute tours of the district are offered for individuals and for groups with a reservation. The tours begin at the Wilson House at 2922 Swiss Avenue. Inside the Wilson House is **Preservation Dallas's In-Town Living Center**, which offers a storehouse of information about older neighborhoods in Dallas. The interactive kiosks feature sites within Loop 12 and include pictures, historical background, and special information about what makes that neighborhood particularly worthwhile. Center hours are 10 AM to 4 PM Monday through Friday and 10 AM to 2 PM on Saturday. Call (214) 821-3290.

THANKS-GIVING SQUARE

1627 Pacific Ave. , P.O. Box 1777, Dallas 75221 (214) 969-1977
Website: www.thanksgiving.org

Located downtown at the intersections of Akard, Pacific, Bryan, and Ervay streets, Thanks-Giving Square is a symbol and a home for America's most beloved tradition, according to former President George H. W. Bush. In 1961 Dallas civic leaders decided to design a place of daily spiritual significance within the busy downtown area, a place of tranquility where citizens could reflect, pray, and count their blessings as Americans have been doing since before the Revolutionary War period.

Entering from Pacific, you can hear the three **Bells of Thanksgiving** ring out at noon on weekdays and every half hour on the weekends. Children are drawn to the courtyard with the rushing waters in the fountains. A good view of the fountains is from the ramp above. In the exhibit room is a series of photographs taken by students at Texas A&M Commerce that illustrate the three truths: "We love God," "God loves us," and "We serve God singing." In the **Hall of World Thanksgiving** is the history of the American tradition of Thanksgiving, beginning with John Adams's original proclamation of 1777 and continuing with presidents since then. Visitors will see a life-sized figure of George Washington kneeling in prayer next to the circular river of life.

The **Chapel of Thanksgiving** is a place for prayer and reflection. The spiraled ceiling with its ring of bright lights and stained glass causes visitors to look upward in praise. Upon leaving, visitors are reminded to "Love your neighbor." Sam Houston, president and later governor of Texas, recommended that Texans celebrate two Thanksgiving Days, one in the spring on March 2 for political independence and another in the fall for expressing thankfulness to God, as Americans have been doing since the 1600s. Visitors may place messages of thanks or prayers in the prayer bowl or submit them online. Check the website for special events.

In 1997 a 15-ton monolith was dedicated to the Texas tradition of thanksgiving. Four hundred years of celebration in Texas are outlined on the stone slab, the last of three monoliths that have been placed at the perimeter of the square. The first words of thanks came from Coronado's exploration of Texas in 1541. It states, "It is right to give Him thanks and praise."

Thanks-Giving Square is free and open Monday to Friday, 9 AM to 5 PM, and on Saturday, Sunday, and holidays from 10 AM to 5 PM. Donations are appreciated. You may want to combine a visit here with a tour of the **underground walkway**, which may be entered from Thanksgiving Tower on the Pacific Ave. side. See **Tours of the Working World** (below).

UNION STATION

400 S. Houston St., Dallas 75202 (214) 939-2700

Built around 1914, Union Station was a center of rail activity in the area but now handles DART's Trinity Railway Express, which goes to Fort Worth, and the Amtrak passenger trains. The DART rail line stops right in front of it before going to Dallas Convention Center. See **Transportation** (below) for trips from Dallas. The Grand Hall has 48-foot ceilings and tall arched windows. It may be rented for special events. At the time of this guidebook's publication, renowned chef Wolfgang Puck is the official caterer. A tunnel connects Union Station to the Hyatt Regency Hotel and the 50-story Reunion Tower.

ON THE HORIZON: GEORGE W. BUSH PRESIDENTIAL LIBRARY

When completed, the George W. Bush Presidential Library will also include a museum and independent public policy institute. George and Laura Bush have moved to the Preston Hollow area of Dallas, and their home is close to Southern Methodist University. The library will be located on the east side of the SMU campus, adjacent to Central Expwy. and SMU Blvd. Its mission is to chronicle the history of the Bush presidency and host scholars and dignitaries for dialogue and study. Website: smu.edu/bushlibrary/.

HISTORIC FARMERS BRANCH

FARMERS BRANCH HISTORICAL PARK

2540 Farmers Branch Lane, Farmers Branch 75234 (972) 406-0184
Website: www.farmersbranch.info/play/historical-park

Farmers Branch Historical Park is the site of the oldest rock structure on its original foundation in Dallas County. This home originally belonged to one of Dallas County's first doctors, Samuel Gilbert, and is furnished and open for tours. Within this 22-acre park are a church, the original Farmers Branch train depot, the home of William Dodson (the first mayor of Farmers Branch), an 1856 dog trot stone house, a single- and a double-crib barn, and an 1847 log house. The single-crib barn has a blacksmith shop. Also on the grounds is an All-America Rose Selection Test Garden.

The park is located near the intersection of I-35 and I-635 on Farmers Branch Lane at Denton Drive. The buildings are handicapped accessible, and picnic tables are available. Operating hours are Monday to Friday, 8 AM to 6 PM; Saturday and Sunday from 12 PM to 6 PM. Check the website for special events, especially near holidays. Groups may take guided tours by appointment. Admission to the grounds is free.

Mustang Trail is a 9.37-mile historic sightseeing trail following city streets and beginning and ending at Farmers Branch Historical Park. For details, call (972) 406-0184.

HISTORIC GARLAND

LANDMARK MUSEUM

4th St. and State, Garland 75040 (972) 205-2780 Website: www.ci.garland.tx.us

Located behind Garland City Hall in Heritage Park, the Landmark Museum is in a three-room Santa Fe railroad depot that houses many interesting artifacts dating from the late 1800s. Visitors may also look over a 1910 Santa Fe Pullman car and two homes (unfurnished) built at the turn of the century. Admission is free, and the depot is open on the first and third Saturday of each month from 10 AM to 2 PM. Please call first for group tours. The Historic Downtown Square is recognized as a Main Street City.

HISTORIC GRAND PRAIRIE

A tour of historic Grand Prairie, which was named after the wide area of grasslands bordered on two sides by lines of timber, should include a look inside a historic home. The **Copeland Home**, 125 S.W. Dallas St., is the recently renovated 1904 home of a former physician that houses antiques of old Grand Prairie families and tools of a physician's office of that period. The Copeland Home is open for tours led by docents on the first Saturday of each month from 12 PM to 4 PM. Contact the Grand Prairie Historical Organization for more information (www.gphistorical.com). Also, you might drive by City Hall Plaza for a look at the replica of the **Liberty Bell** which was hung there during the bicentennial. For further information about Grand Prairie, contact Visitor Information at (972) 263-9588. Grand Prairie Western Days celebrate the Old West with a parade, rodeo, county fair, and more family fun.

HISTORIC GRAPEVINE

The earliest settlers came to Grapevine by wagon train in 1844. Its name comes from the wild mustang grapes that once grew on the Grapevine Prairie, which is now the location of DFW Airport. Grapevine has 75 historic homes and buildings dating from 1865, and the visitors bureau can provide visitors with a list of homes and addresses. Liberty Park Plaza includes the Visitor's Bureau and Torian Log Cabin. Another place of historical interest is Heritage Center, which has the Historical Museum in a 1901 depot, a railroad section farmer's home, and a tenant farmer's home. The museum is open from 9 AM to 5 PM Monday to Saturday, and 12 PM to 5 PM on Sunday. The **Grapevine Opry** is also nearby for a Saturday evening of family entertainment. Main Street Days is a celebration of Grapevine's heritage that is held the third weekend in May, Grapefest is held in September, and Whistle Stop Christmas is the first two weekends in December.

The historic **Grapevine Heritage Railroad** excursion train pulled by an 1896 steam locomotive or a diesel engine leaves from the Cotton Belt Depot at 707 S. Main on its 21-mile route to the Stockyards in Fort Worth. The trip takes about 90 minutes. Passengers have time to visit in Stockyard Station before time for the return trip. Call (817) 410-3123 for hours, rates, and type of engine. Website: www.gvrr.com. The Grapevine Visitor Information Center is inside the depot.

Grapevine is in the midst of a continuing preservation effort downtown. Architexas has recreated the 1891 Wallis Hotel, a drummers' lodging on the south side of Liberty Plaza across Main from the Palace Theater. Look on South Main by the funeral home for the glass-enclosed horse-drawn hearse from around 1900.

Restoration continues on five acres of the **Nash Farmstead** (626 Ball St.) as it operated in the mid- to late1800s. The original house and barn as well as a family cemetery are on the premises. Two festivals held there are Spring into Nash Farm and Fall Roundup. Call (817) 410-3585 to ask questions or to schedule a tour.

Check with the Convention and Visitors Bureau at One Liberty Park Plaza, Metro (817) 410-3185 or (800) 457-6338. Website: www.grapevine texasusa.com

HISTORIC IRVING

Designated a historical landmark, the restored and furnished 1912 **Heritage House Pioneer Home,** located at 303 S. O'Connor, is open on the first Sunday of each month, March to December, from 3 PM to 5 PM or by appointment. The house is not accessible by wheelchair. In the park across the street, find the 1887 Caster Cabin, the original water tower, and a depot. Details about historic trails in Irving are in the book *Irving: A Texas Odyssey,* and the trails map is the model for the mosaic tile map in the DART Station in the Downtown Heritage District on Rock Island at Main. Websites: www.irvingheritage.com; www.irvingtexas.com.

NATIONAL SCOUTING MUSEUM

1329 W. Walnut Hill Lane, Irving (800) 303-3047, (972) 580-2100 Website: www.bsamuseum.org

In addition to Scouting artifacts, the 50,000-square-foot museum has a Cub Scout fort, knot-tying wall, Scout Shop, canteen, six-lane pinewood derby track, laser shooting gallery, and animatronic characters who tell Scouting and campfire stories. The most impressive exhibit is a mountain-like structure that has a screen on which visitors can simulate mountain bike racing and kayaking. Kids can identify animal tracks on one wall and then visit the Norman Rockwall Gallery.

Hours: Monday, 10 AM to 7 PM; Tuesday to Saturday, 10 AM to 5 PM; and Sunday, 1 PM to 5 PM.

Admission: Adults, $8; seniors and children 4–12, $6; Scouts, $5; ages 3 and under, free.

HISTORIC LANCASTER

Located about 12 miles south of Dallas, Lancaster's town square was platted in 1852, modeled by a settler named Bledsoe after his hometown of Lancaster, Kentucky. The visitors bureau can give you a brief walking tour map pointing out historical buildings, as well as a driving tour map of historic Lancaster. The driving tour includes an MKT railroad depot, the site of a Confederate gun factory, and the Lancaster Airport, which was home of the Ghost Squadron of the **DFW Wing of the Confederate Air Force** from 1939 to 1945. At the Lancaster Airport, World War II artifacts and airplanes include the *Corsair,* which was used in WWII in the Pacific, and the *L-5/0Y1*, which is painted in Marine livery and was used in Okinawa. Ask about rides on vintage aircraft. The museum, located at 720 Ferris Rd., is open on Saturday from 9 AM to 4 PM and Sunday from 12 PM to 4 PM. Call (972) 227-9119 for information. Website: dfwwing.org/. Also on the tour is the **Strain Farm**, continuously operated by the same family for more than 100 years. A two-story Victorian farmhouse is on the premises. For educational tours, call (972) 227-1382.

Favorite events include the Second Saturday on the Square, Oktober-Fest, and Christmas in Olde Towne Lancaster. For more information, contact the Lancaster Chamber of Commerce at (972) 227-2579. Websites: www.lancastertx.org; www.visitlancaster.org.

HISTORIC MCKINNEY

Both the county and town were named after Collin McKinney, a member of the Committee of Five who drafted the Texas Declaration of Independence in 1848. The town square, framed by Virginia, Tennessee, Louisiana, and Kentucky streets, is dominated by the **Old Collin County Courthouse** (1875) which now serves as home to McKinney Performing Arts Center. Visitors browse in the antique stores along the square. A favorite place to eat is the Pantry Restaurant at 214 E. Louisiana, well known for its home cooking and fabulous pies. Just northeast of the square is the renovated 1911 Italianate **North Texas History Museum** on East Virginia at Chestnut; it houses memorabilia of Collin County and the world wars, such as an 1891 typewriter and a mill wheel. As you enter the museum, look up to the right at the 1934 triptych mural done by Frank Klepper of an 1862 Civil War scene in McKinney Town Square. The museum is open Monday to Saturday, 11 AM to 4 PM, and Sunday, 12:30 PM to 4:30 PM. Call (972) 542-9457. Websites: www.northtexashistorycenter.org; www.downtownmckinney.com.

Favorite festivals include Mayfair, October's Collin County Fall Festival, Dickens of a Christmas, and Tour of Homes. The Chamber of Commerce has a walk/ride tour map available that points out historic sites, such as the Old Collin County Jail and the Heard Opera House. Contact the Chamber of Commerce at (972) 542-0163. **Chestnut Square** includes nine restored properties dating back to 1854. Houses, a chapel, a schoolhouse, and Dixie's Store may be toured at 11 AM on Tuesday, Thursday, and Saturday. It's located at 315 Chestnut near the town square. Call (972) 562-8790. Website: www.chestnutsquare.org. The 1900 Heard-Craig House/Center for the Arts, located at 205 W. Hunt St., is open for tours of the 7,000-square-foot home on Tuesday and

Thursday at 2 PM, and Saturday at 1, 2, and 3 PM. Call (972) 569-6909. Website: www.heardcraig.org.

West of McKinney is 165-acre **Myer's Park and Event Center**, which includes **Collin County Farm Museum** (7117 CR 166). This developing museum houses agricultural artifacts, such as early tractors and other farm machinery. Acquisitions include a Boll Weevil machine, a windmill, and a 1936 International truck. In addition to the museum, the park has a show and a horse barn, indoor arena, picnic pavilion, wedding gazebo, and Myer's Woods—35 wooded acres with hiking trails. It is a favorite campsite for Scouts. The museum is managed by the North Texas History Center. Call to see if there are regular hours or if it is only open by appointment. For directions and museum hours, call (972) 542-9457. Website: www.collincountytx.gov/parks. Myer's Park: (972) 548-4792. Website: www.myersinfo.com.

While in McKinney, you may also want to visit the **Heard Natural Science Museum**, mentioned in **Chapter 1: Places to Go**. Additional entertainment could include some pedaling in the swan boats on Towne Lake in warm weather (1400 Wilson Creek Pkwy.) and driving the Crepe Myrtle Trails. Website: www.crepemyrtletrails.org/trails. To reach McKinney, go north on Central Expwy. (US 75). Exit 40 (Louisiana) will take you to the square. Call (888) 649-8499. Websites: www.mckinneycvb .org; www.visitmckinney.com.

HISTORIC MESQUITE

In Mesquite, the **Florence Ranch Homestead** operates as a home museum and community park. Donated by the Florence family, the homestead was built in 1891 and was surrounded by 160 acres. Today it is located on five acres at 1424 Barnes Bridge Rd. Most of the furniture is circa 1891 or earlier. The grounds are the site of community meetings and festivals, and tours may be arranged by calling Historic Mesquite at (972) 216-6468. The house is open on the second Sunday of each month. The **Lawrence House**, near downtown in Opal Lawrence Historical Park (701 E. Kearney), is being renovated and will be open for tours upon completion. The 1874 homestead includes the house, a smokehouse, root cellar, and barns. Website: www.historicmesquite.org.

Visitors may wish to stay in Mesquite for a performance at the **Mesquite Arts Center**, located at 1527 N. Galloway. The facility includes a concert hall, art gallery, black box theatre, puppet theater, and courtyard. Call (972) 216-8122. Website: www.mesquiteartscenter.org. The **Mesquite Championship Rodeo** and **Rodeo City Music Hall** are two other popular venues for visitors. For a calendar of events, call the chamber at (972) 285-0211. Website: www.mesquitechamber.com.

HISTORIC PLANO

Traveling north on Central Expwy. just past Richardson takes visitors to Plano. An exit east on 544, 15th St., leads from pavement to a red brick road, taking you back in time to historic Plano. Old Downtown Plano offers shops, tea rooms, services, a theater, skatepark, and restaurants. The Queen of Hearts Costume Shop, at 15th and Avenue K, is a favorite of all ages. The antique/craft mall on the north side of 15th houses interesting shops and a tea room. Cobwebs Antique Mall and Tearoom is located just off 15th at Avenue J and 14th St. Settled by farmers from Kentucky and Tennessee in the 1840s, Plano survived two fires that devastated the downtown area, the last one in 1897. Since 1979, 13 structures have acquired recognition as historic landmarks, and the Chamber of Commerce can provide visitors with background and maps of both the downtown area and other points of historic interest. A favorite stop is Haggard Park on 15th at Avenue H, which has a gazebo, fountain, and the **Interurban Railway Station Museum**, as well as picnic facilities.

The Texas Electric Railway Car once ran from Denison through Plano on its way to Waco, and it has been restored. The Railway Station Museum contains artifacts of the railroad and early Plano and pictures of area settlers. Operated by Plano Parks and Recreation, it is free and open to the public Monday to Friday, 10 AM to 2 PM; Saturday from 1 PM to 5 PM. For more information or to arrange a tour, call (972) 941-2117. The museum is home to the Plano Conservancy for Historic Preservation, Inc. This group sponsors story time for preschoolers on Friday at 10:30 AM.

At 13th St. and Avenue H stands the John Thornton white frame house, which will become the **Plano African-American Museum**. Thornton, a former slave turned entrepreneur, bought the house in the Douglass neighborhood in 1909.

While in Plano, remember the **Heritage Farmstead** and the **Heard Natural Science Museum** mentioned in **Chapter 1: Places to Go**. **Southfork Ranch**, famous TV home of J. R. Ewing, is located on Parker Rd., 5.5 miles east of US 75, and it is open for tours and events. Call (972) 442-7800. Website: www.southfork.com.

Popular events in Plano include the balloon festival and Dickens-style Christmas downtown. For more information, contact the Plano Chamber of Commerce at (972) 424-7547. Websites: www.planotx.org; www.plano.gov.

HISTORIC RICHARDSON

In pre–Civil War days, this community was called Breckenridge, but this changed when a farmer gave free right of way to entice the railroad to come up from Dallas. The railroad accepted his offer, and the town was named after the railroad contractor, E. H. Richardson, in the 1870s. While in Richardson, remember the **Owens Spring Creek Farm's** museum with its collection of artifacts from the turn of the century introduced in **Chapter 1: Places to Go**. Two favorite annual events are the Cottonwood Art Festival and the May Wildflower! festival. Website: www.wildflowerfestival.com. Call the Richardson Visitors Bureau at (972) 744-4100. Website: www.cor.net.

HISTORIC ROCKWALL

Rockwall was named for an ancient stone wall running under the town. Some scientists believe it to be part of the Balcones Fault, but some of its characteristics lead others to speculate that it may have been built by a prehistoric civilization. A small replica of the wall is outside the restored courthouse in the middle of the downtown square. Visitors can access **Old Town Shoppes on the Square** from I-30 by going north on Highway 205 or 740. You could have lunch downtown or at the new entertainment/restaurant/shopping destination, **The Harbor**, located on the shoreline of Lake Ray Hubbard at 2047 Summer Lee Drive, Rockwall, www.theharboratrockwall.com. Check to see if the *Texas Queen* paddlewheel riverboat is in operation to cruise the lake.

The **Rockwall County Historical Foundation Museum**, located at 901 E. Washington, is open Wednesday and Saturday from 10 AM to 2 PM. Guided tours may be scheduled at (972) 722-1507. Call the Chamber of Commerce at (972) 771-5733 for more information. Websites: www.rockwallchamber.org; www.rockwall.com.

HISTORIC TERRELL

Located 35 miles east of Dallas on US 80, Terrell is another Texas town that grew up along the railroad. The attraction for the railroad was a large underground lake that would provide water for the trains. Terrell was established in 1873. The history of the town is preserved in the artifacts housed in the **Terrell Heritage Museum** in the Carnegie Building at 207 North Francis St. Historical items, such as a 1912 Estey pipe organ and Texas-Midland Railroad memorabilia, are on display. Go east on US 80, take the Business US 80 exit, and turn north on North Francis St. to reach the museum. Call Metro at (972) 524-6082 for more information. The **Robert A. Terrell home**, one of two remaining octagon-shaped homes in Texas, is located on Southwestern Christian College campus on 200 Bowser Circle, but the interior is not open to the public. Website: www.terrellheritagesociety.org

Located at Terrell Airport, the **No. 1 British Flying Training School Museum** features a display of newspaper and magazine clippings, model aircraft, World War II uniforms, navigation equipment, and a plaque given in gratitude for the kindness shown to trainees in the flight school. Terrell was home base for about 2,200 British and 138 American cadets in flying training school from 1941 to 1945. The museum plans to move to a new location on the west side of the Terrell Airport. Please call (972) 524-1714 for hours of operation and fees. From I-20, exit north at Texas 34. Turn right on Airport Rd. and go right onto Silent Wings Blvd. It is located at 119 Silent Wings Blvd. From Business 80 in Terrell, go south on Texas 34 (S. Virginia) and east on Airport Rd. Memberships are available.

While in Terrell, shoppers may also want to stop by the **Tanger Factory Outlet** located along I-20. In this chapter under **Farmers Markets**, you'll find the address for Ham's Orchards, a favorite spot for fresh produce and ice cream. A favorite festival in Terrell is the April Heritage Jubilee. Call the Terrell Chamber of Commerce at (972) 563-5703 for information about Heritage Tours of Terrell and copies of the historic trail and marker maps. Website: www.terrelltexas.com.

TOURS OF THE WORKING WORLD

Just as children love to go to their dad's and mom's offices to see what kind of work they do, family or group tours of the working world outside of their immediate family expand their horizons and begin the process in their minds of selecting careers for themselves. Many of these tours satisfy children's natural curiosity about how products are made or how services are performed. Most of the businesses that conduct tours ask that families and groups call ahead for appointments and remember to cancel the appointments if they cannot come, and the very popular ones often require reservations months in advance. If there is a minimum number for a tour, a family can sometimes join a larger group. One other delightful aspect of taking tours is that most of them are free! Tours listed in other locations in this guide are the **Ranger Ballpark in Arlington**, **Legends of the Game Museum**, **Lone Star Park**, **Texas Motor Speedway**, **Dallas Cowboys Stadium**, and the **SPCA**.

Some businesses are reluctant to advertise tours to the public because they do not have staff to guide tours on a regular basis, but if they were approached individually, they might consider it. Many of the tours listed below are for children who are at least school age because they have longer attention spans and would understand more of what they see than would preschoolers. Suggestions for younger folks include local spots, such as a restaurant, post office, bank, veterinarian's office, hospital, police substation, fire department, high school, grocery store, bakery, donut shop, pet store, dog groomer, pharmacy, and nursery or florist shop. Some of the pick-your-own farms listed will lead tours of their trees, fruits, and vegetables.

ARTS DISTRICT PERFORMANCE HALLS

At the time of publication, the newest additions to the Arts District are not completed, but there's a very good chance that when they are up and running, tours of the facilities will be scheduled. They are all downtown, near the Meyerson Symphony Center. Look for these venues:

Dee and Charles Wyly Theatre (Dallas Theater Center)
Margot and Bill Winspear Opera House (Dallas Opera)
City Performance Hall

CALIFORNIA PIZZA KITCHEN

8411 Preston Rd. at Northwest Hwy., Dallas (214) 750-7067 Website: www.californiapizzakitchen.com/

The CPKids Restaurant Tours include a behind-the-scenes restaurant visit, usually held in the morning. Check with the manager about time, age, and size of group that they can accommodate. Additional restaurants in Plano, Frisco, and Grapevine.

CARTER BLOODCARE

2205 Highway 121, Bedford 76021 (800) DONATE-4 Website: www.carterbloodcare.org

Groups who tour Carter BloodCare learn how vital it is for the public to donate blood. Each component can help different patients with various needs; your single donation can help save three lives! Visitors see the journey that each unit of blood takes to get to the patient and see the separation of red blood cells, platelets, and plasma.

Tours are given by request for groups who are in the seventh grade or older; large groups may be divided into smaller groups for touring. The tour takes about an hour, and reservations must be made in advance.

There is time for questions and discussion about career opportunities at Carter BloodCare. Because blood components are so perishable, lifesaving blood donors are needed every day to ensure an adequate supply for patients in need. Contact Carter BloodCare to schedule the outing. Free.

CHANNEL 8/WFAA-TV

606 Young St., Dallas 75202 (214) 748-9631 Website: www.wfaa.com

Although it does not include live broadcasts, a tour of Channel 8 does take visitors through the familiar newsroom as the guide explains how assignments are made, through their broadcasting studios, through the hallway museum, and into the control room. The one-hour tour, scheduled on Tuesday, Wednesday, or Thursday, requires three weeks' written notice. Groups may choose 10:30 AM or 1:30 PM and should range from 5 to 15 people who are 12 years old or older. The tour info line is (214) 977-6020. Wheelchair accessible. Free.

DALLAS CITY HALL

1500 Marilla, Dallas 75201 (214) 670-3322 Website: www.dallascityhall.com

Tours of the impressive Dallas City Hall begin on the first floor and continue up to the sixth floor in City Council chambers. It may include a peek in the mayor's office if it is not occupied. Wednesdays at 9 AM is a good time to tour because City Council meetings are held then. Tours usually last about 30 to 45 minutes. Your **local councilman** can take you on a tour. See the section **History and Politics** (below) for more about City Hall.

DALLAS/FORT WORTH INTERNATIONAL AIRPORT

(972) 973-5555 Website: www.dfwairport.com

A tour of the second most active airport in the world allows guests to see the inside operations. Make reservations at least four to six weeks in advance for groups no larger than 35 people. The tours, which last 90 minutes, are conducted on Wednesdays between 10 AM and 4 PM for ages 5 and older. Families may join a group. Admission is free. DFW is located between Dallas and Fort Worth, north of Hwy. 183 on the western edge of Irving. When making a tour appointment, the guide will help with directions. To schedule a tour, please contact Barbara Pack, DFW Community Relations: bpack@dfwairport.com. Additionally, visitors may want to stop by **Founder's Plaza** to see planes take off and land and hear live feed of the tower communication. Look under **Transportation** in this chapter.

DALLAS PUBLIC LIBRARY

1515 Young St. at Ervay, Dallas 75201 (214) 670-1400 Website: www.dallaslibrary.org

The best place for information about the programs of the Dallas Public Library is in the monthly *Bookmark* published by the library and their website. The downtown J. Erik Jonsson Central Library and all branches are listed in this chapter under **Storytelling, Libraries, and Bookstores**, and announcements about special tours, exhibits, and educational classes are available through each library's activity sheet and online.

Tours of the downtown **Children's Center** for groups of children through sixth grade may be arranged by calling (214) 670-1671, and tours of the Central Library for older students may be arranged by calling (214) 670-1789. User Education Tours for students in grades four through eight may also be arranged through the Children's Center. Free.

KLIF RADIO STATION
3500 Maple St., Ste. 1600, Dallas 75219 (214) 526-2400

Tours of the radio station are sometimes offered and sometimes suspended for awhile. Call ahead to check current policy.

MARY KAY COSMETICS
Website: www.marykay.com

The history of Mary Kay Cosmetics from 1963 to the present is showcased at the **Mary Kay Museum**, which is open Monday through Friday from 9 AM to 4:30 PM. Guided tours of the museum are available at 10 AM and 2 PM, Monday through Friday. For guided tour reservations, call (972) 687-5720. The museum address is Mary Kay World Headquarters Building, 16251 Dallas Pkwy., Addison.

One-hour tours of the **manufacturing plant** are held Mondays at 2 PM, Tuesdays through Thursdays at 10:30 AM and 2 PM, and Fridays at 10:30 AM. These tours must be reserved three days in advance, and visitors must wear closed-toed shoes. Children under 10 must be accompanied by parents. Mary Kay Manufacturing Facility is located at 1330 Regal Row, Dallas (between I-35 and State Highway 183). Both are closed on major holidays. Call (972) 687-5720 for reservations. Free.

MCKINNEY AVENUE TROLLEY
3153 Oak Grove Ave., Dallas 75204 (214) 855-0006 Website: www.mata.org

The historic McKinney Avenue Trolley Barn tour is given by volunteers who explain the history of electric transit and basically what makes the trolley run. Visitors usually then take a 3.6-mile round trip run along McKinney Ave. at Blackburn to Cityplace through the Arts District to the Dallas Museum of Art, Ross and St. Paul, and back to the barn. Sometimes this is included in a **birthday party** tour in which a trolley is rented and decorated for the birthday child and up to 30 friends. There is a shop at the barn that has souvenir T-shirts, visors, caps, and bumper stickers.

Anyone who comes in is welcome to a barn tour. Group tours must be scheduled in advance. Tours are at 10 AM on Monday, Tuesday, Wednesday, and Friday. Call or look online for hours and days of trolley operation. The trolleys are heated in winter, and one is air-conditioned. A round trip takes about 40 minutes. Barn tours are free, but there is a small fee for the trolley ride tour: children, $1. Riding the trolley is free for everyone.

Now you can ride the DART rail line to Cityplace. Get off the train and board the trolley for destinations such as the Dallas Museum of Art, the Magnolia Theater, and uptown restaurants.

MORTON H. MEYERSON SYMPHONY CENTER

2301 Flora, Ste. 100, Dallas 75201 (214) 670-3600 Website: www.meyersonsymphonycenter.com

Tours of the majestic symphony center, located near the Dallas Museum of Art and the Arts District Theater, include a close look at the concert hall, Betty B. Marcus Park with its water wall fountain, and the Wall of Honor.

Public tours are held at 1 PM on selected weekdays (usually Monday, Thursday, Friday, and Saturday), and they last about one hour. Be sure to call ahead to check for days and times. Sometimes the tours are cancelled because of symphony scheduling. Public 30-minute demonstrations of the **Lay Family Concert Organ** are given once a month, followed by a building tour. Private group tours should be scheduled at least six weeks in advance for groups of 15 or more who are in the sixth grade or older. Call (214) 670-3600. Free.

UNDERGROUND DALLAS/DOWNTOWN

Although children will not find any Ninja Turtles in the two miles of underground tunnel networks, they will still enjoy the adventure of seeing how the buildings downtown are connected and eating at one of the restaurants provided for the working world. The **Dallas Convention and Visitors Bureau** may be able to help with the three main areas of connected buildings and what parts of the tunnels are currently open. Call (214) 571-1000. The tunnel is temporarily closed after Renaissance Tower toward the north end of downtown because a building is closed. Visitors can pick it up again at Republic Center. Websites: www.visitdallas.com; www.downtowndallas.org

If the entire tunnel system is open, one good place to start would be Thanksgiving Tower, which is right by **Thanks-Giving Square** on Pacific. Park underground (fee) and take the elevators to the underground. Various shops and restaurants are open during business hours. Children might enjoy lunch at one of the restaurants. Visitors could travel on to the NationsBank building and to One Dallas Center. Enter the tunnel system again at Lincoln Plaza at 500 N. Akard where the steps down are by cascading water wall fountains. This tunnel passes Dakota's restaurant and the Ross Garage before turning right to the Fairmount Hotel, where your group might go up for a look around. Back into the tunnel again will take you to **Fountain Place**, located at 1445 Ross Ave. Children will love this, especially on a warm day. Tiered fountains and waterfalls surround shaded tables, and trees rise from the middle of the pools. A favorite fountain is the one with dancing waters that shoot one- to six-foot sprays up from the ground: 360 high-pressure geysers shoot from holes in the concrete. Watch out because the temptation to run through it may be too great to resist. Website: www.fountainplace.com.

Families could combine a weekday trip to see a play at El Centro with a trek through the tunnels that begin at NationsBank Plaza on Lamar at Elm and go on to One Main Place, Elm Place, Renaissance Tower, and the Holiday Inn Building at Griffin and Elm. You will also be near the Kennedy Memorial Plaza and the West End. Free.

FORT WORTH: MRS. BAIRD'S BAKERY

Ninnie Baird began baking bread in her kitchen in 1908. The first bakery was built in Fort Worth eight years later. Today more than 2 million loaves of bread are made each week. Tours are offered each hour from 10 AM to 4 PM, Tuesdays through Thursdays, by appointments made at least two weeks in advance. One adult must accompany every 10 children who are at least ages 6 and up. Visitors must wear closed-toe shoes during the 45-minute tour. The bakery is at 7301 South Freeway, Fort Worth 76134. Call (817) 615-3050.

BUREAU OF ENGRAVING AND PRINTING: WESTERN CURRENCY FACILITY

9000 Blue Mound Rd., Fort Worth 76131 (817) 231-4000, 1-866-865-1194 Website: www.moneyfactory.gov

Many of us have probably wished we could just manufacture some money, and here is a facility that does just that—but legally. The Bureau of Printing and Engraving offers free 45-minute tours of their money-printing plant Monday through Friday except holidays. Visitors see exhibits of the history of U.S. paper currency, the production process and its technology, an informative 15-minute film that explains the production process, a quarter-mile walkway that overlooks the currency production floor, the Moneyfactory Gift Shop, and three live demonstration exhibits.

Visitors without reservations are taken on a first-come, first-served basis, and everyone is asked to arrive 30 minutes before tour time to clear security. The Tour and Visitor Center is open from 8:30 AM to 5:30 PM, with group and general public tours being conducted every 30 minutes from 9 AM to 2 PM. Times are extended in June and July. Group tours of

10 or more must call to schedule in advance. Press "2" to talk to the tour scheduler. Tours are available in American Sign Language and Spanish.

TEXAS RANGERS BALLPARK

1000 Ballpark Way, Arlington 76011 (817) 273-5099 Website: tours@texasrangers.com

DALLAS COWBOYS STADIUM

Arlington, Website: www.dallascowboys.com

......

TRANSPORTATION

......

The primary means of transportation in Dallas for many years has been the family car. However, with rising costs, overcrowded freeways, fitness awareness, and conservation efforts, other forms of transportation, ranging from bicycles to rail lines, are gaining in popularity. Some are here as pleasant reminders of bygone days, such as trolleys, paddlewheelers, steam engine–driven trains, and surrey rides. Children love vehicles, beginning with the ones that they power with their feet moving along the sidewalk. They like to ring the bells on the boats and honk the horns on the motorcycles at the amusement parks. A wide variety of transportation is available around Dallas, from a short bus ride to a hot-air balloon ride. Some conversation about what causes the vehicle to go makes any trip as educational as it is entertaining.

Several museums in the area are dedicated to preserving and informing the public about various types of transportation. These museums listed in this guide are the **Museum of the American Railroad, Interurban Railway Museum, Frontiers of Flight Museum, Cavanaugh Flight Museum, Ennis Railway Museum, Confederate Air Force Museum, No. 1 British Flying Training School Museum, C. R. Smith Flight Museum**, and **Pate Museum of Transportation**. A website that has a list of flight museums is www.notaam.org.

The natives usually call freeways by names rather than numbers, so here's a little translation for newbies:

Lyndon B. Johnson Freeway (**LBJ**) = I-635
Central = US Highway 75, north of downtown
Stemmons Freeway = I-35, north of downtown
Woodall Rodgers Freeway = north of downtown; connects I-35E with I-75
Carpenter Freeway = State Highway 183 and Highway 114 from I-35E to the north DFW Airport entrance

AIRPLANES, SHUTTLES, HELICOPTERS, AND HOT-AIR BALLOONS

Even though most of today's parents have grown up accepting airplanes as part of daily life, they will still pause to watch an airplane take off and ascend to unknown destinations. Children love to spot airplanes and helicopters and are intrigued by all the contraptions at an airport, from the revolving luggage conveyors to moving sidewalks. A leisurely trip to the airport when no one is in a hurry to check luggage and catch a flight is an inexpensive and entertaining way to introduce a child to aviation.

Most commercial flights in Dallas leave from **DFW** or **Love Field**, but some of the smaller airports will allow tours. Shuttle services are available for families who do not wish to drive in airport traffic or leave cars at the airport.

Helicopters are often kept at the smaller airports, and some owners offer rides to the public for a bird's-eye view of landmarks and homes. Expensive, but fantastic, hot-air balloon rides are also available. A favorite annual event is the hot-air balloon festival in Plano. Museums devoted to the history of aviation are located at Love Field, DFW, Addison Airport, Terrell Airport, and Lancaster Airport. See **History and Politics** in this chapter as well as **Chapter 1: Places to Go** for more details.

The first two discussed below are the major airports in Dallas, but the ones listed after also contribute a great deal to the community and would be worth a visit.

DALLAS/FORT WORTH INTERNATIONAL AIRPORT

DFW Airport 75261 (972) 973-5555 Website: www.dfwairport.com

Dallas/Fort Worth International Airport, aptly named for its location between the two cities, offers flights daily to 173 destinations. It has five terminals (A to E), numerous stores and restaurants and lots of activity for children to watch.

The **Skylink** train connects all five terminals, with two stops per terminal. If you aren't in a hurry, take a round trip and see skylines, planes, and the offerings of all of the terminals. Each station has a travel-themed mosaic floor. One full trip around takes about 20 minutes. Kid stuff is available at KidZoo at A34 and Lone Star Kids at E16. For kids under 6, attractive play areas are located close to gates B14, C12, and D30. Enter the airport from State Highway 183 on the south, or State Highway 114 or I-635 (LBJ) on the north. The airport has one main road, International Pkwy., which runs the length of the airport, north to south. All terminals, parking areas, and on-site hotels are accessible from this road. The website has maps for directions from Dallas and Fort Worth.

Founder's Plaza, located at 1700 N. Airfield Drive at Texan Trail, is a six-acre observation park with shade pavilions, telescopes, a 50-foot-tall rotating light beacon, and the sound of air traffic controllers as they direct planes in and out. Visitors can watch the planes take off and land. It is at the north end of the airport and can be seen from State Highway 114.

DFW hosts flights of American troops coming home for R&R. The USO has a site near gate B15. To volunteer or get details about arrivals, call the USO at (972) 574-0392.

When the airport opened Terminal D and Skylink, it also spent $6 million on art. The Art Program Specialist at DFW will lead a free 60- to 90-minute tour of the art in the airport if you fill out the reservation form on the website, www.dfwairport.com/art, e-mail art@dfwairport.com, or call (972) 973-4614. A small sculpture garden is located just outside Terminal D parking garage on the arrivals level.

The C. R. Smith Museum, which has a restored DC-3 at its entrance, is located adjacent to the AA Flight Academy at the intersection of 4601 Highway 360 and FAA Rd., southwest of DFW Airport in Fort Worth. This American Airlines museum shows visitors what is needed to conduct a worldwide aviation system through interactive displays, hands-on exhibits, and video presentations on a 30-foot-tall screen. Also available is a Scavenger Hunt sheet, and you'll need to ask for the Museum Map and Guide Brochure. Summer aviation-related day camps may be available for children entering the fourth through seventh grades. Group tours are available but must be scheduled at least two weeks in advance. Days and hours are Tuesday to Saturday from 10 AM to 6 PM. Closed most major holidays. Admission fee. Call Metro at (817) 967-1560. Website: www.crsmithmuseum.org

DALLAS LOVE FIELD AIRPORT

8008 Cedar Springs/LB 16, at Mockingbird Lane, Dallas 75235
(214) 670-6073 Website: www.dallas-lovefield.com

Designated as a World War I training base in 1917, Love Field began its first passenger service in 1929 and has been an integral part of aviation in Dallas ever since. The army named it for pilot Lieutenant Moss Lee Love. Until DFW was built, it was the major airport in Dallas. It still serves airlines such as Southwest, Continental Express, and American Airlines/American Eagle, and it schedules more than 100 flights to 17 destinations daily. Passengers may use their Toll Tag to pay for parking. The best place to view take-offs and landings is on the third floor of the airport's parking garage. Frontiers of Flight Museum is on the east side of Love Field. Look in Chapter 1: Places to Go for more information about the museum.

ADDISON AIRPORT: CAVANAUGH FLIGHT MUSEUM

4572 Claire Chennault Drive, Addison 75001 (972) 380-8800
Website: www.cavanaughflightmuseum.com

Addison Airport is the home for the Cavanaugh Flight Museum. Aviation history from World Wars I and II, Vietnam, and Korea is brought to life through more than 35 refurbished aircraft such as the Fokker D VII, P51 Mustang, and MIG 15. Housed in airplane hangers, these planes are polished, kept in flyable condition, and used in air shows. An aviation art gallery and gift shop are at the entrance. For special occasions, such as Father's Day, pilots may offer Warbird Rides for those 18 years old and up. Some of these planes are flown at Addison's Third of July fireworks celebration, called Kaboomtown. Museum hours are Monday to Saturday, 9 AM to 5 PM, and Sunday, 11 AM to 5 PM. Closed major holidays. Admission for adults is $8; children ages 6–12, $4; ages 5 and under, free.

Also at the Addison Airport, **Discovery Flight** will take visitors up to see some of the best views in downtown Dallas. Contact: (972) 931-0345. Website: www.monarchair.com

LOCAL AIRPORTS

Alliance Airport 2250 Alliance Blvd., Fort Worth 76177 Metro (817) 890-1000

Mesquite Airport 1130 Airport Blvd., Mesquite 75149 (972) 222-8536

Lancaster Airport 730 Ferris Rd./P.O. Box 551, Lancaster 75146 (972) 227-5721

A shuttle service that serves both DFW and Love Field is **SuperShuttle** Dallas/Fort Worth. Call (800) 258-3826. The following are businesses that offer helicopter and hot-air balloon rides. To ride hot-air balloons, it is recommended that children be at least 10 years old.

Airventure Balloonport 1791 Millard, Ste. D, Plano 75074 (972) 422-0212

Zebra Air Helicopters Dallas Love Field, 7515 Lemmon, Bldg. J, Dallas 75209 (214) 358-7200

BUSES, TRAINS, AND TROLLEYS

While DART buses and rail lines are taking families downtown and out to Plano and McKinney Avenue trolleys are taking them uptown, the Trinity Railway Express and AMTRAK trains are taking them out of town. Any of these modes of transportation are going to delight and entertain children. If your family has been to the Museum of the American Railroad and the children really want to experience travel by rail, plan to catch AMTRAK at Union Station going either east or west daily or drive down to Palestine to ride the Texas State Railroad round-trip. Look in **Chapter 6: Day Trips** for passenger trains traveling round-trip from Grapevine to Fort Worth and Palestine to Rusk. Six Flags Over Texas has a passenger train that takes visitors around the perimeter of the park.

AMTRAK

Union Station, 400 S. Houston, Dallas 75202 (214) 653-1101, (800) 872-7245 Website: amtrak.com

All aboard! Amtrak's passenger train service departs daily from historic Union Station, travels to Fort Worth, and connects with a daily train that departs for Oklahoma City, stopping at five cities in between. The daily service heading west out of Dallas goes all the way to San Antonio, and three times a week, you can ride all the way to Los Angeles. The daily train going east from Dallas travels to Chicago. Reservations may be made on the website or at the 800 number. Call the 800 number for a copy of the national timetable and copies of their brochures, *Amtrak America* and *Amtrak Vacations*.

DALLAS AREA RAPID TRANSIT

(214) 979-1111. Website: www.dart.org

The wheels on the DART buses go all over Big D and around 13 other communities, providing inexpensive transportation and saving annually an estimated 24 million pounds of carbon monoxide from polluting Texas's blue skies. Students, RideShare commuters, senior citizens, and mobility-impaired passengers take advantage of DART's special programs. At the rail stations, buy tickets at the ticket vending machines. Cash fares for ninety minutes are adults, $1.75; students with ID, disabled passengers, and children (ages 5 to 11), 85 cents; and seniors (65+), 85 cents. A local Day Pass is adults, $3; reduced fare, $1.50. Transfers are free. Call (214) 979-1111 or use the website for information about day and monthly passes, routes, schedules, and fares. Weekend service is limited.

The DART **Red Rail Line** makes stops from Plano's Parker Road Station and passes Northpark Center, Mockingbird Station, Cityplace, the West End, Union Station, Convention Center, and the Dallas Zoo on its way to the end of the line at Westmoreland in Oak Cliff. The ride from the Park Lane Station to the West End takes about 35 minutes.

The **Blue Line** goes from Ledbetter through downtown and on to the city of Garland. When its first four stations are operational (target date 2009), the **Green Line** will travel through Pleasant Grove, by Fair Park, and on to Farmers Branch and Carrollton. Fifteen additional stations will open at a later date. Be sure you have bought your ticket and are on the correct side of the track when waiting for the train. Try out the **online trip planner** at www.DART.org.

The **Trinity Railway Express** leaves from Union Station on its route through Irving, by **DFW Airport**, and on to **Fort Worth**. It takes 70 minutes to travel from Union Station to Fort Worth's Texas and Pacific Station. To get to DFW, take the shuttle that connects DART's Centreport/DFW Airport Station to all airport terminals, Monday to Saturday. Note the interesting **art** at many of the stations. The design reflects the neighborhood where the station is located. For more information, call DART at (214) 979-1111.

DART offers Handiride buses that have wheelchair lifts. At the DART rail line stations are wheelchair lifts.

Presently, DART is carrying out its 20-year plan to include both a light rail system and commuter rail service. DART offers guest speakers, audiovisual presentations, and special exhibits for groups and school classrooms.

"DART About": Create Your Own Itinerary

So many attractions are along the DART rail line that you could have several "DART-About" days and never repeat a venue. Here are some ideas for experiencing an entertaining and educational day while leaving the driving to someone else and helping to green Dallas. The first step is to pick a departure station and purchase an all-day pass. Let's say you start and finish in Richardson at the **Galatyn Park Station** on the **Red Line**. The Red Line and the **Blue Line** (coming from Garland and White Rock) travel the same track starting at Cityplace Station. Available attractions will be a short walk from the stations. It's a good idea to take DART's phone number with you on the off chance that you need to be rescued: (214) 979-1111. Website: www.dart.org.

Park Lane Station. Take a quick shuttle to **Northpark Center**. Choices are on the website. Shopping, restaurants, food court, movies, children's library, art from Nasher collection. Website: www.northparkcenter.com.

Mockingbird Station. Angelica movies, comedy club, shopping, restaurants, ice cream. Website: www.mockingbirdstation.com.

Cityplace Station. Catch the **McKinney Avenue Trolley** and go to the West Village and Uptown Magnolia Theatre movies, Dallas Museum of Art, Nasher Sculpture Center, MADI Museum, art galleries, restaurants, bookstores, shopping. Then take the trolley back to Cityplace and catch the DART rail heading downtown. Websites: www.mata.org; www.westvil.com; www.uptowndallas.net; www.landmarktheatres.com; www.dallasmuseumofart.org; www.nashersculpturecenter.org.

Pearl Street Station. See America's Ice Garden rink at Plaza of the Americas, the Arts District's Center for the Performing Arts including the DMA and Nasher, as well as the new Wyly Theatre, Winspear Opera House, Annette Strauss Artist Square, City Performance Hall, and Sammons Park. Websites: www.icesk8aig.com; www.artsdistrict.org; www.performingartscenter.org

West End Station. Visit museums, restaurants, shopping, festivals, and special events, Dallas World Aquarium, Sixth Floor Museum, Holocaust Museum, Old Red Museum, Dealey Plaza, John F. Kennedy Memorial Plaza. **Victory Park**: American Airlines Center (Mavericks, Stars, concerts, rodeos, ice-skating events), House of Blues, more restaurants, summer outdoor movies. Websites: www.dallaswestend.org; www.dwazoo.com; www.jfk.org; www.dallasholocaustmuseum.org; www.oldred.org; www .victorypark.com; www.americanairlinescenter.com; www.hob.com

Union Station. Tour the historic depot; take the Trinity Railway Express (TRE) to Fort Worth—shuttle to museum district (but not on Mondays) or stockyards; take underground tunnel to the Hyatt Regency Hotel and elevator to the observation deck of Reunion Tower and then to revolving restaurant Five Sixty by Wolfgang Puck. Websites: www.dallascity-hall.com; www.trinityrailwayexpress.org; www.dallasregency.hyatt.com; www.visitdallas.com.

Convention Center Station. Attend a special event, such as an auto show, boat show, bazaar, etc.; walk around the bronze sculptures of longhorns and cowboys in Pioneer Plaza. Websites: www.dallasconventioncenter.com; www.texastreesfoundation.org.

Zoo Station Take a walk on the wild side in this tour of things furry and feathery.

Then, it is back on DART for more adventures along the track back to your departure site. Once at **Galatyn Station** again, try a performing arts event at the Eisemann Center. Or head home with a collage of good memories. Websites: www.dallaszoo.com; www.eisemanncenter.org.

MCKINNEY AVENUE TROLLEY: M-LINE

3153 Oak Grove Ave. at Bowen, Dallas 75204 (214) 855-0006
Website: www.mata.org

Clang! Clang! The bells of the free McKinney Avenue trolleys ring as passengers stop at exciting sites and tempting restaurants all along the 3.6-mile route that begins near the Oak Grove/McKinney Avenue trolley barn and goes on by the Crescent, the Dallas Museum of Art, the Nasher Sculpture Center, the Magnolia Theater, and the West Village. At St. Paul and Ross (by the DMA), the streetcar system connects with a free M-line trolley bus, which proceeds down Ross to the West End and up Main St. and then returns to the Arts District streetcar. The trolley connects to the **DART light rail system** at **Cityplace**. The trolleys, operated by volunteers, are beautifully restored and are heated in winter.

Ninety-year-old "Rosie" is the oldest operating streetcar in North America. A trolley may be rented for birthday parties and other occasions. M-line service operates seven days a week every 15 minutes during peak and lunch hours, every 20 minutes during off-peak hours and weekends, from 7 AM to 10 PM Monday to Thursday, 7 AM to 12 PM Friday, 10 AM to 12 PM Saturday, and 10 AM to 10 PM Sunday. See **Tours of the Working World** for more information.

BOATS

Texas is well known for its large lakes and water sports. See **Chapter 4: Sports and Recreation** for areas to ski, fish, and sail and for boat and jet-ski rentals. One very tranquil boat ride is aboard the *Texas Queen* riverboat on Lake Ray Hubbard in Rockwall, if it is operating. The paddlewheeler usually casts off from the landing at Elgin B. Robertson Park just off I-30 at the Dalrock Road exit, but the economy and new owners may affect its operations.

A popular event at the end of January is the **Dallas Boat Show** held for 10 days at the Dallas Convention Center at 650 S. Griffin. More than 200 colorful fishing boats, water-ski boats, and yachts drop anchor here for all to admire whether interested in buying or not. Children enjoy workshops on topics such as necessities for tackle boxes, and some giveaway items to the first 500 children in the door. Dropping a line into the trout tank is another favorite of hopeful young anglers. Watch the newspapers for announcements. The summer boat show is also very popular with local mariners.

CARS, CAMPERS, AND CARRIAGES

For a teenager living in Dallas, getting a driver's license is the number one rite of passage. Most Texans are accustomed to driving their own cars and transporting large groups of children, as evidenced by the soaring numbers of minivans and Suburbans in carpool lines, beside soccer fields, and on Scout field trips. Dallas does have several taxi and limousine services for visitors. Two **taxicab** services are Cowboy Cab (214-428-0202) and the Yellow Cab Company (214-426-6262). A wide variety of **cars** may be rented from Budget Car Rental (800) 527-0700. **Campers** may be rented from CAMPERS4RENT at (972) 734-3636 in Lewisville and from All Star RV Center, 1700 E. Plano Pkwy., at (972) 516-2222.

Children who are fascinated with driving at an early age would enjoy cars designed with them in mind at amusement parks, such as the antique cars at Six Flags, the mini-virage race cars at Speedzone, and go-carts at Mesquite Go-Carts and Batting Cages, Adventure Landing, and Celebration Station.

Families can step back in time with a **surrey ride** usually during Christmas when the Arboretum, Highland Park Village, and Dallas Heritage Village (214-428-5448) offer carriage tours of lights.

Each April, the Dallas Convention Center is filled with all kinds of new cars, ranging from sports cars and luxury sedans to cars of the future, in the **Dallas Auto Show**. Families enjoy radio personalities and exhibits that include car care products, car phones, and automobile memorabilia. Elementary school students participate in the exhibit of the Car of the Future in a display of their ideas of what cars will look like. The Auto Show lasts five days, and children 12 and under are free. Discount coupons are usually available at car dealerships. For more information, call the New Car Dealers Association at (214) 637-0531. Another very popular annual car show is held at the **Automobile Building** at the State Fair of Texas in late September/early October.

STORYTELLING, LIBRARIES, AND BOOKSTORES

Some people express fear that the magic of storytelling is disappearing with the onset of video games and a bumper crop of TV tater tots, but the art really is alive and well in many homes where parents still read to their children nightly, recite ageless nursery rhymes, and relate favorite tales heard in childhood from their parents and grandparents. Children love this tradition and the cozy, undivided attention of their parents.

Stories are woven weekly in area libraries as children's librarians sit before a semicircle of preschoolers and guide them through exciting tales. The rapt audiences cry for more.

Those who love folk humor and recounting stories have formed at least three guilds in the North Texas area. The **Dallas Storytelling Guild** meets each second Wednesday at 7 PM to share stories at the Churchill Recreation Center. On the Saturday before Thanksgiving, they sponsor **Tellabration**, an evening concert of storytellers in which members tell favorite stories, and they also host December's Winter Jam. Members present workshops, and they have a list of storytellers and the types of stories they like to tell if an individual or group contacts them. Storytelling is popular at children's birthday parties as well as events for adults. Call (214) 821-2562 or e-mail pcarr@electricinsight.com. Website: www.dallasstorytelling.org.

One very active, nationally celebrated storyteller is **Elizabeth Ellis**, who tells stories for both adults and children at a wide variety of occasions. To reach Elizabeth Ellis, call (214) 381-4676. Website: www.eliza-bethellis.com. **Tipi Tellers** tell stories in a full-size tipi. Contact them at (214) 212-1771 or www.tipitellers.org. **Dan Gibson**, the teller with a banjo, includes traditional folktales and ghost stories as well as tall tales and cowboy poetry in his repertoire. Contact him at www.dangibson.net. Locate more storytellers through the Dallas Storytelling Guild website, www.dallasstorytelling.org.

A popular annual event is the **Tejas Storytelling Festival** in March, in which storytellers gather at Texas Women's University in Denton for a weekend of folktales, fantasy, and music. Workshops for the story-tellers are combined with storytelling sessions that the public may at-tend. At Friday evening's Olio, participants tell stories to introduce themselves, and on Saturday afternoon a Family Olio and Traditional Texas Tales are also open to the public. Some performances are inter-preted for the deaf. For details, write the Tejas Storytelling Association, P.O. Box 2806, Denton 76202, or call (940) 382-7014. Website: www.tejasstorytelling.com.

LIBRARIES

DALLAS PUBLIC LIBRARY

Twenty-six branches stem from the J. Erik Jonsson Central Library to form the Dallas Public Library system. Daily, children discover a love of reading from the story times, educational user classes (including free computer classes), reading clubs, and special events designed to inspire and encourage them. Patrons who live in Dallas may apply for a free li-brary card, but those who live outside the city limits must purchase a fee card: $20 for 5 items checked out, $50 for 15 items, $75 for 25 items, and $200 for unlimited checkout for one year. Most books and maga-zines may be checked out for three weeks and may be renewed. Videos, DVDs, books, music on CDs, large-print books, ESL CDs, and paintings may be borrowed for one week. Books may be returned to any Dallas li-brary branch. To renew by phone, call (214) 670-1740 on weekdays; pa-trons can also renew online. Fees are charged for overdue items. Free Internet access is available at all locations. The Dallas Public Library's home page is www.dallaslibrary.org.

Bookmarks is a kid-friendly library for infants to age 12, located in-side Northpark Center, Ste. 1514. It has books, audiobooks, DVDs, CDs, and parenting items as well as free wireless Internet access and lap-top computers for children. All sorts of cubbies invite children to crawl in and enjoy their books. Story time for preschoolers as well as other ac-tivities for older children and their parents are scheduled. Call (214) 671-1381. Website: www.dallaslibrary.org/bookmarks.htm.

J. ERIK JONSSON CENTRAL LIBRARY

1515 Young St. at Ervay, Dallas 75201 (214) 670-1400
Information and Reference: (214) 670-1700
Children's Center: (214) 670-1727
Website: www.dallaslibrary.org

Families who make regular trips to the downtown library like the exhibits, usually displayed on the lobby level, in the fourth-floor gallery, and in the seventh-floor O'Hara exhibit hall, as well as the multitude of books from which they may choose their favorites. The best guide to special exhibits, programs, tours, and events is the *Bookmark* or the individual library's calendar. Families who are puzzled by a subject at home should call Information and Reference at (214) 670-1700. An annual program greeted with enthusiasm each year is the **Summer Reading Club**. Certificates and rewards are given for the number of hours a child reads or is read to, and it is climaxed with a recognition party. Upper elementary students could combine this program with reading the year's new Bluebonnet book selections so they can vote for their favorite during the school year if their school library participates.

The imagination of children is stimulated by the second-floor **Children's Center** with its storytelling forest, a "village" to read in, and the Kahn Pavilion used for plays, puppet shows, films, and story times. The computers are very popular. Preschool stories in both English and Spanish are offered regularly. Call (214) 670-1671 for information about children's activities. See **Tours of the Working World** for information about special tours and user education classes for both children and adults.

Annually, the library sponsors a **Youth Poetry Competition** for Dallas students in grades 2 to 12. Call (214) 670-1671 or visit the website www.dallaslibrary.org and click on "Kids' Page." The **Dallas Children's Book Fair and Literary Festival** usually takes place in the fall at the Central Library.

Consider a family ride on a DART bus to the library for an outing. Be sure to browse in **BookEnds: Used and Rare Books** for great bargains on books, audio books, and magazines. Call (214) 670-1727. The downtown library is open daily: Sunday, 1 PM to 5 PM; Monday to Thursday, 9 AM to 9 PM; and Friday to Saturday, 9 AM to 5 PM.

The following are the 26 branches of the Dallas Public Library. Regularly there is discussion at City Hall about cutting back branch library services as a way to save money. If you enjoy the service of your branch library, please let your local representative know how vital its services are to you and your neighborhood. Contact each library or look online for days and hours of operation. Some branches are closed on Sunday.

Summer hours may be different from the rest of the year. All libraries are located in Dallas.

Arcadia Park, 1302 N. Justin, (214) 670-6446
Audelia Road 10045 Audelia Rd., (214) 670-1350
Bachman Lake, 9480 Webb Chapel, (214) 670-6376
Bookmarks, Northpark Center, Ste. 1514, Central Expwy. at Northwest Hwy., (214) 671-1381
Casa View, 10355 Ferguson Rd., (214) 670-8403 (moving 11221 Lochwood at Garland Rd.)
Dallas West, 2332 Singleton Blvd., (214) 670-6445
Dunbar Lancaster-Kiest, 2008 E. Kiest, (214) 670-1952
Forest Green, 9015 Forest Lane, (214) 670-1335
Fretz Park, 6990 Belt Line Rd., (214) 670-6421
Grauwyler Park, 2146 Gilford, (214) 670-1447
Hampton-Illinois, 2951 S. Hampton, (214) 670-7646
Highland Hills, 3624 Simpson Stuart Rd., (214) 670-0987
Kleberg-Rylie, 1301 Edd Rd., (214) 670-8471
Lakewood, 6121 Worth St., (214) 670-1376
MLK Library, 2922 Martin L. King Blvd., (214) 670-0344
Mountain Creek, 6102 Mountain Creek Pkwy., (214) 670-6704
North Oak Cliff, 302 West 10th St., (214) 670-7555
Oak Lawn, 4100 Cedar Springs Rd., (214) 670-1359
Park Forest, 3421 Forest Lane, (214) 670-6333
Pleasant Grove, 1125 South Buckner Blvd., (214) 670-0965
Polk-Wisdom, 7151 Library Lane, (214) 670-1947
Preston Royal, 5626 Royal Lane, (214) 670-7128
Renner-Frankford, 6400 Frankford Rd., (214) 670-6100
Skillman/Southwestern, 5707 Skillman, (214) 670-6078
Skyline, 6006 Everglade Rd., (214) 670-0938
Timberglen, 18505 Midway, (214) 670-1365

BOOKSTORES

Children love to read their favorite books over and over. Being able to write your own name and the date that you acquired it in the book is a special pleasure. Some of the most unique collections of books for children are not housed in a bookstore but in a museum gift shop specializing in science or nature.

Many of the retail chain bookstores house a wonderful collection of fiction and nonfiction books, CDs, and DVDs for children of all ages. These include **Borders, Barnes & Noble,** and **Waldenbooks. Half Price Books,** which has multiple locations, saves families some dollars. Bookstores with a Christian family emphasis are **Logos, Lifeway Christian**

Stores, Mardel Christian, and Cokesbury. A new huge independent bookstore is Plano's Legacy Books, located in the Shops at Legacy at the Tollway and Legacy Drive. Large discount warehouses like Sam's or department and grocery stores, such as Target, Wal-Mart, and Tom Thumb, often carry entertaining children's books at reasonable prices. The addresses and phone numbers for these bookstores are listed under "Book Dealers Retail" in the Yellow Pages. For announcements about local literary events, look each Sunday in the *Dallas Morning News* "Books" section for the literary calendar. The Friday *Guide* lists literary events at bookstores and library events for children.

Summer reading clubs are a traditional form of summer entertainment. These clubs often offer prizes for a designated number of books read or hours spent in reading or being read to. Look for these clubs at bookstores, public libraries, church libraries, and movie theaters. Premiere Video, 5400 E. Mockingbird, also has an extensive selection of audio books for adults as well as classic videos. Call (214) 827-8969. Half Price Books stocks used books on tape and CDs.

SMALL ART MUSEUMS, GALLERIES, CENTERS, AND STUDIOS

Artists agree that the earlier children are exposed to art, the more they will appreciate it throughout their lives. They are attracted to colors and designs at a very early age, and a home with easy access to crayons, watercolors, and art paper encourages creativity in budding artists.

Art is all around you in Dallas. It is hanging in the halls in school buildings, in the sculptures in the parks, in the center aisles at the malls, and in the gallery at City Hall. Sometimes a small art center or gallery is just the right speed for younger children who do not have long attention spans or like to walk long distances. Most of the area community colleges and universities have small galleries that feature local artists, and personnel will be happy to mail information about the exhibits scheduled. Many city halls, libraries, community cultural centers, performing arts centers, and museums display changing exhibits regularly, and local art groups regularly sponsor art exhibits and offer classes for both children and adults. Many art museums and community colleges hold summer art classes and day camps.

The Friday "Guide" of the *Dallas Morning News* lists museums and galleries and their current exhibits, and many of these also have mailing lists. See Festivals and Special Events for Artfest and Dallas Arts Fair, popular art festivals. Richardson's Cottonwood Art Festival is another favorite event. More art fun is listed under Shopping and Hobbies (just below).

Helpful artsy websites:
www.dallasculture.org. City of Dallas Office of Cultural Affairs site. Overview of Dallas arts community, mailing and newsletter, events at cultural centers, neighborhood touring.
www.artsdistrict.org. Dallas Arts District Alliance site. Keep up with established and newly opening art venues in the Arts District downtown, events, tours, newsletter.
www.dallasartsrevue.com. Visual art news, reviews, calendars, links.
www.dallasartdealers.org. Dallas Art Dealers Association site. Information about galleries, links to additional arts-related sites, sponsor of two free gallery walks annually.
www.artiststuff.com. Artist and Elaine Thornton Foundation site. Sponsors programs such as the Young Photographers Workshop and the Young Photographers Competition, theater festivals, and other art-related programs.

ARLINGTON MUSEUM OF ART

201 West Main, P.O. Box 114, Arlington 76010 (817) 275-4600 Website: www.arlingtonmuseum.org

The AMA showcases Texas contemporary art. Call about special events, summer day camps, gallery tours, birthday parties, and children's classes. Parking is available at nearby City Hall. Hours: Wednesday to Friday, 1 PM to 5 PM; Saturday, 10 AM to 5 PM; Sunday, 12 PM to 5 PM.

ARTCENTRE OF PLANO

1039 E. 15th St., Plano (972) 423-7809 Website: www.artcentreof-plano.org

The galleries and classrooms of ArtCentre of Plano are dedicated to promoting art and art education in both visual and performing arts. Business hours are Tuesday to Saturday, 10 AM to 5 PM.

BATH HOUSE CULTURAL CENTER

521 E. Lawther Drive, Dallas 75218-0032 (214) 670-8749 Website: www.bathhousecultural.com

Located on the eastern shores of White Rock Lake in northeast Dallas, the Bath House beach was a popular place in the 1930s for swimming. Chain-link fences ran on both sides of the building and down into the water to mark off a swimming area. Today, no swimming is allowed in the lake, and the Bath House has been converted into a cultural center that fosters the growth, development, and quality of multicultural arts within the city of Dallas.

Part of the City of Dallas Office of Cultural Affairs, the Bath House includes a 105-seat theater, the Main and Hall Galleries, and several workshops. Plays, concerts, art exhibits, and workshops for both children and adults are regularly scheduled. Classes for children include printmaking and weaving, and student art exhibits are often displayed in the galleries. It also houses **White Rock Lake Museum**. Website: www.whiterocklakemuseum.org. Write or call the center to be on their mailing list for advance notice of activities.

Visitors might like to bring a picnic lunch and plan to spend some time on playground equipment at White Rock Lake while there. To reach the Bath House from North Buckner Blvd., turn west on Northcliff. Signs are there to guide you.

Hours: Office hours are Tuesday to Saturday, 12 PM to 6 PM.

MUSEUM OF BIBLICAL ARTS

7500 Park Lane, Dallas 75225 (214) 691-4661 Website: www.biblicalarts.org

In 2005, an electrical spark caught the 120-foot-long *Miracle at Pentecost* painting on fire, and the flames spread throughout the museum. It is undergoing an $8 million reconstruction. Call to see if the new museum has opened. The center will include a Golden Ziggurat, reminiscent of ancient stepped pyramids from the time of Abraham, surrounded by 36 windows providing light to the atrium. The museum will provide art galleries, a religious architecture archive, Damascus Gate and Ceremonial Entryway, and a restoration room where visitors may watch conservators restore religious artifacts.

Its focus is to help all people better understand the places, events, and people of the Bible through artwork and historical artifacts, theater, music, and film. It is located west of Northpark Center.

CRAFT GUILD OF DALLAS

14325 Proton, Dallas 75244 (972) 490-0303 Website: www.craftguildofdallas.org

Classes for children and adults in fiber arts, book binding, paper art, jewelry, ceramics, surface design, and other mediums are offered by the Craft Guild of Dallas. Fees vary, with discounts available to members. A family membership is $100, and a student membership is $25. Classes in clay throwing and hand building are open for ages 3 to 12. A holiday craft fair is offered in November and children's camps in the summer. Shop for great gifts at the Craft Guild Store.

CROW COLLECTION OF ASIAN ART

Trammell Crow Center, 2010 Flora at Olive, Dallas 75201 (214) 979-6430 Website: www.crowcollection.org

Located by the Dallas Museum of Art, the Crow Collection of Asian Art includes more than 300 pieces from Japan, China, India, and Southeast Asia, dating from 3,500 BC to the early 20th century. A Sculpture Garden surrounds Trammell Center. On the website is "Passport to Asia for Kids." Two pictures are available to print out and then color. Schedule group tours two weeks in advance. Call (214) 979-6435 for reservations.

Hours are Tuesday, Wednesday, Friday, Saturday, and Sunday, 10 AM to 5 PM; Thursday, 10 AM to 9 PM. Free admission.

DALLAS CONTEMPORARY

2801 Swiss Ave., Dallas 75204 (214) 821-2522 Website: www.the-contemporary.net

Dallas Contemporary (about the fourth name change) is a nonprofit agency that exists to provide community access to and education about the art and artists of Texas. Located in the **Wilson Historic District**, the center provides year-round exhibitions, art classes, and a resource room of art-related periodicals and art organization materials. Information concerning the center's latest exhibition may be found on the center's website and the "Art Centers: Openings" listing in the newspaper each Friday.

The gallery plans to expand its youth programs, family days, and tours. Following a visit to the center, children might enjoy a picnic at the scenic **Central Park Square** and a stroll down Swiss Ave. along the row of Victorian and Queen Anne–influenced houses in the Wilson Historic District. Hours are Tuesday to Saturday, 10 AM to 5 PM.

JESUIT DALLAS MUSEUM

12345 Inwood, Dallas 75244 (972) 387-8700

Housed in Jesuit College Preparatory School, the museum's collection includes 375 pieces by artists such as Henry Moore, Joan Miro, and Eduardo Chillida. Call for information about viewing the exhibit, and the school office will give you the name of a docent who can lead a tour.

THE BLACK ACADEMY OF ARTS AND LETTERS, INC.

Dallas Convention Center Theater Complex, 650 S. Griffin, Dallas 75202 (214) 743-2440 Website: www.tbaal.org

Dedicated to promoting and preserving the works of black Americans, the TBAAL presents workshops, exhibitions, seasonal events, concerts, summer art programs for kids, youth choirs and orchestras, comedy night, a 24-hour film festival, and seminars. It is located near City Hall on the corner of Canton and Akard. Call for a brochure of events and concerts. Hours: Monday to Friday, 9 AM to 5:30 PM and Saturday, 11 AM to 4:30 PM. The Academy stays open later for special events.

SOUTH DALLAS CULTURAL CENTER

3400 S. Fitzhugh, Dallas 75210 (214) 939-2787 Website: www.dallasculture.org/

The South Dallas Cultural Center is a multipurpose arts venue near Fair Park. It has a visual arts gallery and studios for two-dimensional art, ceramics, printmaking, and photography. Also, it features a 100-seat black box theater and studios for dance, as well as classes in digital recording technology for youth and adults. **Summer Arts at the Center** is a five-week arts institute for school-aged kids that is taught by local and visiting artists.

LATINO CULTURAL CENTER

2600 Live Oak, Dallas (214) 670-3320 Website: www.dallasculture.org

Opened in 2003, the Latino Cultural Center has galleries for art exhibitions and workspace for artists. The Center wishes to present opportunities for education and experience in visual, literary, media, performance, and traditional arts. In the 300-seat theater are musical and children's theater performances and films in Spanish.

THE ICE HOUSE CULTURAL CENTER

1000 W. Page St., Dallas 75208 (214) 670-7524 Website: www.dallasculture.org

Providing a Latino-focused venue to promote the arts and cultural events that reflect the diversity of Oak Cliff and nearby areas, the Ice House Cultural Center works with the Dallas Museum of Art and Arte Oak Cliff and provides visual art exhibitions and workshops as well as theater and dance workshops.

MEADOWS MUSEUM

Southern Methodist University, 5900 Bishop Blvd. at Schlegel St., Dallas 75275 (214) 768-2516. Website: meadowsmuseum.smu.edu

The Meadows Museum houses the most comprehensive collection of Spanish art in the United States, including paintings, sculpture, and works on paper from the 10th through the 21st centuries. Artists represented in the collection include Velasquez, Murillo, Goya, Picasso, and Miro. The museum offers a variety of programs for visitors of all ages, including docent-led tours, art classes, and Family Days. Free admission and free public gallery tours are offered Thursdays at 6 PM. The gallery tour is free on Sundays at 2 PM, but museum admission fee must be paid. Private tours of the museum's permanent collection and special exhibitions may be scheduled for groups of 10 to 60 people Tuesday to Saturday by calling (214) 768-2740. Group tours are available for ages 5 to adult, and reservations must be made at least three weeks in advance.

The Meadows Community Education Program hosts children's art classes throughout the year to introduce students to a variety of media and techniques. **Family Days** are scheduled regularly in conjunction with special exhibitions or events. Family Day activities and programs are designed especially for children and include live performances by musicians, dancers, or performing artists; studio art activities; and story-telling in the galleries.

Visit the Meadows Museum Store for a wide selection of books, gifts, and educational materials with a Spanish flair. Admission to the museum is free; special exhibitions, group tours, and classes may incur additional fees. Hours: Tuesday, Wednesday, Friday, Saturday, 10 AM to 5 PM; Thursday, 10 AM to 8 PM; Sunday, 12 PM to 5 PM. Closed Monday and some holidays. The **Gates** restaurant is open Tuesday to Friday, 11:30 AM to 2 PM. For reservations, call (214) 768-3928. Free parking is available in the museum garage.

PAN AMERICAN ART PROJECTS

1615 Dragon St., Dallas 75207 (214) 522-3303 Website: www.panamericanart.com

Pan American Art Projects specializes in the art of the Americas, featuring work from Canada, the United States, the Caribbean, and Latin America. They have a large collection of Cuban, Haitian, and Jamaican art. The gallery includes avant-garde and contemporary works, as well as ceramics, photography, folk art, and sculpture.

MADI MUSEUM AND GALLERY

Kilgore Law Center, 3109 Carlisle, Dallas 75204 (214) 855-7802 Website: www.madimuseum.org

Kids are immediately attracted to the bright facade of the building. Dedicated to a movement founded in Argentina in 1946, the MADI collection is distinguished by asymmetrical geometric influences, polygonal forms, and contoured surfaces. It includes bright visual art, music, poetry, and three-dimensional parts that move. Hours of operation are Tuesday to Saturday, 11 AM to 5 PM; Sunday, 1 PM to 5 PM. Free admission.

ART STUDIOS

The following is a list of visual art centers that offer varying types of art lessons, some for kids and some for ages up to adult. Additionally, most offer summer camps, birthday parties, drop-in art, family art days, workshops, after-school and holiday activities, and exhibitions.

Kid Art, 3407 Milton Ave., Dallas 75205 (214) 750-7118 Website: www.kidartdallas.com

J's Art Studio, 17822 Davenport, Ste. C, Dallas 75252 (972) 931-1933 Website: www.jsartstudio.com

Studio Arts Dallas, 10051 Shoreview, Dallas 75238 (214) 827-1222 Website: www.studioartsdallas.com

Artistic Gatherings, 9440 Garland Rd., Ste.138, Dallas (214) 821-8383 Website: www.artisticgatherings.com

Purple Glaze, Inc., 6128 Berkshire, Dallas 75225 (214) 987-1440. Ceramics.

Smashing Times Mosaic Art Studio, 308 Preston Royal Shopping Center, Dallas (214) 363-2088. Website: www.smashingtimes.com

Paint Yer Pottery, 17194 Preston at Campbell, Dallas 75248 (972) 248-0001 Website: www.paintyerpottery.com

Quiggly's Clayhouse: Painters and Potters, 1344 E. Beltline at Plano Rd., Richardson 75081 (972) 234-2644 Website: www.quigglys.com

Pee Wee Picasso Art Studio, 15757 Coit Rd., Ste. 324 at Arapaho, Richardson (972) 980-4600 Website: www.peeweepicasso.com

The Artist Within/Painting, Sculpture, Clay, 2001 Coit Rd., Ste. 206, at Park, Plano 75075 (972) 596-6077 Website: www.artistwithin .com

Art-A-Rama, 1610 Ave. J, Plano (972) 423-4554 Website: www.ar-taramaplano.com

Kidsarts, Irving Arts Center, 3333 N. MacArthur Blvd., Irving 75062 (972) 256-4270 Website: www.irvingartscenter.org/kidsarts

OUTDOOR SCULPTURE AND MURALS

Visitors to downtown might want a copy of the Dallas Convention Center's guide to the 32 sculptures located there. They include some lifelike pieces, such as the elderly lady who is knitting while sitting on a park bench at Olive and Ross. Many other pieces located throughout the Dallas area are also catalogued. Call (214) 571-1000 for details.

Other sections of the guide list Metroplex outdoor sculpture locations, such as the garden at the Dallas Museum of Art, Dallas City Hall, the Pump House at White Rock Lake, the Dallas Zoo (tallest outdoor sculpture in Texas), the Fort Worth Stockyards, Northpark Center, the Mustangs at Las Colinas, DFW Airport, and Irving Arts Center garden.

Northpark Center developer Raymond Nasher constructed a two-acre sculpture garden on land across Harwood from the Dallas Museum of Art. The **Nasher Sculpture Garden** is the setting for 30 to 40 sculptures at a time from his collection, which consists of more than 250 master-works. See **Chapter 1: Places to Go** for more details. A few of his sculptures are in the walkways at Northpark Center.

In the Quorum Business Center in Addison is a sculpture that is an **equinox marker**—it marks the equinox twice yearly when fall and spring begin. The sun shines through the metal arch and aligns with marks on a metal ball below it. John V. House's sculpture is located west of the Tollway and south of Belt Line Rd. in a traffic circle at the Quorum.

Huge **murals** are being painted in downtown Dallas by artists from Eyecon Inc. Some are painted on the sides of parking garages and may take up a city block. Three locations and titles are *Mass Transit* at Griffin and Pacific, *Resources* at St. Paul and San Jacinto, and *The Storm* (12 stories high) at San Jacinto and Leonard. *Whaling Walls* by Wyland is located at 505 Akard St. near San Jacinto. On the nine-story brick wall of the old Sanger Building section of El Centro College is *We Are One*, depicting a Native American pipe-smoking ceremony that includes the points of the compass, Mother Earth and Father Sky, animal symbols, and the four elements: earth, fire, air, and water.

TRUETT HOSPITAL/BAYLOR

On permanent display at Baylor's Truett Hospital are more than 86 casts of hands that are the work of orthopedic surgeon Dr. Adrian Flatt. Famous hands in the display are those of U.S. presidents, actors, athletes, writers, and more. The hands of Nolan Ryan hold a baseball.

DALLAS CONVENTION CENTER

650 S. Griffin, Dallas (214) 658-7000 Website: www.dallascvb.com

The $9 million **Pioneer Plaza** includes a 19th-century cattle drive with a herd of 40 bronze longhorns and attending cowboys on horseback heading downhill to water. The historic Shawnee Trail ran through the area near today's Reunion Arena, and the sculptures celebrate it as well as the introduction of longhorn cattle to our land more than 500 years ago. This is a definite photo opportunity.

TRAMMEL CROW CENTER

2001 Ross Ave. at Olive, Dallas 75201 (214) 979-6430

Located near the Dallas Museum of Art downtown, the Trammel Crow Center includes the **Crow Collection of Asian Art**. Children especially like the sculptures that surround the building. Call for information about current exhibits or read the gallery listing in the Friday newspaper.

FREEDMAN'S MEMORIAL CEMETERY

Central Expwy. (75) at Lemmon Ave., S.W. corner, Dallas

The cemetery, which is more than 135 years old, is the burial ground for about 7,000 former slaves. Sculptor David Newton designed the 20-foot marble-and-stone entry arch and the bronze sculptures. On the left of the entrance is a bronze African warrior who protects those who are buried there; on the right is an African historian/storyteller called a "griot." A sculpture of an African couple who are comforting each other following enslavement is located at the reflection area. A male in chains and a sorrowful woman, the "Struggling Soul" and the "Violated Soul," are at the back of the arch. Erykah Badu performed a song she wrote for Freedman's Cemetery when the new memorial was dedicated in 1999.

HORSES

Dallas Soars! is the Pegasus art project based on the Dallas landmark **Flying Red Horse** on the Magnolia Building downtown. About 80 Pegasus sculptures, decorated by both professional and amateur artists, can be spotted around Dallas. One is in front of the Dallas Children's Theater.

The Freedom Horses, a stallion and a mare by Veryl Goodnight, Dallas North Tollway and Loop 12

Pegasus, by Booker T. Washington art students, 2501 Flora, Dallas

Traveler and Robert E. Lee, Lee Park, Dallas

Colts in Motion, Anna Debska, 2001 Bryan at San Jacinto, Maxus Energy Tower Garage

TEXAS SCULPTURE GARDEN

Hall Office Park, 6801 **Gaylord Pkwy., Frisco (after Hwy.** 121 **on the Dallas North Tollway). Exterior open dawn to dusk. Lobby hours: weekdays,** 9 AM **to** 5 PM, **Saturday,** 9 AM **to** 12 PM. **Websites: www.texassculpturegarden.org;** www.hallofficepark.com

Forty-one contemporary sculptures by Texas artists make up the Texas Sculpture Garden, part of a collection of 165 works of art displayed in Hall Office Park at Gaylord and the Tollway. Some pieces are in lobbies, and some are outdoors. A brochure that includes a map of the location of each sculpture, a thumbnail picture, and the names of each artist and sculpture is available from the Frisco Visitors Bureau, (877) 463-7472. Guided tours are available for groups of 15 or more. Call (972) 377-1152. It is located near Stonebriar Centre, Gatti Town amusement center, and the Heritage Center Museum. While in Frisco, see the **cattle sculptures** at Central Park, 3155 Parkwood Drive, and the **Bronze Cattle Drive** in which longhorns, cowboys, and a chuck wagon resurrect the Shawnee Trail in The Centre at Preston Ridge, 8400 Gaylord Pkwy.

SHOPPING AND HOBBIES

SHOPPING

Shopping is such a favorite pastime in Dallas that the city is able to claim that there are more shopping centers per shopper than any other city in the United States. "Shop til ya drop" is more than a motto. However, this is accurate only for teenage mall dwellers on up. Most 5-year-olds would not place a trip to the mall as a top-10 activity, but there are usually some shops at the malls or centers that focus on the younger set and some fast-food restaurants that are just their speed. Many shopping centers have fountains and displays with flags that catch the eye of little ones, especially during holiday seasons.

Check with the malls near you for a calendar of special events. Health fairs, children's art exhibits, puppet shows, petting zoos, Santa, and the Easter Bunny are often part of mall activities. The mall or a particular restaurant may offer breakfast and photos with the latter two. Hobby shops are great places to spend time with your young shopper. Starting a collection or craft at an early age makes a real adventure out of shopping, as kids try to find a certain baseball card or add to their dollhouses. One of the most entertaining family shopping days can be found at local flea markets and trade days, such as the one at Canton.

Listed below are only some of the Metroplex area's malls and their shops and fast-food restaurants that would appeal to children. Look under "Hobbies" and "Toys" in the Yellow Pages for additional shops. Near most of the wonderful shops is sure to be a place to make the necessary stop for ice cream or another rejuvenating snack.

SHOPPING MALLS AND OUTLET CENTERS

ALLEN PREMIUM OUTLETS

US 75 N. at Stacy Rd., Exit 37
Allen (972) 678-7000
Website: www.premiumoutlets
.com

Carter's
The Children's Place
Cinnamonster

Claire's
Dallas Cowboys Pro Shop
Gap Kids and Baby
Gymboree
KB Toys
Little Me
NauticaKids
Oshkosh B'gosh
Polo Ralph Lauren Children
Stride Rite Keds Sperry

Stroller Rental
Tommy Kids

COLLIN CREEK MALL
811 Central Expwy.
Plano 75075 (972) 422-1070
Website: www.collincreekmall
.com

Amazing Jake's Amusement Park
The Children's Place
Claire's
The Disney Store
Express Train Rides
Gymboree
Justice
McDonald's
Soft Play Area (by Dillard's)
Stride Rite
Stroller Fit Exercise Class

GALLERIA
I-635 (LBJ) at 13350 Dallas
Pkwy.
Dallas (972) 702-7100
Website: www.galleriadallas.com

abercrombie kids
Adopt-A-Bear
Amazing Toy Creations
American Girl Boutique and
    Bistro
BabyGap and GapKids
The Children's Place
Children's Play Place
Chuck E. Cheese's
Gymboree
Ice Skating Center and Playplace
Limited Too
McDonald's
Pumpkin Patch

Slappy's Puppet House
Strasburg Children

GRAPEVINE MILLS OUTLET CENTER
Hwy. 121 North and 3000
Grapevine Mills Pkwy.
Grapevine (972) 724-4900
Website: www.grapevinemills.com

AMC Movie Theater
Bass Pro Shops Outdoor World
Build-A-Bear Workshop
Candy HQtrs.
(on perimeter)
Carters
The Children's Place
Choo Choo Station
Cowboys Pro Shop
Disney Store
Disney's Rainforest Cafe
Dr Pepper Stars Center Ice Rink
Games Workshop
GameWorks Arcade
Gap Outlet
Go! Toys and Games
Gymboree
Icing/Claire's
Island Carousel
Kid's Foot Locker
Lunar Mini Golf
Old Navy
Oshkosh B'Gosh
Sanrio
Simon Kidgits Clubhouse—
    Events and Activities
The Sports Authority
Tommy Kids Company Store
Woodward Skatepark

NORTHPARK CENTER
8080 N.Central Expwy. at
Northwest Hwy.

Dallas (214) 361-6345

Website: www.northparkcenter
.com

abercrombie
Bookmarks Public Library
Build-A-Bear Workshop
Chick-fil-A
Claire's
Gamestop
GapKids
Gymboree
Hanna Anderson
Jacadi
Janie and Jack
Lacoste
Lily Pulitzer
Limited Too
Oilily
Peek
Planet Funk
Puzzle Zoo
Ralph Lauren
Sweet Factory
TGI Fridays
Playhouse Parade in May, SPCA
   in Dec.
Model Train Display in Decem-
   ber
Safety Pin Sculpture outdoors

TANGER OUTLET MALL

I-20 and Hwy. 34, Exit 501

301 Tanger Drive, Terrell 75160

(972) 524-6034

Website: www.tangeroutlet.com

Bass Company Store
Claire's
Gap Outlet
KB Toys
Levi's

Nova Cinemas
Old Navy
OshKosh B'Gosh
Reebok

TOWN EAST MALL

2063 Town East Blvd. at LBJ
Frwy. (I-635)

Mesquite 75150 (972) 270-
4431

Website: www.towneastmall.com

abercrombie
A+ School Uniforms
Champs
Chick-fil-A
The Children's Place
Children's Play Area (by
   Dillard's)
Claire's
Dallas Cowboys Pro Shop
Game Stop
Gymboree
Journeys Kidz
Kid's Foot Locker
Limited Too
Payless Kids
Pet Zone
Stride Rite Shoes
Town East Express train

STONEBRIAR CENTRE

Hwy. 121 and 2601 Preston
Rd., Frisco (972) 668-6255

Website: www.shopstonebriar.com

abercrombie
AMC 24 Movie Theater
BabyGap and GapKids
Build-A-Bear Workshop
California Pizza Kitchen and
   CP Kids School Programs

Candy World
Carousel at the food court
Chick-fil-A
The Children's Place
Claire's
Climbing wall
Dick's Sporting Goods
Gamestop
Gymboree
Ice skating rink
Journeys Kidz
Limited Too
Safari Time shop and play
Soft playground
Stride Rite Shoes

VALLEY VIEW CENTER
Preston Rd. at LBJ Fwy. (I-635)
Dallas (972) 661-2424

Website: www.shopvalleyview
center.com

Camp Valley View Kid's Club
Camp Valley View soft play area
Champs
Chick-fil-A
Claire's
Carousel
Disney Store
Food court
Game Chest
Game Stop
Gameworks
Journeys Kidz
Justice
Kids' Foot Locker
Sweet Factory
Waldenbooks

HOBBIES AND COLLECTIONS

In addition to the hobby and collection shops in the malls, some very interesting and helpful shops are located all around the city. Two stores with multiple locations that specialize in craft and hobby items but also carry toys, party supplies, and a variety of other items are **Michaels** and **Hobby Lobby**. Below are some more popular shops that have personnel who are very interested in your hobby or collection and have some genuine expertise to offer.

AMERICAN GIRLS BOUTIQUE AND BISTRO
13350 Dallas Pkwy. at Galleria
Dallas (888) 777-0010
Website: www.americangirl.com

COLLECTIBLE TRAINS AND TOYS
13615 Welch at Alpha (N.W. corner)
Dallas 75244 (214) 373-9469
    Trains and related items.

DISCOUNT MODEL TRAINS
4641 Ratliff Lane
Addison (972) 931-8135
    Trains and related items.

HOBBYTOWN USA
N.E. corner of Central (75) and 8041 Walnut Hill
Dallas (214) 987-4744
N.E. corner of 3033 W. Parker and Independence
Plano (972) 758-7875

LONE STAR COMIC BOOKS, GAMES, AND TOYS

Website: www.mycomicshop.com
6465 E. Mockingbird at Abrams
Dallas (214) 823-0934
3100 Independence at Parker
Plano (972) 985-1593
3600 Gus Thomason at Town East. Blvd.
Mesquite (972) 681-2020

QUEEN OF HEARTS COSTUME AND MAGIC SHOP

1032 E. 15th and Ave. K
Plano (972) 578-1969

RECOLLECTIONS SCRAPBOOKING

5500 Greenville Ave., Ste. 3866 at Lover's Lane,
Dallas (214) 572-1112

ROCK BARRELL BEADS

13650 TI Blvd., Ste. 104 at Sherman
Dallas (972) 231-4809
Website: www.rockbarrell.com

SPLENDOR IN THE GRASS BEADS

1900 Abrams Pkwy. at Gaston
Dallas (214) 824-2777

BEADING DREAMS

5629 W. Lover's Lane
Dallas (214) 366-1112
Website: www.beadingdreams.com

TEXAS R/C MODELERS

230 W. Parker, Ste. 180, at Central
Plano (972) 422-5386
Website: www.planorc.com

MIKE'S HOBBY SHOP

1201 N. I-35, Carrollton
Near Sandy Lake Rd. (972) 242-4930
Website:www.mikeshobbyshop.com
  R/C models, aircraft/cars/boats.

TANDY LEATHER FACTORY

10220 E. NW Hwy.
Dallas (214) 342-2282
Website: www.tandyleatherfactory.com

TRIPLE CARDS AND COLLECTIBLES

2452 Ave. K at Park Blvd.
Plano (972) 509-5263
  Sports cards.

NICK'S SPORTS CARDS

7522 Campbell Rd. at Coit
Dallas (972) 248-2271
Website: www.nickscards.net

THROUGH THE KEYHOLE

625 Preston Forest Shopping Center, SE corner
Dallas (214) 691-7467
  Miniatures and dollhouses.

THE ENCHANTED COTTAGE

202 N. Greenville at Tyler
Richardson (972) 234-5500
Dolls, bears, and surprises.

HOME DEPOT KIDS WORKSHOP

Saturdays/Multiple locations

COOKING CLASSES

Kids Cooking Company, Dallas (214) 265-9949
Young Chefs Academy, Plano (972) 473-9090
Central Market, Dallas (214) 361-5754
Sur la Table, Dallas (214) 219-4404
Viking Cooking School, Dallas (214) 526-3942

TOY STORES AND LEARNING STORES

Most children are willing to take time out from whatever they are do-ing for a trip to the toy store. The aisles of Toys R Us are almost over-whelming with their array of games, dolls, skates, books, bicycles, school and party supplies, and other toys as well as many items for ba-bies and preschoolers. Toys R Us has several locations around Dallas. Some of the other toy stores listed below are also not located in the malls and often carry popular toys as well as some challenging and edu-cational toys, collectible items, and nature-related projects. Nature stores, museum gift shops, and bookstores listed earlier in this chapter often have some fascinating toys to help children learn more about the world around them.

US TOY

3115 W. Parker Rd.
Plano (972) 964-8600

4760 Preston Rd., #226
Frisco (214) 387-8697
4900 Eldorado Pkwy., #148
McKinney (972) 542-8697

LEARNING EXPRESS

www.learningexpress.com
6818 Snider Plaza
Dallas (214) 696-4876
Willow Bend Market
5964 W. Parker Rd. #120
Plano (972) 473-8697
1314 W. McDermott at Alma
Allen (214) 383-2610

LAKESHORE LEARNING STORE

13846 Dallas Pkwy.
Dallas (972) 934-8866
Website: www.lakeshorelearning-store.com

TOYS UNIQUE

5600 W. Lover's Lane, #130
Dallas (214) 956-8697

FROGGIE'S 5 & 10
3211 Knox St.
(near Wild About Harry's)
Dallas (214) 522-5867

THE TOY MAVEN
6025 Royal, Ste. 223, at Preston
Dallas (214) 265-9971
Website: www.thetoymaven.com

AMAZING TOY CREATIONS AT IN-DOOR SAFARI PARK
13350 Dallas Pkwy., Ste. 3870
Galleria, Dallas (972) 661-2990
Website: www.indoorsafaripark.com

LEGO EDUCATION CENTER
2315 E. Southlake Blvd., # 110
Southlake (888) 728-LEGO
Website: www.LEGOeducation-centers.us

PARTY SUPPLIES

Sometimes nothing else will do for your child's birthday but the face of his or her favorite character on invitations and party plates. A wide assortment of paper goods, decorations, party favors, and invitations may be found at the area's stores devoted solely to helping you organize a fun and hassle-free party. Party Universe, Party City, Michaels, Hallmark, Target, Wal-Mart, and Hobby Lobby have multiple locations around the city. Other favorite party suppliers are listed below.

PARTY BAZAAR
4435 W. Lovers Lane
Dallas (214) 528-4795

THE SOCIAL BEE
5960 W. Parker Rd. #256
S.E. corner at Tollway
Plano (972) 781-0151

FLEA MARKETS AND TRADE DAYS

CANTON FIRST MONDAY TRADE DAYS
P.O. Box 245, Highway 19, Canton 75103 (903) 567-6556
Website: www.firstmondaycanton.com

The tradition of trading and swapping goods and animals began at the turn of the 20th century in Canton around the courthouse in the square. Farmers and vendors would come on the first Monday when court was in session. The popularity of the trade day outgrew its surroundings, so in 1965 it was moved to a location a little north of town that could accommodate the crowds and provide 100 acres for vendors. Be prepared for a great deal of walking. Mobility scooter rentals. No admission fee. Parking fee.

Hours: Canton Trade Days are Thursday to Sunday before the first Monday of every month, 7 AM until dark, rain or shine. Many of the vendors are in covered pavilions.

Directions: Take I-20E about 60 miles. Exit on Hwy. 19 or FM 859 and go about one mile south.

Splash Kingdom, a family water park, is open seasonally on I-20 near Canton. The park offers a wave pool, a river pool, a children's play castle, five slides, miniature golf, arcade games, and party areas. The park is located at I-20 and FM 859, Exit #526. Mailing address: P.O. Box 876, Canton 75103 (903) 567-0044. Website: www.splashkingdomwater park.com.

TRADE DAYS USA

at Texas Motor Speedway, 3601 Highway 114, Fort Worth 76177 (800) 946-7009. Website: www.tradedaysusa.com

This 200-acre trade days venue, opened in 2008 on the grounds of Texas Motor Speedway, offers a flea market, arts and crafts, food and drinks, farmers market, children's play area, plant nursery, and live entertainment. Admission fee. Parking fee.

Hours: Trade days are on Saturday and Sunday before the fourth Monday of each month. 9 AM to 5 PM.

Directions: Go west on I-635. Merge onto TX-121S via Exit 36A on the left toward DFW Airport. Merge onto TX-114W toward Fort Worth. End at 3601 Highway 114.

TRADERS VILLAGE AND RV PARK

2602 Mayfield Rd., Grand Prairie 75052 (972) 647-2331 Website: www.tradersvillage.com

More than 1,800 dealers set up shop in the 106-acre flea market every Saturday and Sunday. Traders Village also has great festival foods, kiddie rides, and arcade games. Special events include the Prairie Dog Chili Cookoff in April and the National Championship Indian Pow Wow on the weekend after Labor Day, as well as other family activities. This market is not like Canton. Most of the vendors sell new, inexpensive products. There are few craft items. No admission fee. Parking fee.

Hours: 8:00 AM until dark.

Directions: Traders Village is located just off Hwy. 360 on Mayfield, one mile north of I-20 or five miles south of I-30. RV Park: (972) 647-8205.

THIRD MONDAY TRADE DAYS

4550 University Drive, McKinney (972) 562-5466 Website: www.tmtd.com

Both indoor and outdoor treasures abound at the nearly 300-vendor flea market in McKinney. Smaller than Canton, but a great three-hour-plus shopping day. No admission fee. Parking fee.

Hours: 8 AM to 5 PM; Friday, Saturday, Sunday preceding the third Monday of each month.

Directions: Hwy. 380 (W. University), two miles west of Hwy. 75.

HOTEL HIATUS

If your family enjoys staying in hotels, letting someone else cook and make beds, lounging by the pool (or splashing wildly in it), but you hate the long rides in the car that it often takes to reach vacation spots, try a weekend at one of our local hotels. Sometimes discount rates are available because the business folks have flown home and the rooms are empty and waiting. If it is winter, pick one with an indoor pool, such as the Embassy Suites Hotel–Market Center or the one by Dallas Love Field, both of which also have rooms with refrigerators, ranges, and two televisions. Others with indoor pools include Intercontinental Dallas, Holiday Inn Select North Dallas, Sheraton Suites Market Center. Many even offer a complimentary breakfast.

Some are within walking distance of major attractions, and others, like the Westin by the Galleria, are attached to shopping centers. The Galleria has an ice rink and wonderful shops, and the Crescent is on the trolley line to the Arts District. In Las Colinas, the Omni Mandalay is on the canal that winds by the famous Mustangs sculpture. Not far away is the Las Colinas Equestrian Center.

Sunday brunch at the hotels is a family treat. What appears to be acres of beautifully displayed breakfast/lunch dishes are bound to encourage even the pickiest eaters. Hotels with scrumptious Sunday brunch include Four Seasons Resort, Hilton Anatole, Wyndham Garden Hotel, the Rosewood Crescent Hotel, Doubletree Hotels at Campbell Center and at Dallas Market Center, the Mansion on Turtle Creek, and Five Sixty in the tower at Hyatt Regency Reunion. Watch the weekend newspapers around holidays for other special meals and surprise visits from characters like the Easter Bunny.

HYATT REGENCY AT REUNION

300 Reunion Blvd., Dallas 75207-4498 (214) 651-1234 Website:
www.dallasregency.hyatt.com

One of the favorite landmarks of the downtown skyline that children love to spot, especially at night, is the sight of the ball atop Reunion Tower. The multifaceted glass facade of the hotel reflects the growing downtown area and fantastic Texas sunsets.

Children enjoy riding the glass-fronted elevator up 50 stories whether or not they are treated to lunch at Five Sixty (formerly Antares), the revolving restaurant with a panoramic view of the city. At night the dome dances in a computer-operated light show. Inside the hotel is an 18-story atrium, an interesting mineral ball, and more glass elevators. Just outside the hotel are fountains cascading into a serene pool. Those staying at the Hyatt have access to the outdoor swimming pool, three tennis courts, jogging track, health club, and four restaurants. A three-story collection of art, photographs, and memorabilia salutes Dallas history from its early days to today. Reunion Arena, which is also part of the complex, is home to ice-skating performances, concerts, circuses, and a variety of other entertainment. Reunion is so named because of its location as the site of an early settlement, so it is part of the historic district that includes Union Station next door. Union Station, once a thriving railway station, now is the site of a DART rail stop, Trinity Railway Express, and Amtrak.

GAYLORD TEXAN RESORT AND CONVENTION CENTER

1501 Gaylord Trail, Grapevine 76051 (866) 782-7897 Website:
www.gaylordhotels.com/gaylordtexan/

Opened in 2004 by the owners of Nashville's Opryland Hotel, the Gaylord Resort, located on the southern tip of Lake Grapevine, is a $328 million luxury hotel. A striking four-acre indoor atrium features familiar elements of the Texas landscape, such as Texas limestone and lush native plants, as well as waterfalls and a babbling brook. A Lone Star, which can be seen from airplanes flying over it, tops off the atrium. Amenities include an indoor lap pool and an outdoor pool, four restaurants, shops, jogging and biking trails, workout facilities, and an indoor entertainment complex. Sections of the hotel have different Texas themes, such as the oil boom. A nine-story oil derrick is the showpiece of that area. Visitors also have access to the Cowboys Golf Club and water sports on Lake Grapevine. Nearby are DFW Airport, Grapevine Outlet Mall, and Bass Pro Shops.

GREAT WOLF LODGE

1400 East Highway 26, Grapevine 76051 (800) 693-9653 Website: www.greatwolf.com

A definite kid-magnet, the Great Wolf Lodge grabs them at the entrance with the wolf sculptures and a peek at the rushing water in its indoor waterpark tube slides. Water fun is found in the 80,000-square-foot indoor park that features six pools, nine slides, whirlpool, and a four-story interactive water fort. Outdoors is an 84,000-square-foot park with a water basketball pool, a family whirlpool, and two body slides. Additionally, the hotel offers four restaurants, an interactive MagiQuest game, redemption arcade, kids spa, story time at the big clock tower, and Wolf Walks where kids hike around the lobby to learn about wolves, bears, and other wildlife.

RESTAURANTS WITH MORE

Dallas has so many restaurants that a family could easily eat out every night without dining in the same restaurant twice. The staple foods for children, such as pizza, hamburgers, and fried chicken strips, are readily available, as well as Dallas's famous Tex-Mex and many other delicious ethnic foods. But some of the area restaurants don't just satisfy hunger; they also entertain with the addition of small rides, music, arcades, play areas, and costumed characters.

When asking the very young where they would like to go for lunch, the first reaction is likely to be McDonald's, Braum's, or Burger King because of the soft-floored play areas with slides and other toys to play on, as well as little prizes to take home if you buy the child's meal. Some Burger Kings and McDonald's also have indoor play parks. However, as children grow older, they notice that in addition to these great restaurants, Dallas has many others designed with their entertainment in mind. They also are good places for birthday parties.

PIZZA AND MORE

CRYSTAL'S PIZZA
930 W. Airport Fwy.
Irving (972) 579-0441
  Arcade, room to show a team video.

CHUCK E. CHEESE'S PIZZA
Dallas (972) 392-1944
Allen (972) 396-7825
Arlington (817) 861-1561
Garland (972) 681-1385

Irving (972) 256-1600
Grand Prairie (972) 660-6799
Rides, video games, music.

MR. GATTI'S PIZZA
5941 Greenville Ave.
Dallas (214) 691-2222
Video games.

PETER PIPER PIZZA PARLOR
729 W. Jefferson, Oak Cliff
Dallas (214) 943-6582
Video games.

PLANET PIZZA
3000 Custer Rd., S.E. corner
Plano (972) 985-7711
Many indoor rides, soft play.

HAMBURGERS, CHICKEN, STEAKS, AND MORE

BALLS HAMBURGERS
4343 W. Northwest Hwy. at
Midway
Dallas (214) 352-2525
Sports theme, TV, video games.

BENIHANA
7775 Banner Drive
Dallas (972) 387-4404
Food cooked at your table
with a flourish, pricey.

COACH'S BURGERS
362 Abrams-Forest Center
Dallas (972) 342-2622
Burgers, great grilled cheese,
salads, chicken strips, shakes.
TVs, large party room, a few arcade games.

CHUCK'S
15757 Coit, Ste. 502
Richardson (972) 386-7752
Hamburgers, chicken, salads;
seven arcade games, video screen,
party room.

DAVE & BUSTER'S
10727 Composite
Dallas (214) 353-0620

8021 Walnut Hill at Central
Expwy.
Dallas (214) 361-5553
1202/2220 Stonebriar Center
Frisco (214) 387-0915
Large arcade; redeem prizes; in-
sist adult accompany each child.

THE DREAM CAFE
2800 Routh St. at Quadrangle
Dallas (214) 954-0486
5100 Belt Line Rd.
Dallas (972) 503-7326
Small outdoor playground area.

FUDDRUCKER'S
5500 Greenville
Dallas (214) 360-0146
4520 Frankford Rd.
Dallas (972) 818-3833
Also Garland, Plano.
A few video games.

HARD ROCK CAFE
Victory Park
2211 N. Houston St., Dallas
Website: www.hardrockcafe.com
Rock memorabilia, music, sou-
venir store.

JOE'S CRAB SHACK

10250 E. Technology Blvd.
Near Loop 12-35E split and
Lombardy (214) 654-0909
3320 Central Expwy.
Plano (972) 423-2800
Also Mesquite, Lewisville,
Grapevine

Outdoor playground, loud music; go early to avoid a large crowd.

MAGIC TIME MACHINE

5003 Belt Line
Addison (972) 980-1903

Costumed waitpersons, unique dining rooms.

THE PURPLE COW

6025 Royal Lane
110 Preston Royal Shopping
Center
Dallas (214) 373-0037

Famous for purple milkshake, hot pimento cheese sandwich.

RAINFOREST CAFÉ

Grapevine Mills Outlet Center
Hwy 121 N. and 3000
Grapevine Mills Pkwy.
Grapevine (972) 539-5001

Jungle rainforest theme, sounds of rainstorm, jungle animals; Wednesday Family Night.

SCOTTY P'S

11661 Preston Rd. Ste. 131 at
Forest
Dallas (972) 398-6767

Also in Garland, Frisco, Plano, Allen, McKinney

Hamburgers, chicken, hot dogs, salads.

WILD ABOUT HARRY'S

3113 Knox St.
Dallas (214) 520-3113

Great hot dogs, cold custard, close to Froggie's Toys.

COOK YOUR OWN

MELTING POT

4900 Belt Line
Addison (972) 960-7027

Fondue; cook at table, pricey.

SIMPLY FONDUE

2108 Lower Greenville
Dallas (214) 827-8878

Cook at table, pricey.

DINNER THEATER

MEDIEVAL TIMES DINNER AND TOURNAMENT

2021 Stemmons at Market Center, Dallas (214) 761-1800

Return to the age of chivalry and knighthood as you come to Medieval Times Dinner and Tournament. As you feast on a sumptuous four-course banquet, you will witness feats of skill and daring adventure. See

127

the beautiful Andalusian stallions dance and the graceful falcon soar. Cheer as six brave knights compete in the Tournament Royale, a joust and combat to determine the true champion of the castle. Call for reservations or group discounts.

THE POCKET SANDWICH THEATER

5400 E. Mockingbird, east of Central Expwy., Dallas (214) 821-1860 Website: www.pocketsandwich.com

Dine on sandwiches, nachos, etc., while watching the fun at Pocket Sandwich Theater. A variety of performances are scheduled, but the favorites seem to be the melodramas (popcorn to throw at the villain available) and spoofs. Thursdays to Sundays.

COMMUNITY COLLEGES

The **Dallas County Community College District** offers both credit and noncredit courses for adults, but it is also a place for children. Each college has a different program, but most offer a few classes during the school year and a wide variety of classes and day camps in the summer. The classes vary according to interest and availability of instructors. If the college has a drama department, there will probably be some plays for the family included, and some of them are free. Each campus also has literary and music festivals, art exhibits, guest lecturers, and sports events. Some campuses have mailing lists to which community members may be added by calling **Student Programs** or **Continuing Education**. If the college you are interested in does not mail out, then stop by those offices and pick up their schedule of events periodically. Listed below are the colleges and numbers to call for continuing education classes/camps for kids. Most classes are during the summer months.

BROOKHAVEN

3939 Valley View Lane, Farmers Branch 75244 (972) 860-4600 Theater box office: (972) 860-4118

CEDAR VALLEY

3030 N. Dallas Ave., Lancaster 75134 (972) 860-8210

EASTFIELD

3737 Motley, Mesquite 75150 (972) 860-7113 Theater.

EL CENTRO
Downtown: Main and Lamar, Dallas 75202 (214) 860-2147
Some children's theater productions.

MOUNTAIN VIEW
4849 W. Illinois Ave., Dallas 75211 (214) 860-8680

NORTH LAKE
5001 N. MacArthur Blvd., Irving 75038 (972) 273-3360

RICHLAND
12800 Abrams Rd., Dallas 75243 (972) 238-6144
Pretty trail around pond, ducks; tree farm, horticulture area; theater.

3. PERFORMING ARTS FOR CHILDREN

Alex DeLange ©

Although not all of us are blessed with a beautiful singing voice, an unfailing sense of rhythm, limber joints, and the ability to convincingly assume the personality of a character in a play, we are able to sit back at a performance and appreciate the talents of others and leave with the feeling that we are better for it—whether the music is opera or opry and the play *Romeo and Juliet* or *Snow White*. Encouraging creative expression in children is an important part of parenting. The arts in the Dallas area have numerous avenues to help parents introduce their children to many types of theater, music, and dance. Opportunities for children to attend stimulating classes and become performers themselves are available in all of the arts to help children develop skills and self-confidence. Performing arts festivals held throughout the year enable families to relax together and to be thoroughly entertained by live performances, far away from televisions and video games.

In the Friday "Guide" of the *Dallas Morning News*, notices are given of performances, visual arts presentations, and festivals for families. The website www.guidelive.com gives the name, location, phone, price, and date of current productions. Also a good source for Dallas arts and cultural organizations is the website of the **Dallas Office of Cultural Affairs**: www.dallasculture.org. OCA lists links for public art, cultural centers, performance organizations, and events. The **Sammons Center for the Arts** is home to various nonprofit performing arts groups, and www.sammonsartscenter.org provides helpful links. The downtown **Arts District Friends** provide an Events Calendar on www.artsdistrict.org, or you may call (214) 953-1977. A very useful website for teachers, schools, and parents is **Dallas ArtsPartners**, www.dallasartspartners.org, a collaboration between DISD, Dallas Office of Cultural Affairs, Young Audiences of North Texas, A.R.T.S. for People, and more than 60 additional cultural and community arts agencies. Produced by KERA public media in North Texas, www.artandseek.org is another site for arts, culture, and creative people, and it offers a list for kids and family.

If parents are not sure if a performance is appropriate for their children, they should call the performing arts group and ask what ages would most enjoy the performance. Many arts organizations and performing arts centers have mailing lists and websites that can keep you up-to-date on their schedules. Usually discounts are given for children, students with ID, and groups. Some performances are free.

A matinee is a good time to introduce younger children to classical music and dance because the atmosphere is more informal. Shorter performances are often presented at the Dallas Museum of Art, Texas Discovery Gardens, and libraries. Many of the performing arts groups have outreach programs that allow them to perform in schools, and some of the Dallas County Community Colleges and other area colleges include children's theater in their season. Listed below are some of the major performing arts centers in the area that include performances for families. Your chamber of commerce/visitors center can give you the phone numbers of performing arts groups in your community.

Tickets for many performances may be purchased through **Ticketmaster** at (214) 373-8000 or (800) 745-3000 or online at www.ticketmaster.com.

DALLAS CENTER FOR THE PERFORMING ARTS

Administrative offices: (214) 954-9925
2403 Flora St.
Dallas
(from Woodall Rodgers Freeway, exit Pearl St.)
Website: www.dallasperformingarts.org

New venues opening fall 2009 (See "Arts District" in **Chapter 1:** Places to Go.)

Dee and Charles Wyly Theatre
Home to Dallas Theater Center, Anita N. Martinez Ballet Folklorico, Dallas Black Dance Theatre.
Margot and Bill Winspear Opera House
Home to Dallas Opera and Texas Ballet Theater.
City Performance Hall
Theater, dance, music, film, lectures.

METROPLEX PERFORMANCE VENUES

ADDISON THEATRE CENTRE
15650 Addison at Mildred
Addison (972) 450-6232
Website: www.watertowertheatre.org

ARTCENTRE THEATRE
1039 E. 15th St.
Plano (972) 423-7809
Website: www.artcentreofplano.org

DALLAS CONVENTION CENTER
650 S. Griffin
Dallas (214) 939-2700
Website: www.dallasconvention center.com

GRANVILLE ARTS CENTER
300 N. Fifth St.
Garland (972) 205-2780
Website: www.garlandarts.com

HOUSE OF BLUES
White Swan Building
2200 N. Lamar St.
Dallas (214) 978-BLUE

KALITA HUMPHREY'S THEATER
3636 Turtle Creek Blvd.
Dallas (214) 526-8210
Website: www.dallastheater-center.org

SAMMONS CENTER FOR THE ARTS
3630 Harry Hines
Dallas (214) 520-7788
Website: www.sammonsarts center.org

MAJESTIC THEATRE
1925 Elm
Dallas (214) 880-0137
Website: www.dsmmanagement group.com; www.liveatthe majestic.org

MEYERSON SYMPHONY CENTER
2301 Flora, Ste. 300
Dallas (214) 670-3600
Website: www.dallassymphony.com

IRVING ARTS CENTER
3333 N. MacArthur
Irving (972) 252-ARTS; (972) 252-7558
Website: www.irvingartscenter.com

LATINO CULTURAL CENTER
2600 Live Oak
Dallas (214) 670-3320
Website: www.dallasculture.org

MEADOWS SCHOOL OF THE ARTS
SMU, Hillcrest and Binkley
Dallas (214) 768-2880
Tickets (214) 768-ARTS
Website: www.meadows.smu.edu

MUSIC HALL
Fair Park, 909 First St. and
Parry
Dallas (214) 565-1116
Website: www.liveatthemusichall
.com

POCKET SANDWICH THEATER
400 E. Mockingbird
Dallas (214) 821-1860
Website: www.pocketsandwich
.com

NOKIA THEATRE
1001 Next Stage Dr.
Grand Prairie (972) 854-5111
Website: www.nokialivedfw.com

THEATRE ARLINGTON
305 W. Main
Arlington (817) 275-7661
Website: www.theatrearlington
.org

MESQUITE ARTS CENTER
1527 N. Galloway
Mesquite (972) 216-6444
Website:
www.cityofmesquite.com

SUPERPAGES.COM AMPHITHEATER
Fair Park
Dallas (214) 421-1111
Website: www.fairpark.org

THEATRE THREE
2800 Routh, Quadrangle
Dallas (214) 871-3300
Website: www.theatre3dallas.com

EISEMANN CENTER FOR PERFORMING ARTS
2351 Performance Dr.
Richardson (972) 744-4600
Website: www.eisemanncenter
.com

DALLAS CHILDREN'S THEATER
Rosewood Center for Family Arts
5938 Skillman
Dallas (214) 740-0051
Website: www.dct.org

AMERICAN AIRLINES CENTER
2500 Victory Ave.
Dallas (214) 222-3687
Hotline: (214) 665-4200
Website: www.americanairlines
center.com

TEXAS THEATRE
231 West Jefferson
Dallas (214) 565-1116
Website: www.liveatthetexas
theatre.com

DANCE

One good source for keeping up with dance-related activities in the Metroplex is through the Dance Council publication *Dance* and their website: www.thedancecouncil.org. The Dance Council number is (214) 219-2290. Scholarships for ages 13 to 21 and memberships are available.

TITAS

Office: 3625 N. Hall St., Ste. 740, Dallas 75219 (214) 528-5576
Website: www.titas.org

TITAS is a nonprofit organization dedicated to bringing the best performances in dance and music to the Dallas area. To encourage families to attend performances together, TITAS offers $5 youth tickets for kindergarten to grade 12, as well as 50 percent off student rush tickets for college students. Call the box office or look online for details on these programs as well as series subscription information.

ANITA N. MARTINEZ BALLET FOLKLORICO DANCE STUDIO

4422 Live Oak, Dallas 75204 (214) 828-0181
Website: www.anmbf.org

The performance season for this professional Hispanic dance company runs from May through September and includes both public and private performances. Some dancers also teach in the Anita M. Martinez Ballet Folklorico Academy and train children 6 years of age and up to perform regional folk dances of Mexico. Their performances are mainly at the Wyly Theatre in the Dallas Center for the Performing Arts.

DALLAS BLACK DANCE THEATRE

2627 Flora St., Dallas 75201 (214) 871-2376
Website: www.dbdt.com

The Dallas Black Dance Theatre, a modern contemporary dance company, has entertained local, national, and international audiences since 1976. During each performance season, they schedule performances at the Wyly Theatre in the Arts District. The group also performs in the September *Dallas Morning News* Dance Festival. As part of an outreach program, the company presents Schoolday Matinee Performances for area schools and other groups. In their **Dallas Black Dance Academy**, students ages 4 to adult study dance onsite at the Arts District facility and offsite for DISD, private schools, and other youth centers. Their repertory consists of jazz, modern, ethnic, and spiritual works by well-known choreographers. Boys and girls ages 9 to 16 are offered the opportunity to audition for their summer dance program, providing the dancers have had some experience. Look for the annual Dance Africa Festival and African Marketplace.

TEXAS BALLET THEATER
Winspear Opera House, Dallas Center for the Performing Arts, Dallas
6845 Green Oaks Rd., Fort Worth 76116 (817) 763-0207
Website: www.texasballettheater.org

This dance company, formerly Fort Worth/Dallas Ballet, now presents its season from October to May mainly at the Winspear Opera House in the Arts District. **Texas Ballet Theater School** enrolls students ages 4 and up.

MUSIC AND CHORUS

THE CHILDREN'S CHORUS OF GREATER DALLAS
400 N. St. Paul St., Ste. 510, Dallas 75201 (214) 965-0491
Website: www.thechildrenschorus.org

The Children's Chorus of Greater Dallas offers Metroplex children the opportunity to experience musical artistry and excellence through choral singing in a group that reflects Dallas's diversity. This tuition-based ensemble includes fourth- through eighth-grade girls and boys with unchanged voices. Tuition assistance is available. Qualifications are a good voice, a good sense of pitch, and a commitment to regular attendance at rehearsals and performances. Auditions are held in April. Current membership is 415 children singing in seven children's choruses and one youth chorus. CCGD gives its own three-concert series at the Meyerson Center; performs frequently across the area; and tours regionally, nationally, and internationally.

DALLAS CHAMBER ORCHESTRA
P.O. Box 600954, Dallas 75360 (214) 321-1411
Website: www.dallaschamberorchestra.org

An award-winning orchestra of 15 strings, the Dallas Chamber Orchestra presents a diverse repertoire and highlights local soloists and world-class artists in a comfortable and less formal atmosphere. The orchestra presents two concert series each season: the Traditional Series of five concerts and the Sunset at the Lake Series of six concerts. The Lake series is held at White Rock Lake's Dreyfus Club. Check the website for other North Dallas concert locations.

THE ALLEGRO GUITAR SOCIETY

Sammons Center, 3630 Harry Hines, Ste.15, Dallas 75219 (888) 553-7387, (972) 243-1199 Website: www.guitarsociety.org

The Allegro Guitar Society presents five concerts by international touring artists in various venues. The majority of their work is outreach programming that they perform in schools throughout North Texas, reaching about 12,000 children every year. Additionally, they have a Guitar in the Schools program that allows them to visit and teach guitar clinics in schools so the students have a one-on-one class with a concert artist. Annually, they work with the Acoustic Music Camp, mainly for ages 13 and older.

DALLAS JAZZ ORCHESTRA

P.O. Box 743875, Dallas 75374 (214) 521-8816
office: Sammons Center for the Arts,
3636 Harry Hines, Dallas 75219
Website: www.djo.org

The Dallas Jazz Orchestra, a 20-piece Big Band, plays original and traditional Big Band jazz music. It performs regularly at The Village, 8310 Southwestern, and high school age and older really enjoy attending. Once each July the orchestra performs with DISD's Dallas Area Youth Orchestra and college groups at The Village. Families are more familiar with their free summer Sunday afternoon performances at Lee, Samuell, and Kidd Springs parks. Several recordings are available.

A popular jazz event at the Sammons Center in the fall and spring is Sammons Jazz, the only regular ongoing jazz performance series in the area featuring local jazz artists. Call ahead for tickets.

DALLAS/MUSIC

Snider Plaza, 3415 Milton, Dallas 75205 (214) 363-4980
Website: www.dallas-music.net

Dallas/Music has classes in piano, guitar, Suzuki flute, Suzuki violin for ages 4 or 5 to adult. Classes for ages 3 months to kindergarten include "Music, Mommy, and Me," "First Movement," and "Wee Music Makers." Recitals, festivals, and other activities round out the music experience. Adult instruction is also offered.

THE DALLAS SCHOOL OF MUSIC

2650 Midway Rd., Ste. 204, Carrollton 75006 (972) 380-8050
Website: www.dsminfo.com

The Dallas School of Music has been providing award-winning and innovative music education for both children and adults since 1992.

Individual instruction is available for piano, guitar, and voice, plus all woodwind, brass, percussion, and stringed instruments. Year Round, School Year, Semester, and Flex plans offer families a wide variety of enrollment options. Optional performance programs occur throughout the year and include student showcases, holiday recitals, and a uniquely designed event called "Musicking," which creates a friendly and comfortable cabaret-like atmosphere for adult students. The school is open Monday through Thursday from 10 AM to 9 PM and Saturdays from 9 AM to 4 PM. Many events are free and open to the public.

DALLAS SYMPHONY ASSOCIATION, INC.

Morton H. Meyerson Symphony Center, 2301 Flora St., Ste. 300, Dallas 75201 (214) 871-4000 Websites: www.dallassymphony.com; www.dsokids.com

The Dallas Symphony performs year-round in the internationally acclaimed Meyerson Symphony Center. In addition to Classical, Pops, and Summer Festival series, the DSO presents numerous concerts throughout the year for children and their families. The Cecil and Ida M. Green Youth Concert Series features the DSO performing educational programs approximately 45 minutes in length. Daytime concerts are offered for children pre-K to second grade and grades three to six. The DSO also presents an annual high school concert featuring a side-by-side performance with the Greater Dallas Youth Orchestra.

In addition to the youth concert series, the Dallas Symphony offers numerous free concerts throughout the year. The summer concert series each late March through June features free concerts in Dallas parks. Two favorite family concerts are the Easter concert on the lawn at Lee Park and the Memorial Day concert at Flag Pole Hill. Other concerts in the Meyerson Center include the annual Festival Latino Concert and the African American Festival Concert. On the website, look under "Community and Education." For ticket information, please call (214) 692-0203 or check the website. The DSO Kids site is audiovisual fun.

DALLAS WIND SYMPHONY

P.O. Box 595026, Dallas 75359 (214) 565-9463 Website: www.dws.org

Fifty woodwind, brass, and percussion players make up the Dallas Wind Symphony, whose style ranges from Bach to Bernstein and Sousa to Strauss. They perform at the Meyerson Symphony Center and have an annual concert subscription series. An exciting event is the DWS Invitational Windband Festival in May. A link to a list of area community bands is on their website.

FINE ARTS CHAMBER PLAYERS

Sammons Center for the Arts, 3630 Harry Hines Blvd., Dallas
75219 (214) 520-2219 Website: www.fineartschamberplayers.org

The Fine Arts Chamber Players include musicians from the Dallas Symphony, Dallas Opera, and music teachers who perform many free concerts annually. Every Sunday afternoon in July in the Basically Beethoven Festival series, musicians present classical music designed for family entertainment at the Texas Discovery Gardens at Fair Park. These free performances begin at 3 PM and end at 5 PM, with one intermission. Doors open at 2 PM, and For Love of Music Youth Recitals begin at 2:30 PM and last 30 minutes. These performances are free, but a reservation is required.

A good format for children to be exposed to classical music in a more informal setting is the **Bancroft Family Concerts** in October and November and January through May. These concerts, held at the Dallas Museum of Art's Horchow Auditorium, begin at 3 PM and last for one hour with no intermission.

GREATER DALLAS YOUTH ORCHESTRA ASSOCIATION, INC.

Sammons Center for the Arts, 3630 Harry Hines Blvd., Dallas
75219 (214) 528-7747 Website: www.gdyo.org

The Greater Dallas Youth Orchestra offers a wonderful opportunity for children to experience other children and youth performing music. The six orchestras, involving more than 400 talented musicians, perform a variety of concerts at various locations throughout the school year and tour nationally and internationally. Four concerts, performed at the Meyerson by the top orchestra, are two-hour symphony concerts similar to what you would experience in a Saturday evening Dallas Symphony classical concert. They may be beyond the attention span of younger children but could be very inspiring for older elementary children.

The afternoon concerts performed by the younger orchestras are accessible to all ages and can be "come and go" affairs, depending on the child's attention span. Details about auditions and concerts are available on the website.

KINDERMUSIK INTERNATIONAL

Various locations in the Metroplex; Website:
www.kindermusikdfw.com

Kindermusik instructors lead a group of parents and children in fun, musical play that is designed to promote self-esteem, improve coordination and balance, and develop creative skills. Ages newborn to 7 years old are included in Kindermusik classes. The classes may be held in private studios, music stores and studios, schools, community centers, churches, and other types of locations. Go to the website to find classes and summer camps in your area.

MUSIC TOGETHER

Dallas: Temple Emanu-El. Other locations: Plano, Frisco (972) 267-4452 Website: www.musictogetherdallas.com

Music Together is an early childhood music program for ages birth to 6. It builds on children's natural enthusiasm for music and movement. In the weekly 45-minute classes, students learn songs, rhythmic rhymes, movements, and instrument play.

SCHOOL OF ROCK MUSIC

5606 Dyer St., Dallas (214) 363-ROCK Website: www.SchoolOfRock.com

The Paul Green School of Rock Music offers a core program for students ages 7 to 18. It includes weekly private lessons in guitar, bass, drums, vocals, and keyboards, as well as weekly three-hour supervised and organized rehearsals.

MEADOWS SCHOOL OF THE ARTS

P.O. Box 750356, Southern Methodist University, Dallas 75275 (214) 768-ARTS Website: www.meadows.smu.edu

Meadows School of the Arts performances in music, dance, and theater are held at the Meadows School of the Arts. The *Dallas Morning News* Community Arts Calendar on Sunday lists performances, and SMU has an arts line to call. Student presentations of classic, modern, and musical productions are usually held in the Caruth Auditorium, Bob Hope Theatre, and Margo Jones Theatre.

MUSIC MILL AMPHITHEATRE

2201 Road to Six Flags, Arlington 76010; Metro (817) 640-8900 Website: www.sixflags.com/texas

Pop, country, gospel, and many other types of superstar concerts are enjoyed during the Six Flags summer season as well as throughout the year. Concert ticket prices are usually in addition to the park entrance fee.

RICHARDSON SYMPHONY ORCHESTRA

2100 N. Collins, Ste. 310, Richardson 75080 (972) 234-4195 Website: www.richardsonsymphony.org

The Richardson Symphony Orchestra usually holds seven evening performances at Richardson's Eisemann Center. The orchestra also sponsors the Lennox Young Artists Competition in January. Young musicians from all over the country come to compete in three categories, and the winners of the top honors perform with the RSO in the March concert. A Sounds of Freedom patriotic program is held annually on July Fourth, and they also present a free Sounds of Class concert at UTD in late September. A Symphony Days concert is presented for RISD third-graders in November. The orchestra offers discounted tickets for children and their families.

PLANO SYMPHONY ORCHESTRA

2701-C W. 15th St., Ste. 187, Plano 75075 (972) 473-7262
Website: www.planosymphony.org

In addition to their regular concert season, the Plano Symphony Orchestra presents an orchestral series of five symphonies during October to March called Family Symphony Sundays at Plano's Courtyard Theater, 1509 Avenue H, and at the Eisemann Center for the Arts in Richardson. The symphony offers educational programs for elementary-age children and supports the Collin County Young Artist Competition. Look online or call about appearances at Barnes & Noble bookstores for music and story time.

SUPERPAGES.COM CENTER

1818 First Ave. at Fair Park, Dallas 75210 (214) 421-1111
Website: www.ticketmaster.com

Superpages.com Center amphitheatre presents concerts by popular musicians and singers year round, but the summer season is a favorite. This outdoor theater can seat 20,000 people, and concessions are available. Tickets are available at Ticketmaster outlets or by calling (214) 373-8000 or (800) 745-3000. Tickets may also be purchased on the Web.

TEXAS BOYS CHOIR

3901 S. Hulen St., Fort Worth 76109 (817) 924-1482
Website: www.texasboyschoir.org

Founded in 1946 in Denton, the Texas Boys Choir moved to Fort Worth in 1957. The 50-voice choir is the top-level choir of the Texas Boys Choir organization, and it performs both nationally and internationally. The school has become a publicly funded co-ed school with 350 students in grades 3 to 12; it offers music, dance, and theater in conjunction with an academic core curriculum. The Fort Worth Academy of Fine Arts owns the campus where both classes and some performances are held. The repertoire of the Texas Boys Choir includes early classical, sacred, folk, patriotic, international, and Broadway music.

TEXAS GIRLS CHOIR

4449 Camp Bowie, Fort Worth 76107 (817) 732-8161
Website: www.texasgirlschoir.org/

The 200-voice Texas Girls Choir has been an active performance group for more than 30 years. The talented girls, ages 8 to 12, audition to become members. The choir performs locally and also takes two tours each year, one primarily in the South and the other abroad. The concert choir includes approximately 40 of the girls, and the remainder are in a preparatory choir. Choir members are drawn primarily from Tarrant, Dallas, Johnson, and Parker counties. Concerts are usually held in October, December, February, and May. Call for locations or look on the website.

YOUNGER GENERATION CHORUS

2828 W. Parker Rd., Ste. 202F, Plano 75075 (972) 596-9620
Website: www.youngergeneration.org

The Younger Generation Chorus of Plano consists of Collin County–area students in fourth to eighth grades who audition and then participate in a premier chorus. The choir performs locally and tours.

OPERA

THE DALLAS OPERA

Winspear Opera House, Dallas (214) 443-1043
Website: www.dallasopera.org

The Dallas Opera season, November through March, consists of approximately five operas with easy-to-read English subtitles and an additional holiday presentation, held at their new home in the Arts District, the Winspear Opera House. The Sunday matinee would be a good time for a family with older children to attend. One hour before the performance on Saturday is Opera Overtures, in which background information about the opera is given. Call (214) 443-1000 for tickets, or visit their website.

The Dallas Opera usually hosts **summer opera camps** for students who want to sing, write, design, or work in opera.

OPRY

The oprys in Texas should be on each country music lover's list of family entertainment. They are smaller but similar to Nashville's Grand

Ole Opry. They provide great singers and bands and a wholesome, lively atmosphere, free from the smoke and liquor of honky-tonks. Concessions are provided, and some offer group rates and dinner and show combinations. Some recommend reservations. Dress casually and get ready for a toe-tappin' good time.

GRAPEVINE OPRY

300 S. Main St., Grapevine; Metro (817) 481-8733
Websites: www.grapevineopry.com; www.grapevinetexasusa.com

Grapevine Opry, which has a lower floor and a balcony, is usually packed at its 7:30 PM Saturday performance. Sometimes, talented youngsters appear to sing, clog, and fiddle. The second half of the program is often arranged around themes such as Waltz across Texas, gospel songs, and patriotic songs. Dinner and show combinations for groups are offered. Occasionally, the singers and musicians in Grapevine will rotate with performers from other oprys. Gospel music is presented on the fourth Friday of each month. A concession stand is available. Reservations are made by telephone. If you must cancel, do so 24 hours in advance, or you forfeit your money.

PUPPETRY

The antics of puppets have entertained all ages for hundreds of years. In the Dallas area, the public libraries often present free puppet shows for children. Shopping malls, such as Northpark, sometimes offer December puppet shows, and groups who offer series for children often include puppet shows. KIDSarts, the summer program of the Irving Arts Center, sometimes offers classes in puppetry.

DALLAS PUPPET THEATER

Office: 3905 Main St., Dallas
Performances: The Women's Museum, Fair Park
(214) 515-0004 Website: www.puppetry.org

The Dallas Puppet Theater offers family performances, guest artists, school programs, outreach programs, puppetry gift shop, and birthdays. Geared toward ages 3 to 10, the performances at Fair Park's Women's Museum include familiar fairy tales, fables, holiday stories, and more to delight youngsters and their parents.

SLAPPY'S PUPPET PLAYHOUSE

13350 Dallas Pky., Ste. 3860, Dallas 75240 at Galleria Mall by Nordstrom's, third floor. (214) 369-4849 Website: www.slappysplayhouse.com

Slappy's Puppet Playhouse presents delightful European-style marionette shows with full-scale string puppets. It also offers summer activities such as circus camp, clown workshops, and birthday parties as well as vaudeville-style variety shows with clowns, magicians, and children's entertainers.

KATHY BURK'S THEATRE OF PUPPETRY ARTS

Dallas Children's Theater, 5938 Skillman, Dallas 75231 (214) 740-0051 Websites: www.kathyburkspuppets.com; www.dct.org

The Rosewood Theater houses Kathy Burk's collection of antique puppets and studio. Kathy Burk's Theatre of Puppetry Arts presents two original puppet plays each year as part of the Dallas Children's Theater's regular season and collaborates with DCT when puppets represent characters in a play, as in *The Velveteen Rabbit*. Some shows, such as *The Nutcracker*, are offered for onsite performances. It also offers birthday parties and create custom puppets.

THEATER

WATERTOWER THEATRE AT ADDISON THEATRE CENTRE

15650 Addison Rd., Addison 75001 (972) 450-6232 Website: www.watertowertheatre.org

The WaterTower Theatre offers a season of 11 productions and holiday shows in the Addison Theatre Centre. A yearly favorite is the Out of the Loop Fringe Festival of theater, dance, music, and visual arts. For students it offers the Summer Performing Arts Conservatory—two weeks of acting, singing, and dancing for ages 6 to 18. An after-school drama program, student rush tickets, and a summer internship program for college students are available.

CAPERS FOR KIDS

381 Casa Linda Plaza, Ste. 122, Dallas 75218 (972) 661-ARTS Website: www.capersforkids.com

Capers for Kids is an educational creative arts school that offers a faculty of degreed teachers who teach classes in drama and visual arts in preschools, private schools, and public schools in the area, for mainstream students and also those with learning differences. The half-day Summer Arts Camps are held in the morning and afternoon on Monday to Friday for two-week sessions.

CREATIVE ARTS THEATRE AND SCHOOL

1100 West Randol Mill Rd., Arlington 76012; Metro (817) 265-8512 Website: www.creativearts.org

The Creative Arts Theatre is a youth theater that includes year-long classes for age 4 to grade 12 in dance, acting, creative dramatics, technical theater, and more. The theater presents Spotlight shows in the main season. Six shows plus a fundraiser are presented in its season. A special two-week summer program is offered for out-of-town gifted students. Regular summer classes are in two-week sessions.

DALLAS CHILDREN'S THEATER, INC.

Rosewood Center for Family Arts, 5938 Skillman St., Dallas 75231 (214) 978-0110; box office (214) 740-0051 Website: www.dct.org

With a company of professional adult actors, Dallas Children's Theater (DCT) delights and enlightens young audiences and teenagers with an 11-play season based on classic literature, folk tales, myths, and contemporary stories. It also commissions original works and stage adaptations of literary sources relevant to today's families. Contact DCT or see the website for suggested age appropriateness for each show. Much of the season is presented in the Rosewood Center, and also includes El Centro College Performance Hall at Main and Market streets in downtown Dallas.

Most plays have an intermission, and drinks and snacks may be purchased. Season tickets and group rates are available. Other programs include a national touring company, a year-round theater academy for ages 3 to 18, school matinees, a teenage youth council, and arts-in-education programs for North Texas public and private schools. Special event parties and clubs provide family philanthropic opportunities. DCT was recognized by *Time* magazine as "one of the top five in the U.S."

THE DALLAS SUMMER MUSICALS

Box office: 542 Preston Royal Shopping Center, Dallas 75230 (214) 691-7200 (no phone sales)
Ticketmaster phone orders: (214) 631-ARTS (2787) or www.ticketmaster.com

Administrative offices: The Music Hall at Fair Park, 909 First Ave., Dallas 75210 Mailing address: P.O. Box 710336, Dallas 75371 (214) 421-5678
Websites: www.dallassummermusicals.org. Academy: www.dsmschool .org

The Dallas Summer Musicals is a nonprofit organization dedicated to bringing the very best of American musical theater and Broadway shows to the Dallas area. Since 1941, it has produced a summer season of entertainment, outdoors for 10 years, moving indoors to the air-conditioned Music Hall in 1951. The organization also presents six shows in the **Broadway Contemporary Series** in the winter at both the Music Hall and the Majestic Theater. The summer season is usually eight shows. Dining is available in Dining at the Music Hall buffet (214-413-3940) as well as at the more casual Bistro Café.

Of special interest to children and parents is their **Kids Club**, a free-to-join club that rewards kids with free events and prizes for coming to the shows. Also, the **Dallas Summer Musicals School of Musical Theatre**, located in the Majestic Theatre, is a school for ages 7 to adult. It offers some evening and Saturday classes as well as an intensive three-week summer camp for ages 12 and up. Recent student productions include *School House Rock* and *The Jungle Book*. **Satellite locations** of the Academy are listed on the website. For more information about the school, call (214) 969-7469, or visit the website above.

DALLAS THEATER CENTER

Dee and Charles Wyly Theatre at Flora and Leonard streets
Dallas Center for the Performing Arts (214) 252- 3918
Website: www.dtcinfo.org

The Dallas Theater Center opened its doors in 1959; it continued to hold performances in the Kalita Humphreys Theater, designed by Frank Lloyd Wright, until 2009 when it moved from the Turtle Creek Blvd. location to its new home downtown in the Dallas Center for Performing Arts. Usually, the theater center kicks off each season with an evening festival in late August called **Neighborhood Nights**. A family favorite during the regular season, which runs from September through April, is the annual performance of *A Christmas Carol*. For information about touring the theater, rehearsal halls, and costume shop, please call the theater (that information was not available by the publication date of this guide). The Dallas Theater Center also offers year-round classes in theater for children ages 4 to 18, taught by professional actors and teachers with extensive theater experience. In **The Lab**, these students have the opportunity to audition for children's parts in the professional productions, such as *A Christmas Carol*. The teen company does a summer production.

SOUTH DALLAS CULTURAL CENTER

3400 S. Fitzhugh at Second Ave., Dallas 75210 (214) 939-2787
Website: www.dallasculture.org/SDCCinfo.cfm

The South Dallas Cultural Center near Fair Park has a wide variety of activities for all ages and income groups. It provides a 120-seat black box theater, visual arts gallery, studios for dance, two-dimensional arts, ceramics, printmaking, photography, and a digital recording studio. Classes are available for children and adults. A summer program is included in the activities.

HARTT AND SOUL STUDIO

4105 Brook Tree, Dallas 75287 (972) 788-1150
Website: www.harttandsoul.com

Located between the Dallas North Tollway and Midway, Hartt and Soul Studio offers exciting classes in acting, improv, on-camera auditions, and master scenework for ages 4 to adult. It offers one-on-one private coaching, small group sessions, summer camps, and one- and two-day weekend workshops.

DRAMA KIDS INTERNATIONAL

Locations in Rockwall, Rowlett, Richardson, Garland, Mesquite: (972) 772-3233 Locations in McKinney, Allen, and Frisco: (214) 592-4066
Website: www.dramakids.com

Drama Kids mission is to develop children's speaking skills, acting skills, and confidence. For ages 3 to 18, it offers one-hour classes weekly throughout the school year and camps in the summer. Locations are usually elementary schools, community centers, and churches.

EISEMANN CENTER FOR PERFORMING ARTS

2351 Performance Drive, Richardson (972) 744-4600
Website: www.eisemanncenter.com

The Eisemann Center for Performing Arts offers an annual **Family Theatre Series** consisting of six shows that are presented on Sunday afternoons at 2:30 PM. Favorites include shows such as *Pippi Longstocking* and *Stellaluna*. The Eisemann's regular season includes dramas, comedies and comedians, musical theater, bands, orchestras, holiday performances, and more. The center is located by the DART rail line.

GARLAND CIVIC THEATRE'S CHILDREN ON STAGE

108 N. Sixth St., Garland 75040 (972) 485-8884;
box office (972) 205-2790 Website: www.garlandcivictheatre.org

Young people audition for and perform in the plays produced by Children On Stage. Two shows, such as *Bridge to Terabithia* and *Joseph and the Amazing Technicolor Dreamcoat*, are presented in the summer, one in the fall, and another in the spring. These performances are at the Performing Arts Center in downtown Garland on the east side of the town square. Theater classes are offered for ages 8 to 18 in the fall and spring, with two-week camps held during the summer.

The Garland Civic Theatre's main season is listed on the website, or you may call (972) 485-8884 for production titles and dates.

JUNIOR PLAYERS

4054 McKinney Ave., Dallas 75204 (214) 526-4076
Website: www.juniorplayers.org

The Junior Players is the oldest children's theater group in Dallas. Its goal is to introduce children ages 7 to 18 to theater, dance, music, and art and to help them develop self-confidence and self-esteem through after-school, Saturday, and summer programs. Junior Players holds free summer camps at recreation centers and other locations in the area. During the summer it also works with high school actors and the **Shakespeare Festival of Dallas** to present a Shakespearean play in late July or early August at Samuell-Grand's amphitheater. Call their office for specific dates and times.

KD STUDIO ACTORS CONSERVATORY

2600 N. Stemmons, Ste. 117, Dallas 75207 (877) 278-2283
Website: www.kdstudio.com

KD Studio offers classes for ages 4 to adult who want to learn the fundamentals of acting for film, TV commercials, and theater. The studio schedules eight-week courses for children and teens on Saturdays and weekday evenings. In addition, it offers summer camps and **fashion and modeling** Saturday classes. The studio offers 15-month Career Acting and Musical Theater programs.

PLANO CHILDREN'S THEATRE

Plano Community Theatre, 1301 Custer Rd., Ste. 706, Plano 75075
(972) 422-2575 Website: www.planochildrenstheatre.com

The Plano Children's Theatre (PCT) is an active nonprofit educational theater that offers skill classes for ages 3 to 18 in acting, creative drama, art, voice, and musical theater, puppetry, and improv. The PCT also has production classes in which every child in the class gets a part in a play that is produced as a finale. In addition, PCT has a touring performance series for children that is performed by adults, as well as workshops, camps, and special holiday shows that are performed by adults and children together. Performances are usually Thursday to Sunday.

POCKET SANDWICH THEATRE

5400 E. Mockingbird, Dallas 75206 (214) 821-1860 Website: www.pocketsandwichtheatre.com

Many of the performances by the Pocket Sandwich Theatre are suitable for families, but if you have a question, just call the theater and someone who is familiar with the play can discuss it with you. Melodramas, in which the audience can hiss, boo, cheer, and throw popcorn, are favorites for families and birthday parties. Performances are held Thursday, Friday, and Saturday nights at 8 PM with food service open at 6:30 PM, and on Sunday at 7 PM with food service open at 5:30 PM. There is table seating, and the optional menu consists of sandwiches, soups, salads, nachos, and individual pizzas. Prices for the plays are $10 to $18 depending on the evening you attend. A $2 discount is offered for seniors and children. It is located in the corner of the L-shaped shopping village. Reservations are recommended.

REPERTORY COMPANY THEATRE

650 N. Coit, Promenade Center, Richardson 75080 (972) 690-5029 Website: www.rcttheatre.com

Repertory Company Theatre is a nonprofit theatre producing quality family theatre for the Dallas area for more than 20 years. Each season, special weekday morning performances are offered at reduced rates for area school groups. Most performances are held at the RCT's Promenade Theatre. RCT's **School of Musical Theatre and Dance** offers year-round theatre arts education for all ages. Classes focus on all aspects of musical theatre from entry-level classes to advanced programs and are taught by professional performers. Spring break and summer camps are available for children. RCT's **Arts in Education Classes** are available for school field trips.

ROVER DRAMAWERKS

Cox Building Playhouse, 1039 East 15th St., Ste. 202, Plano 75074 (972) 849-0358 Website: www.roverdramawerks.com

Rover Dramawerks is the resident theatre group at the Cox Building Playhouse. Presenting a six-show season, they are "searching for treasures, new and rediscovered, for theatre 'off the beaten path.'" Their children's programs consist of classes and camps at spring break and in the summer. Adult classes are also available.

SHAKESPEARE FESTIVAL OF DALLAS

Mailing address: 3630 Harry Hines, 3rd floor, Dallas 75219 (214) 234-4195

Performances:

Samuell-Grand Park Amphitheater, 5808 East Grand, Dallas

Addison Circle Park, 4970 Addison Circle, Addison 75001

Annette Strauss Artists Square, Dallas Performing Arts District, downtown Dallas

Website: www.shakespearedallas.com

Three of Shakespeare's plays are performed each June and July. The **Junior Players** perform in July. An additional play is offered in September and October. Families may bring picnics and have dinner before the performance. Those with blankets and sand chairs sit closer to the front while those with lawn chairs are nearer the back, but the sound system is excellent and you will be able to hear and see no matter where you sit. The gates open at 6:45 PM for members, 7 PM for groups and advance ticket holders, and 7:30 PM for general admission, and the play begins at 8:15 PM. There is an intermission, and the play ends around 11:15 PM. Most people bring a picnic supper but concessions are available, as well as T-shirts and other souvenirs. Sand chairs may be rented. Restrooms are provided, and bringing insect repellent is recommended. The amphitheatre is located behind Samuell-Grand Recreation Center and across from Tennyson golf course. Once the sun goes down, it's usually very pleasant outside even in July.

Fee parking is beside the amphitheatre, and security is provided. Free parking is along the park roads. Don't leave valuables in sight. Admission: Friday and Saturday, $10; Tuesday to Thursday and Sunday, $10 donation is requested. Seniors and students are $7. Children under 12 are free. Children need to be very familiar with the characters and plot before they go and have a two-hour attention span. Shakespeare Dallas has an educational outreach program called Shakespeare to Go, which consists of educational entertainment and instruction for all grades. Memberships are available.

TEATRO DALLAS

1331 Record Crossing Rd., Dallas 75235 (214) 689-6492 Website: http://teatrodallas.tix.com

Teatro Dallas is dedicated to the presentation of theater that reflects the culture of Latino communities. Most performances are held at the Latino Cultural Center. It presents works by classical and contemporary playwrights and hosts the International Theater Festival. Classes, taught in both English and Spanish, include dance, theater, improv, theater crafts, and makeup. The programs end with two presentations. Children's summer theater classes are for ages 6 to 15. Adult classes for ages 16 and older are ongoing.

THEATRE THREE

2800 Routh St., Ste. 168/The Quadrangle, Dallas 75201 (214) 871-3300 Website: www.theatre3dallas.com

Theatre Three has some performances each season that are suitable for families with older children. "Three" stands for its emphasis on the playwright, the performers, and the audience. Theatre Too presents its own season in the basement of the Theatre Three building. Hookey Theatre is for students, and plays are usually presented on Wednesdays at 2 PM. Study guides are available for teachers. Performances are held from Thursday to Sunday. Free parking is offered in the Quadrangle Tower garage, entered from Laclede or Howell streets. Nearby is a popular restaurant called Dream Café, which has a small playground outside.

YOUNG ACTORS STUDIO AND PERFORMING ARTS CENTER

11496 Luna Rd., Ste. G, Dallas 75234 (972) 401-2090 Website: www.youngactors.org

The Young Actors Studio (YAS) has been encouraging young actors and actresses through classes that have an emphasis in television, film, and commercials. YAS offers programs for ages 6 to 19 year-round, including classes, workshops, summer camps, and much more. The YAS offers a large amount of on-camera experience. With state-of-the-art production equipment, each child can develop his or her individual talents. Courses are divided into two semesters during the school year, but students may join any month. YAS also has a program for special needs children.

MOVIE THEATERS

While not the same caliber of entertainment as live performances, movies have their place in a youngster's world. Movies can feed and free their imagination. Dallas has movie ratings for parents to use to decide the appropriateness of a film for their children.

On Friday in the *Dallas Morning News* is a list of current movies with a delineation concerning language, violence, nudity, etc. Online, www.guide

live.com lists movie theaters in the area, their movies, and times. Some theater chains sponsor summer reading clubs. A different sort of theater that kids enjoy is **Studio Movie Grill**, where they can have a meal and watch a movie at the same time. For a trip back in time, load up the family and head for the **Galaxy Drive-in Theatre** in Ennis (972) 875-5505. Many questions that visitors ask are answered on the website: www.galaxydriveintheatre.com. Below is the description of a favorite annual film festival called **KidFilm**.

ANNUAL CONCERTS AND
PERFORMANCES AND FILM FESTIVALS

JANUARY

KidFilm. Angelica Theater. KidFilm is a film and video festival for kids sponsored by the USA Film Festival. It includes features, shorts, and animation, and offers tributes to greats in children's arts. Selections are viewed on Saturday and on Sunday afternoon. Admission fee. (214) 821-FILM Website: usafilmfestival@aol.com.

African American Read-in. Majestic Theatre. Dallas County Community College. District annual gathering featuring readings of black literature by performers, writers, celebrities, and storytellers. Ages 8 and up. (214) 378-1819. Website: www.readin.dcccd.edu.

Black Music and the Civil Rights Movement Concert. Meyerson Symphony Center. Film, narration, choral music, and dance. Presented by the Black Academy of Arts and Letters. (214) 743-2440. Website: www.tbaal.org.

FEBRUARY

Dallas Art Fair. Fashion Industry Gallery by Dallas Museum of Art. Features paintings, sculpture, prints, drawings, and photographs. (214) 220-1278. Website: www.dallasartfair.com.

Texas Black Film Festival. Studio Movie Grill, 11170 N. Central, Dallas. Filmmakers' conference and juried film exhibition: shorts, TV pilots, features, music videos, documentaries, animated films. (214) 379-7444. Website: www.texasblackfilmfestival.com.

Chinese Festival. Crow Collection of Asian Art. Family Days series. Art, food, dance. (214) 979-6430. Website: www.crowcollection .org.

MARCH

North Texas Irish Festival. Fair Park. Showcase of Irish cultural arts, including lively Irish dancing and music. (972) 943-4616. Website: www.ntif.org.

Tejas Storytelling Festival. Denton Civic Center Park. An annual event with family folio; master storytellers weave their tales for audience. Workshops. (940) 387-8336.

APRIL

Lee Park Annual Easter Concert. Corner of Lemmon Ave. and Turtle Creek Blvd. A Dallas Symphony Association free performance is held annually at Lee Park. Families are invited to the park on Sunday afternoon for a picnic and music. (972) 380-7390. Website: www.turtlecreekassociation.org.

North Texas Jazz Festival. Crowne Plaza Hotel, Addison, and UNT. Jazz artists performing in the area for a week. (972) 450-6251.

Main St. Fort Worth Arts Festival. Main St. in downtown Fort Worth. A celebration of visual and performing arts. (817) 336-8791.

Scarborough Faire Renaissance Festival. 2511 FM 66, Waxahachie. Opening this month on weekends through Memorial Day. Includes music, dancing, food, costumed characters, short theatrical performances. (972) 938-3247. Website: www.scarboroughrenfest.com.

Denton Arts and Jazz Festival. Denton's Civic Center Park. (940) 565-0931.

AFI Film Festival. Held in several theaters. Screenings from around the world and discussions with those who are involved in filmmaking. Some films are family friendly. (214) 720-0555.Website: www.afidallas .com.

Dance for the Planet. Annette Strauss Artist Square, downtown Dallas. (214) 219-2290. Dance festival featuring 140 dance groups from North Texas on three stages. Website: www.thedancecouncil.org.

Scottish Society of Dallas Tartan Day *Ceildh*. Winfrey Point at White Rock Lake. An afternoon of Celtic music and demonstrations of highland dancing. Website: www.scotsindallas.org.

Spring Fling Art Festival. Irving Arts Center Sculpture Garden. Children's art projects, two performance stages, visual arts area. (972) 252-7558. Website: www.irvingartscenter.com.

Barefoot Brigade Dance Festival. Bath House Cultural Center at White Rock Lake. Modern and contemporary dance and performance art. (214) 559-3993. www.cdfw.org.

MAY

Memorial Day Concert. Flag Pole Hill, E. Northwest Hwy. at Buckner Blvd. Free outdoor concert by Dallas Symphony Orchestra. Bring kids and a picnic. (214) 692-0203.

Folklorico Festival. Latino Cultural Center. Latino music, dance, art, food, workshops, classes. (214) 670-3687. Website: www.folkloricofestivalofdallas.com/festival.html.

Cottonwood Art Festival. Cottonwood Park, Richardson. Includes more than 200 artists, music, and children's activities. Website: www.cottonwoodartfestival.com.

Wildflower! Arts and Music Festival Richardson's Galatyn Park. Spring festival with music acts, arts and crafts, and children's entertainment. (972) 744-4580. Website: www.wildflowerfestival.net.

Asian Festival. Annette Strauss Artist Square, downtown or Dallas City Hall Plaza. Features cultural music, dance, art, and more. (972) 241-8250. Website: www.gdaacc.com.

Jazz under the Stars. Dallas Museum of Art. Series of outdoor jazz concerts on Thursday nights, beginning at 8 PM. (214) 922-1200.

Artfest. Fair Park. For more than 30 years, Artfest has entertained with hundreds of artists and included great music and food. (214) 565-0200. Website: www.artfest500.com.

SUMMER

City Arts Celebration. Downtown Arts District, various locations. Performing and visual artists, culinary demonstrations, children's activities, free admission to the DMA, Nasher, and Crow Museum, storytelling, and more. (214) 571-1376. Website: www.dallascityarts.com.

Basically Beethoven. Texas Discovery Gardens at Fair Park. Every Sunday in July at 2:30 PM , the Fine Arts Chamber Players perform selections from Beethoven and other composers. (214) 520-2219.

Saturday Night in the City. Nasher Sculpture Center. Concert series begins at 8 PM. Bring a blanket. (214) 242-5100. Website: www.nashersculpturecenter.org.

Cool Thursdays. Dallas Arboretum. Music on Thursdays at 7 PM, May to July. (214) 515-6521. Admission and parking fees. Website: www.dallasarboretum.org.

Dallas Jazz Orchestra. City parks. (972) 644-8833. These free concerts are held on Sunday afternoons at 3 PM at various city parks. (972) 644-8833.

Dallas Summer Musicals. Music Hall at Fair Park. The Dallas Summer Musicals present spectacular dramas, comedies, Las Vegas–type shows, and many others in both matinee and evening performances. There are usually five plays in the summer, one during the state fair, and one in March. (214) 691-7200.

Jazz under the Stars. Dallas Museum of Art. For more than 10 years, the museum has provided entertainment for visitors with concerts each Thursday evening at 8 PM at the Ross Avenue Plaza. (214) 922-1200.

Patriotic Pops Concert. Las Colinas, Irving. The Irving Symphony Orchestra presents this free evening concert in Williams Square, site of the famous Mustangs sculpture. Lawn chairs, blankets, and picnics are encouraged, and fireworks follow the concert held on July 4. (972) 831-8818.

Shakespeare Festival of Dallas. Samuell-Grand Park Amphitheatre. Three of Shakespeare's plays are performed each June and July. See earlier entry.

July Fourth Concert. Richardson Symphony Orchestra. Patriotic program for families. (972) 234-4195. Website: www.richardsonsymphony.org.

Festival of Drums and Bugles. Lake Highlands High School Stadium, 9449 Church Rd. This lively performance festival by high school players is sponsored by the Lake Highlands High School Band Club annually on an evening in latter July. Around seven groups from throughout the United States compete, and a clinic is held earlier in the afternoon. All seats are reserved. Website: www.dci.com.

Texas Scottish Festival and Highland Games. UTA's Maverick Stadium. Dance competitions, Celtic music, and games. June. (800) 363-7268. Website: www.texasscottishfestival.com.

Annual Festival of Independent Theatres. Bath House Cultural Center at White Rock Lake. An ongoing theater four-week festival in July that features smaller theater companies. (214) 670-8749. Website: www.bathhousecultural.com.

Sounds of Lewisville Summer Concerts. Old Town Lewisville, Wayne Ferguson Plaza. Four July concerts. (972) 219-3401. Website: www.cityoflewisville.com.

SEPTEMBER

TITAS Music and Dance Series Kickoff. Winspear Opera House. Music and dance artists featured. (214) 528-5576. Website: www.titas.org.

Addison Oktoberfest. Addison Circle Park. Re-creation of the festival in Munich with German entertainment and food. (800) 233-4766. Website: www.addisontexas.net.

Greek Food Festival. Holy Trinity Greek Orthodox Church. Greek dancing, arts, and food. (972) 233-4880. Website: www.greekfestivalofdallas.com.

OCTOBER

Harambee Festival. Martin Luther King Jr. Center. All-day family festival. (214) 670-8355.

White Rock Lake Artists' Studio Tour. Includes more than 40 studio locations, art school tours, and exhibitions, near White Rock Lake. Saturday and Sunday. (214) 354-3104. Website: www.dallasartsrevue.com/whiterock.

Plano International Festival. Haggard Park, Plano. Parade of nations, food, crafts, music, and dance; naturalization ceremony. (214) 495-7838. Website: www.planointernationalfestival.org.

Cottonwood Art Festival. Cottonwood Park, Richardson. More than 200 artists with paintings, sculpture, ceramics, fiber art, woodwork, photography. Hands-on art for children. (972) 744-4581. Website: www.cottonwoodartfestival.com.

Addison World Fest. Addison Circle park. Art, dance, food, cultural activities from around the world. (800) 233-4766. Website: www.addisontexas.net.

NOVEMBER

South Dallas Dance Festival, South Dallas Cultural Center. Dance and workshops. (214) 939-2787. Website: www.dallasculture.org.

Texas Stampede. American Airlines Center. Combination of country music and rodeo. Activities for children. Benefits Children's Medical Center. (214) 520-8874. Website: www.texasstampede.org.

Family Day. Meadows Museum at SMU. Storytelling, art, dancing. (214) 768-2516.

DECEMBER

A Christmas Carol. Dallas Theater Center, Wyly Theatre, Arts District. This family favorite is presented each year . (214) 526-8210. Website: www.dallastheatercenter.org. Many Metroplex theater companies perform this annual favorite.

Christmas Celebration Concerts. Meyerson Symphony Center. The Dallas Symphony Orchestra presents **Deck the Halls**, a magical afternoon of family fun focused on ages 3 to 12. They also present family-oriented Christmas concerts of a pops nature, which includes soloists and chorus, called Joy of Christmas. (214) 692-0203.

Christmas in the Branch. City Hall Plaza, Farmers Branch. Farmer's Branch Chamber of Commerce holds a free concert for families, followed by Santa's arrival on Friday evening at City Hall Plaza on William Dodson Pky. at Valley View Lane.

Dallas Children's Theater. 5938 Skillman St. Each Christmas the Dallas Children's Theater presents a wonderful holiday program, such as *The Best Christmas Pageant Ever.* (214) 978-0110. Website: www.dct.org.

Most of the **local children's theaters** and **choruses** have holiday performances.

The Night before Christmas. McFarlin Auditorium at SMU. Fanciful, full-length ballet performed by adults and children of the Dallas Metropolitan Ballet during two December weekends. (214) 631-2787.

The Nutcracker. Various groups perform this traditional favorite. One of the best ways to enhance its enjoyment by young children is to read them the story first so they are familiar with the story line and anticipate the entrance of the characters. Some of the performing companies are the Texas Ballet Theater, Tuzer Ballet, Ballet Ensemble of Texas, Dallas Repertoire Ballet, and Dallas Ballet Center.

Greater Dallas Youth Orchestra. Meyerson Symphony Center. GDYO is joined by the **Children's Chorus of Greater Dallas** and the **Youth Chorus of Greater Dallas** to present holiday music. (214) 528-7747.

Texas Boys Choir. Check for location. Musical holiday performance. (800) 848-6443.

Holiday Sing. UTD's University Theatre, Campbell and University in Richardson. Annual Sing with children's concert in the afternoon. Free. (972) 883-2787.

Look for more **holiday music** from the Women's Chorus of Dallas, Dallas Bach Society, Cross Timbers Youth Orchestra, Richardson Symphony Orchestra, Dallas Wind Symphony, The Vocal Majority, Turtle Creek Chorale, and Rich-Tones Women's Chorus.

Also, look for holiday **puppet shows** at the three local theaters and Northpark Center.

4. Sports and Recreation

Observing a generation of children often referred to as couch potatoes or tater tots because of their sedentary lifestyle in which they are parked endlessly in front of TV sitcoms, rented movies, and video games, more and more parents are recognizing the need to get these children outdoors and moving. The Dallas area has abundant opportunities for physical exercise and fun for individuals, teams, and families. Finding activities that the family can enjoy, such as hiking, bicycling, or fishing, will not only aid in physical fitness and an appreciation of the world outdoors, but also create some wonderful memories as well.

Area sports information is available on www.dallasnews.com. For your particular community sports on this website, choose "Local News" and then select option "City-by-City." For recreation information in Dallas, look online at www.dallascityhall.com.

SPECTATOR SPORTS

MAJOR LEAGUE SPORTS

Dallas Cowboys (National Football League). Preseason and regular season games for the silver and blue team begin in August and end in December. The Cowboys play home games in their new stadium in Arlington. Sales office: (817) 404-0100. Address: 925 North Collins St., Arlington Website: www.dallascowboys.com. **Tours** of the new stadium should be available as soon as the team settles in.

Dallas Mavericks (National Basketball Association). The Dallas Mavericks season runs from October through April. Home games are played at American Airlines Center, 2500 Victory Ave. For a schedule or ticket information, call (214) 747-MAVS. The Mavs also offer summer basketball camps to kids ages 8 to 18. Campers ages 8 to 12 may apply to be honorary ballkids. Kids ages 13 and under may join **Mavs Kids Club** on-line or at a game. Birthday packages are available. Mailing address: 2909 Taylor, Dallas 75226. Website: www.dallasmavericks.com.

Texas Rangers (American League). This baseball team is now playing at the Rangers Ballpark in Arlington. See **Chapter 1: Places to Go** for more information about the stadium and the season, which runs from April through October. Special promotion nights allow all children ages 13 and under with a paid admission to receive items such as baseball gloves, backpacks, and jerseys. The Rangers usually hold an open house for fans during the winter. While at the park, visitors may want to see baseball memorabilia in the **Legends of the Game Museum** (817) 273-5600 and have a ballpark hot dog. For information about schedules, tickets, or membership in the **Junior Rangers Club** (ages 13 and under), call Metro (817) 436-5934. Mailing address: 1000 Ballpark Way, Arlington 76011. Call (817) 273-5100 for tickets, (817) 273-5222 for Rangers. Website: www.texasrangers.com.

FC Dallas (Major League Soccer). FC Dallas soccer team begins its season in March and plays into October. Games are played at Pizza Hut Park, located at Main Street and North Dallas Tollway in Frisco. Kids ages 14 and under are eligible for the **Kids' Club**, and ages 6 to 18 may be interested in the MLS soccer camps. For information, look up their website: www.mlscamps.com. One of their outreach programs is Get a Kick Out of Reading. For tickets, call Ticketmaster or call (888) 323-4625 for their office. Mailing address: 9200 World Cup Way, Frisco 75034. Website: fcdallas.mlsnet.com.

AMERICAN ASSOCIATION BASEBALL

Frisco RoughRiders (Texas Rangers AA affiliate). The RoughRiders play in very family-friendly Dr Pepper Ballpark. Besides the stands, fans can watch the game from Leslie's Pool Zone. They offer a Play Ball Art Contest for kids to design the cover of a Play Ball game program. Tours of Dr Pepper Ballpark are held Monday through Friday and last one hour. Online is a tour request form. Mailing address: 7300 RoughRiders Trail, Frisco 75034. (972) 731-9200. Website: www.ridersbaseball.com.

Grand Prairie Airhogs (American Association). The Airhogs take the field in Quicktrip Park during their season from May through July. Kids enjoy the large play area and the Airhogs Knothole Club (ages 14 and under). Little League teams may apply to take the field with the Airhogs during the national anthem. Quicktrip Park is located at 1600 Lone Star Pky., Grand Prairie 75050. Mailing address: P.O. Box 530251, Grand Prairie 75053. (972) 504-9383. Website: www.airhogbaseball.com.

ARENA SPORTS

Dallas Desperados (Arena Football League). An expansion team of Dallas Cowboys owner Jerry Jones, the Desperados play at American Airlines Center on a hockey-rink-sized arena. Eight men play on each side. The 2009 season was suspended for restructuring. For information about their season and tickets, look online. Website: www.dallasdesperados.com.

Dallas Dragoons (National Polo League). The Dragoons play arena polo and give lessons for ages 10 and up at Bear Creek Polo Ranch, 550 Bent Trail, Red Oak 75154. The Dragoons play eight matches in the spring and eight in the fall. Call (214) 979-0301 for more information. Website: www.dallaspoloclub.org .

Dallas Stars (National Hockey League). The Dallas Stars ice hockey team plays home games at American Airlines Center in a season that runs from October through April. The Dallas Stars' new affiliate will play minor league hockey in the 6,200-seat Allen Event Center, which is under construction at North Central Expressway and Stacy Rd. This team and another in Austin will prepare players for the Dallas Stars. Online, young fans may apply to be Stick Kids. Fans may watch the Stars practice at the Dr Pepper Star Center in Frisco. Summer camps are offered there. Call (214) GO-STARS for information. Tickets may be purchased online, by phone, at American Airlines Center, or at any of the seven Dr Pepper StarCenter locations. Mailing address: Dr Pepper StarCenter, 2601 Avenue of the Stars, Frisco 75034. Website: www.dallasstars.com.

COLLEGIATE SPORTS

Cotton Bowl. Fair Park. Annually the Cotton Bowl is the site for at least two exciting collegiate football games, the state fair matches between the University of Texas and the University of Oklahoma and between Grambling University and their opponent. The New Year's Day Cotton Bowl classic has moved to the new Cowboys Arlington Stadium. State high school playoffs are also scheduled here.

Southern Methodist University (Conference USA). SMU. The only division I athletic program in Dallas, SMU sponsors 17 sports. Mustang football is played at Gerald Ford Stadium on the SMU campus. Ages 12 and under are invited to join the **Mustang Kids Club**, and birthday packages may be reserved. Check online for announcements of clinics for kids. "The Boulevard" offers food and music during games, as well as a kids' area with inflatables and other interactive games. Call (214) SMU-GAME for tickets or purchase them online at www.smumustangs.com .

Other popular sports include men's and women's basketball played at Moody Coliseum and swimming, baseball, track, and soccer. Summer sports camps for youth are held on campus, as well as cheerleading camps and camps for talented and gifted students. Moody Coliseum is the site for the annual SWC Women's Post-Season Basketball Classic and the SWC Post-Season Men's Basketball Classic, usually held in March. The SMU Swim Center is the site for the *Dallas Morning News* Swimming Classic held in late January. SMU invites the top five finishers in the NCAA Swimming Championship to compete with the SMU team.

Other College Sports. Many other colleges in the Metroplex have sporting events open to the public. Here are some phone numbers if the family is interested in going to cheer them:

Dallas Baptist University, (214) 333-5324

Dallas County Community College District: Eastfield, Brookhaven, Richland, Mountain View, North Lake, Cedar Valley

University of Dallas, (972) 721-5009

University of North Texas, Denton, (940) 565-2662

University of Texas at Arlington, (817) 272-2261

AUTO RACING

Devil's Bowl (972) 222-2421. This dirt track raceway is located at 1711 Lawson, off Hwy. 80, in Mesquite. Races are usually on Saturday night from mid-March through October. Website: www.devilsbowl.com.

Texas Motor Speedway (817) 215-8500. NASCAR racing is held here in April and November on a 1.5-mile track. The 150,000-seat facility is located on SH114 and I35W in Roanoke. The cars average more than 180 mph. Track officials advise sunscreen, earplugs, comfortable shoes, and plenty of liquids. Fans may bring a 14-inch cooler.

The Alliance Raceway Ministries provides children's activities in the campground areas at every major race event at TMS. The fun includes a carnival with games, Pinewood Derby racing, inflatables for bouncing, crafts, and snacks on selected days. Website: www.txarm.org.

The park also hosts concerts and other events. **Tours** are available daily except during racing events. To make a reservation, call toll free (888) 816-TMS1. Concessions and souvenirs are available. Traffic is usually awful, so leave very early and wear shoes made for walking. Ticket office: 3601 Highway 114, Fort Worth 76177. Website: www.texasmotorspeedway.com.

GOLF

GTE Byron Nelson Classic (972) 717-0700. Held at the Four Seasons Resort and Club at Las Colinas, Irving, the activities in this PGA tour May golf tournament usually extend for one week. A free youth clinic is usually scheduled on one afternoon, and there are door prizes and giveaways and a free golf club after the exhibition is over. Look for the statue of Byron Nelson. Website: www.pgatour.com.

Colonial National Invitational. The PGA tournament is held at Colonial Country Club in Fort Worth on a 7,010-yard, par-70 course in late May.

RODEOS, HORSE RACING, AND HORSE SHOWS

Rodeo events and horse shows, such as the **Texas Black Invitational Rodeo** (Fair Park Coliseum) and the **Big D Charity Horse Show** (Las Colinas Equestrian Center), both in May, are annual events. The **Mesquite Rodeo** and Rodeo Parade are covered in **Chapter 1: Places to Go**. See Fort Worth in **Chapter 6: Day Trips** for more rodeo events. Horse shows and competitive exhibitions, such as the SW Classic Grand Prix, are held at **Las Colinas Equestrian Center**, 600 W. Royal, Irving (972) 869-0600. Website: www.lascolinasequestrian.com. A yearly favorite that combines rodeo and music is **Texas Stampede** held at American Airlines Center.

Lone Star Park (972) 263-RACE. 1000 Lone Star Parkway, Grand Prairie 75050. The 315-acre Lone Star Park has races for quarter horses Thursday to Sunday, October to November. The thoroughbred horses race Thursday to Sunday from mid-April through July. Simulcasting is used the rest of the year. Up to 8,000 fans may sit in the Grandstand and 1,500 in the Post Time Pavilion. During special events, a playground, picnic tables, petting zoo, and pony rides are offered in a family area. Dining is in the Pavilion and outdoor patio. On the LSP grounds is **Alliance Skate Park and Entertainment Center**. LSP is located one-half mile north of I-30 just off Belt Line Road in Grand Prairie. Website: www.lonestarpark.com.

HOT-AIR BALLOONING

A spectacular hot-air balloon festival is held each year in Plano's Oak Point Park, (972) 422-0296. In late September, colorful hot-air balloons fill the skies over a weekend. In addition to the races, there are usually arts and crafts, exhibits, foods, and carnivals. See the **Transportation** section of **Chapter 2: Tidbits** for information about taking private balloon rides. Website: www.planoballoonfestival.com.

TENNIS

The **Dallas Tennis Association**, (972) 387-1538 or www.dta.org, and the **Dallas Professional Tennis Association**, www.dptatennis.org, can provide information about tennis tournaments to watch in Dallas. A Texas link is at www.usta.com.

INDIVIDUAL, FAMILY, AND TEAM SPORTS

ARCHERY

The **National Field Archery Association** sponsors archery for youth. There are Cubs (ages 4 to 10), Youth, and Young Adult levels in lessons and competition. In the Yellow Pages, look up "Archery Equipment and Supplies" for the location of outdoor and indoor ranges, and the proprietor can give you information about clubs near you. Also on the Web, look up www.texasfieldarchery.org and www.nfaa-archery.org.

The **Texins Archery Club** invites the public to come by on Wednesday evenings and Saturday mornings for an introduction to archery. Family memberships and birthday parties are offered. The address is 8880 Restland Blvd., Dallas (214) 827-7000. Website: www.dallasarchery.com.

BASEBALL, SOFTBALL, AND T-BALL

Youngsters all over the Metroplex begin warming up in April for baseball season, which lasts into July. Recreation centers, churches, the YMCA, and athletic associations field hundreds of recreational teams, with players ages 4 and up. Baseball camps are offered in the summer. Very popular with boys who are serious about the game is **Boys Baseball Inc.** for ages 8 to 18, (972) 682-1444. Website: www.bbidallas.org. Baseball card collecting is a popular hobby for some fans. For a list of stores that sell cards, look in the Yellow Pages for "Baseball—Sports Cards and Memorabilia." All across town are **batting cages** so players can practice their swings, but some may have height requirements. Baseball camps in the area may be found on America's Baseball Camps Website: www.baseballcamps.com.

Celebration Station, 4040 Towne Crossing Blvd., Mesquite (972) 279-7888

Mesquite Go-Carts and Batting Cages, 1630 E. Hwy. 80, Mesquite (972) 288-4888

Top Golf, 8787 Park Lane, at Abrams Rd., Dallas (214) 341-9600, www.topgolfusa.com

Adventure Landing, 17717 Coit, Dallas (972) 248-4653

Sportsplex, 5702 Alpha Rd., Dallas (972) 385-5416. Indoor.

Scout Training Facility. 301 Hilltop, Richardson (972) 994-0101. Indoor.

BASKETBALL

Basketball is usually offered for third grade and up at recreation centers, the YMCA, athletic associations, and churches. Practice usually begins in December and play in January to early March. Basketball clinics are often advertised through the Dallas Mavericks website, the newspaper, or city athletic clubs, and summer camps are abundant.

The **Hoop-It-Up** is a three-on-three street basketball tournament held for children (around age 10 and up) and adults, and wheelchair teams are included. Each team should play at least three games. The event is free for spectators. For time and place, look online at www.hoo-pitup.com.

BICYCLING

Bicyclists of all ages and skill levels enjoy Dallas area bike trails. Covering more than 500 miles of city streets, the bike routes are marked by blue and white signs with a bicycle on them, or Pegasus on wheels signs. Bike trail maps may be obtained from the Department of Transportation. Maps are also available at bike shops. The east-west routes are the three-digit even numbers, and north-south routes are two-digit odd numbers. A helpful bicycling book is *Bicycling in the Dallas/Ft. Worth Area*, by Bill Pellerin and Ralph Neidherdt. Call your parks and recreation department for bike routes in your area. For Dallas hike and bike trails, look online at www.dallascityhall.org/parks. Bikes may be rented at Richardson Bike Mart by White Rock Lake: 9040 Garland Rd. (214) 321-0705. Remember your helmet! Website: www.greendallas.net. Select "Biking."

The **Greater Dallas Bicyclists** is an active club that sponsors more than 60 rides each month. For information, call (214) 946-BIKE or look up their website: www.gdbclub.com. Online you will find information about rides, rallies, festivals, clinics, bike care, and trails.

Another local bicycling group is **Dallas Offroad Bicycling Association**: www.dorba.org. It has information on mountain biking at good beginner places, such as L. B. Houston Park, Cedar Hill State Park, and Dinosaur Valley State Park. May is National Bicycle Month, and special events are planned. Texas Parks and Wildlife has a free brochure called *Bike Texas* that provides information about trails in Texas state parks. Website: www.tpwd.state.tx.us.

Metroplex BMX in DeSoto is a covered year-round track enjoyed by racers ages 3 and up. Most competitors start with a 20-inch street bike and a helmet. It's located at 500 E. Centre Park Blvd., DeSoto 75115 (972) 224-6664. Website: www.metroplexbmx.org. Another BMX track is at **The Edge at Allen Station Park**, 201 East St. Mary, Allen (214) 509-4860.

Dallas Bike Trails:
Bachman Lake (3.08 mi.) 2750 Bachman
Katy Trail (3.5 mi.) American Airlines Center to Mockingbird Station
    Website: www.katytraildallas.org. (214) 303-1180
Trinity Park (.66 mi.) 3700 Sylvan
Glendale Park (1.7 mi.) 1300 E. Ledbetter
Samuell/Elam/Crawford 8700 Elam (2.13 mi.)

White Rock Creek Greenbelt 7000 Valley View (7.5 mi.)
Juanita J. Craft Park 4500 Spring (1.41 mi.)
White Rock Lake (11.1 mi.) 8300 Garland Road
Kiest Park (2.4 mi.) 3000 S. Hampton
L. B. Houston (5 mi./mountain bike) 1600 California Crossing

BOWLING

Children have become so much a part of bowling that most bowling lanes have designated youth directors, and young bowlers take lessons and play in leagues and tournaments under the leadership of the **Youth American Bowling Alliance**. The website is www.bowl.com. Youth leagues usually play two games on Saturday mornings in mixed leagues for ages 6 to 8 and three games for ages 9 to 11 and 12 to 14. The Pee-Wee bowlers may begin lessons and leagues as early as age 3. Local winners play in a state tournament. Some centers have youth-adult leagues.

Bowling is a great family sport, and children as young as 3 may play using six-pound balls. Bumpers may be added so very young bowlers don't get discouraged. Birthday parties at the bowling lanes are great fun, and some lanes will take party members behind the scenes so they can see how the pins are loaded and balls returned. Some amusement centers, such as **Main Event**, have bowling lanes and offer laser-light bowling some nights.

USA Bowl, 10920 Composite, Dallas (214) 358-1382
AMF Garland Lanes, 1950 Plaza Drive, Garland (972) 613-8100
AMF Jupiter Lanes, 11336 Jupiter Rd., Dallas (214) 328-3266
AMF Richardson Lanes, 2101 North Central Expressway, Richardson (972) 231-2695.
Plano Super Bowl, 2521 Ave. K, Plano (972) 881-0242.
300 Bowling Center, 3805 Belt Line Rd., Addison (214) 431-3282
Strikz, 8789 Lebanon Rd., Frisco (972) 668-5263

With an opening planned in 2010, **The International Bowling Museum and Hall of Fame** has moved from St. Louis to 621 Six Flags Drive in Arlington. The three-story history museum will display artifacts from the early days of bowling to today and promote the sport.

DANCING

Dance lessons are a part of many young girls' and boys' education. Ballet, tap, modern, ballroom, and jazz, as well as cultural dances such as Irish dancing, are all very popular with children. In the Yellow Pages, look under "Dancing" for schools near you. Some dance companies with classes for children are listed in **Chapter 3: Performing Arts for Children**. Dancing is also offered through cultural centers, recreation centers, and some community colleges. Cotillion classes are sometimes offered at country clubs. The Plano Sports Authority Dance Team is open to all girls from second to fifth grade. Website: psaplano.org.

DISC GOLF

A Frisbee, a pretty day, and a good arm are all that are needed to participate in one of the Dallas parks' disc golf courses. Call the parks and recreation department for the location of one near you. Tournaments are sometimes scheduled. The following are some courses in the area: Audubon Park, Northwest Drive at Oates Drive, Garland (map available in recreation center); B. B. Owen Park, Kingsley and Plano Rd.; Shawnee Park, near Avenue P and Parker Rd., Plano; Fritz Park, Britain Rd. one block south of Shady Grove, Irving; Victoria Park, Northgate at Pleasant Run, Irving; Greenbelt Area 2, Southern Oaks and Josey Lane, Carrollton; Myers Park, 815 E. Washington, Rockwall. For more local courses and dates of tournaments, look online at www.texasdiscgolf.org.

FENCING

Fencing for youth usually begins at 6 years old in a local fencing club. Classes are held for ages 6 through adult at the **Dallas Fencers Club**, Oak Hill Academy, 9407 Midway Rd., Dallas 75220 (214) 629-5358. Students may belong to the United States Fencing Association and compete on local, divisional, sectional, and then the National Junior Olympic Competition level. Wheelchair tournaments are included in national competition. Contact www.dallasfencers.com and www.usfencing.org for more information.

FISHING

Look under **Lakes** in this chapter for some great fishing in the Metroplex and surrounding area, and see **White Rock Lake** in **Chapter 1: Places to Go** for fishing in the city. Anyone 17 years old or older is required to have a fishing license, which costs about $28, or a temporary one-day license, which is $10. Fishing supply stores usually have them. Texas Parks and Wildlife has a *Texas Fishing Guide* that may be obtained online. The first Saturday in June is the annual **Free Fishing Day**. Contact Texas Parks and Wildlife Department online to find a park and their facilities and events. Website: www.tpwd.state.tx.us/.

Information about lakes operated by the Fort Worth District of the U.S. Army Corps of Engineers may be accessed through the website ww.swf-wc.usace.army.mil/index.htm. Texas lakes usually have fishing guides, such as G. A. Miller's Fishing Guide Service on Lake Texoma, (903) 786-9866, website: www.fishtexoma.com. Another guide is Tom Redington's Lake Fork Guide Service at (214) 683-9572.

FOOTBALL

Youth football is offered through private associations, such as Spring Valley Athletic Association, for fourth-, fifth-, and sixth-graders, and the teams play other teams on their grade level. Look under "Athletic Organizations" in the Yellow Pages. Football in school begins in the seventh grade, and many coaches feel that is soon enough. Some YMCAs offer flag football for elementary grades. Some youth teams in the area are organized by **Pop Warner Football** (www.popwarner.com). Peewee football is played in suburban cities, such as Garland, Carrollton, Mesquite, and Grand Prairie. Sports International sponsors football camps for ages 8 to 18 that include NFL players. In the Dallas area the player has been Jay Novacek of the Dallas Cowboys. To find out dates and locations, call Sports International at (800) 555-0801 or look online at www.football-camps.com.

The **Dallas Cowboys Youth Football Academy** offers non-contact football instruction, games, and contests for boys and girls ages 7 to 14, at sites in the D/FW area. Website: www.dallascowboys.com. Select "Community."

GOLF AND MINIATURE GOLF

Northern Texas PGA Junior Golf Foundation (972) 429-1111, ext. 110. The JGF sponsors the junior tours, the Texas State Junior Championship, PGA Junior Qualifying, and the Junior Tournament of Champions and Cup Matches. Many area recreation centers and country clubs offer lessons, youth rates, summer golf programs, and tournaments. Kevin Johnson, of Texas Junior Golf Academy, gives lessons to ages 5 and up and holds clinics and camps for ages 6 to 15 at DA's Spring Creek Golf in Plano. Website: www.texasjrgolf.com. Some driving ranges also offer lessons. A junior golf clinic is offered at the Byron Nelson each year. Some young golfers ages 12 and up who aspire to play golf in college also join the **American Junior Golf Association**. Website: www.ajga.org. The five public golf courses in Dallas that offer youth programs are listed below. Website: www.golfindallas.net.

Cedar Crest, 1800 Southerland (214) 670-7615
Grover Keaton, 2323 N. Jim Miller (214) 670-8784
L.B. Houston, 11223 Luna Rd. (214) 670-6322

Stevens Park, 1005 Montclair (214) 670-7506
Tenison Park, 3501 Samuell Blvd. (214) 670-1402

The following are more family amusement parks and miniature golf parks:

Celebration Station, 4040 Towne Crossing Blvd., Mesquite (972) 279-7888
Speedzone, 1130 Malibu Drive, I-35E and Walnut Hill, Dallas (972) 247-RACE
The Zone, 1951 Summit, Lewisville (972) 317-7373
Sandy Lake Park, I-30E North at Sandy Lake Rd., Carrollton (972) 242-7449
Adventure Landing, 17717 Coit, Dallas (972) 248-4966
TopGolf, 8787 Park Lane, Dallas (214) 341-9600
The Practice Tee, 2950 Waterview Parkway, Richardson (972) 235-6540
Golden Bear Golf Center, 2538 Golden Bear Dr., Carrollton (972) 733-4111

At **TopGolf**, golfers of all ages and skill levels can swing at balls that have chances to score points, rain or shine, in the two-level driving range. There are four competitive games to play, and loaner clubs are available. Also on the premises is a restaurant and nearby are 54-hole mini-golf and nine-station batting cages. Lessons may improve skills at the Academy, which sometimes offers an after-school program. TopGolf is located at Park Lane and Abrams. Website: www.topgolfusa.com.

GYMNASTICS AND TUMBLING

Gymnastics and tumbling help children with flexibility, control, and confidence. Young gymnasts in Dallas take lessons through recreation centers, the YMCA, summer camps, sports complexes, and private gyms. Ridgewood Recreation Center in Dallas is well known for its gymnastics program. Many offer USGF competitive teams, and some Dallas youths have national ranking. Classes for tots and older are available through these centers: Gymboree (www.gymboree.com), The Little Gym, Gymstar, Nexgym, PowerKids, AWTC, University of Gymnastics, and My Gym. Popular gymnastics centers are ASI Gymnastics (www.asigymnastics.com), Kurt Thomas Gymnastic Center of Frisco (www.kurtthomas.net), Dallas School of Gymnastics, and Metroplex Gymnastics (www.metroplexgymnastics.com). Some private gyms offer birthday parties and parents' night out. In the Yellow Pages, look under "Gymnastics Instruction."

HIKING AND VOLKSMARCHING

Look under **Nature** in **Chapter 2: Tidbits** for beautiful, woodsy places to hike in the Dallas area. Groups such as the Sierra Club and Audubon Society regularly publish calendars of hiking and backpacking adventures. The Dallas Parks Hike and Bike map has helpful information about the trails. Website: www.dallascityhall.org/parks.

Volksmarchers, who often trek through nature areas, belong to clubs that measure routes, set trail markers, bring water, sign walkers in and out, and give medals and stamps indicating completion of walks. Youths and adults earn special awards for participating together in volkssporting events, and special programs are designed for Girl Scouts. One Dallas club is **Dallas Trekkers Inc.**: www.dallastrekkers.org . The American Volkssport Association has a list of Texas walks: www.ava.org.

Not exactly considered "hiking" but still good exercise for mom and entertaining scenery for baby is **StrollerFit**, where moms and babies in strollers get together for walking classes. Check this website for a class near you: www.strollerfit.com.

Northpark Center offers a map of walking loops on the first and second levels. Website: www.northparkcenter.com. Look under "Directory" for walking maps.

HUNTING AND SPORTING CLAYS

As a sideline of the Texas Wildlife Association, the **Texas Youth Hunting Association** serves ages 9 to 17 who pay a membership fee of $12. Other requirements include buying a hunting license, signing a medical release, and passing a hunter education course. The association tries to find a place for each young hunter to hunt at least once a year. Sometimes this is before the official season begins. For more information, call (800) 460-5494 or look online: www.tyhp.org.

Designed to stimulate different types of wild bird–hunting conditions, **sporting clays** is a shotgun clay target game. Target speeds, shooting positions, and angles change, unlike skeet and trap where clay targets are thrown from standardized speeds and positions. Sub-junior and junior competitions are held at various locations. A course in the area is Elm Fork Shooting Park Inc., 10751 Luna Rd. (972) 556-0103. Website: www.elmfork.com.

ICE HOCKEY, ICE SKATING, AND BROOMBALL

Sign-up time for **ice hockey** for ages 4 to 19 is in September, and ice skating lessons are not required for younger players but are recommended for older divisions. The season lasts from October to March. For information about ice hockey teams in the area, contact the **Dallas Junior Hockey Association** or call the ice rinks. Website: djha.com. A hockey-only facility, which hosts leagues and camps, is **Ice Training Center-Richardson**, 522 Centennial Blvd., Richardson, TX (972) 238-1803.

Ice skating is fun any time of year, but in the heat of a Texas summer, it is the coolest spot in town. Ice skating rinks offer public skating, lessons and competition in the U.S. Figure Skating Association, ice hockey, and broomball. Birthday party packages and group rates are available, and the rinks may be rented for broomball. The Galleria rink is particularly beautiful in December, with a huge Christmas tree in the center.

The **Dr Pepper StarCenter** (Website: www.drpepperstarcenter.com) offers skate school, hockey academy, and figure skating. They also offer public skating, hockey leagues, laser tag, and an arcade. Look for them at the following locations:

4020 West Plano Parkway, Plano (972) 758-7528
1700 S. Main, Duncanville (972) 283-9133
12700 North Stemmons, Farmers Branch (214) 432-3131
2601 Avenue of the Stars, Frisco (214) 387-5600
3000 Grapevine Mills Pkwy., Grapevine (972) 874-1930
1400 S. Pipeline Rd., Euless (817) 267-4233
PSA StarCenter, 6500 Preston Meadow, Plano (972) 208-5437

More area ice skating rinks:

Americas Ice Garden, Plaza of the Americas, 700 N. Pearl at San Jacinto, Dallas (214) 720-8080
Addison Square Garden, 15100 Midway Rd. at Belt Line, Addison (972) 960-7465
Galleria Ice Skating Center, 13350 Dallas Pkwy., Dallas (972) 392-3363
The Ice at Stonebriar Centre, 2601 Preston Rd., Frisco (972) 731-9600
Polar Ice, Grapevine Mills Mall, 3000 Grapevine Mills Pkwy., Grapevine (972) 874-1930
Ice at The Parks, The Parks at Arlington Mall, 3815 S. Cooper St., Arlington (817) 419-0095

KITE FLYING

Kiters in the **Dallas Area Kiteflying Association** meet monthly to share information about kite construction and flying techniques and to fly their extraordinary kites. Children are welcome with parental supervision. Three locations where they fly kites are Richardson's Breckenridge Park and Rockwall's Elgin B. Robertson Park at Lake Ray Hubbard.

Contact them online: www.mackite.com/clubs.htm. **Flag Pole Hill** at Northwest Highway and N. Buckner is a favorite spot to fly kites.

LACROSSE

To locate a lacrosse team in the area, summer camps and clinics for grades five to eight, look online at www.uslacrosse.org to contact the **North Texas Youth Lacrosse Association.** One very active association is Plano Junior Lacrosse. Website: www.dallaslacrosse.com. In lacrosse, 10 players in protective gear are on the field at a time, and they are trying to move the ball toward the opponent's goal by running with the ball in the basket of the stick. They run, pass, and change direction in this full-contact sport.

MARTIAL ARTS

Those who love karate and other martial arts believe that they not only foster physical fitness but also build a positive self-image, self-discipline, confidence, and respect for others. Classes are offered at recreation centers, YMCAs, athletic centers, and some schools. It's a good idea to observe a class before enrolling. Popular centers include Highland Park Black Belt Academy, Lee's White Leopard Kung-Fu and Tai Chi, Kim's College of Tae Kwon-Do, Plano Martial Arts, and Dallas Karate Academy. Look in the Yellow Pages under "Martial Arts" for private instruction near you.

MOTOR SPORTS: CARS, MODEL PLANES, GO-CARTS, MINI-VIRAGE CARS, ATVS

Celebration Station, I-30 and I-635, Mesquite (972) 279-7888
Speedzone, 11130 Malibu, Dallas (972) 245-RACE
Mesquite Go-Carts, 1630 E. Hwy. 80, Mesquite (972) 288-4888
Adventure Landing, 17717 Coit Rd., Dallas (972) 248-4966
Precision Karting, 2525 Southwell, Dallas (972) 243-0714
North Texas Kartway, I-35 at Exit 474, North of Denton Website: www.ntkarters.com
Barnwell Mountain Recreation Area, trails for ATVs, jeeps, motorcycles; Gilmer (903) 738-0002. ATV safety course, (800) 887-2887 Website: www.barnwellmountainra.com

Many hobbyists in the area enjoy remote-controlled cars and planes, and model rockets. Supplies for all sorts of RC vehicles may be found at **Texas RC Modelers,** 230 W. Parker Rd., Plano (972) 422-5386; **A-1 Hobby Shop** at 1425 Gross Rd., Mesquite (972) 289-1160; and **Mike's Hobby Shop Superstore** at 1201 N. I-35 E, Carrollton (972) 242-4930.

The Academy of Model Aeronautics (Website: www.modelaircraft.org) has lots of helpful information and lists clubs. Three in this area are the Dallas Radio Control Club, the North Dallas Radio Control Club, and the Richardson Radio Control Club. The clubs usually offer classes for beginners, and it is fun just to watch their events. After some instruction, you will be less likely to crash your plane on its maiden flight or watch it fly away into the wild blue yonder.

ORIENTEERING

In orienteering, hikers use a compass and topographical map to go from one point to another. Many children learn this skill through Boy Scouts or Girl Scouts. Orienteering clubs with members of all skill levels sometimes have theme meets or canoe trips. Youth ages 14 to 20 may join an Orienteering Venture Crew with no experience required. The **North Texas Orienteering Association** offers a family membership. Website:www.ntoa.com. Their mailing address is P.O. Box 832464, Richardson 75083-2464.

PAINTBALL

Probably best for families or youth groups with junior high school students, paintball is a team game in which team members eliminate other team players while they try to capture the other team's flag and protect their own. They carry air-powered guns that shoot colored paint pellets and wear masks, goggles, and long-sleeved shirts. Two local paintball games locations are at:

Fort Paintball in Allen (972) 442-77. Website: www.fortpaintball.com.
Official Paintball Games of Texas in Forney (972) 564-4748. Website: www.officialpaintball.com.

RAFTING, CANOEING, TUBING, AND KAYAKING

Although the area around New Braunfels, San Marcos, and Glen Rose has some great tubing and rafting, there are a few popular spots closer to home. Canoes, kayaks, and rafts may be rented from **High Trails Canoe**, 3610 Marquis Drive, Garland (972) 2-PADDLE. Website: www.high-trailscanoe.com. One recommended Trinity River trip is on the Elm Fork from TX 121 near the dam at Lake Lewisville to I-35 bridge (5.5 mi.) or on to McInnish Park on Sandy Lake Rd. in Carrollton (9.4 mi.).

Single or family memberships are offered at **Dallas Downriver Club** (Website: www.down-river.com). The address is P.O. Box 820246, Dallas 75382-0246. They participate in the annual Trinity River Challenge, an 11-mile paddlesport race in September, starting and finishing at Carrollton's McInnish Park.

Canoes and kayaks may be rented on area lakes. See **Chapter 6: Day Trips** for information about Glen Rose and Tyler State Park. Some of the community colleges, such as Eastfield and Richland, offer canoeing trips.

ROCK CLIMBING

The only way is up at local rock-climbing gyms. Kids can scale boulders using safety equipment and also take classes. Gyms may require parents to sign an insurance liability release form. Some gyms offer classes and after-school climbing for youth.

Dallas Rocks, 9201 Forest Lane, Dallas (972) 231-7625.
Website: www.DallasClimbing.com
Exposure, 2389 Midway #B, Carrollton (972) 732-0307.
Website: www.exposurerockclimbing.com
Stone Works Indoor Rock Gym, 1003 Fourth Ave., Carrollton (972) 323-1047. Website: www.stoneworkssilos.com
Dyno-Rock, 608 E. Front St., Arlington (817) 461-3966.
Website: www.dynorock.com

Texas Mountaineers Club promotes outdoor climbing in Texas and other states. Members must be 18 years or older, but the club website gives information about sites to climb, such as **Mineral Wells State Park**. Website: www.texasmountaineers.org.

ROCKETRY

The **Dallas Area Rocket Society** has a full calendar of events. Sites for launches are at Frisco Parks field and Plano's Bob Woodruff Park, and the general public is welcome. The society also has a science education outreach program, and it can be reached online at www.dars.org/rockets. The website www.flyrockets.com offers helpful information for beginners, a discussion of many aspects of rocketry, and a list of local clubs and links.

ROLLER SKATING AND ROLLER (IN-LINE) HOCKEY

In the Dallas area, both roller-skating and ice-skating rinks are listed in the Yellow Pages under "Skating Rinks." Skaters may bring their own skates, but that usually does not affect admission prices. Most rinks will let preschoolers wear their Fisher-Price skates if the skates are in good condition. On Sunday, some rinks let parents skate free with their children, and some have special preschool skating hours during the week. Lessons, group rates, and birthday parties are usually offered.

White Rock Skate Center, 10055 Shoreview, Dallas (214) 341-6660
Thunderbird Roller Rink, 3200 Thunderbird, Plano (972) 422-4447
Westlake Skate Center, 413 S. Yale, Garland (972) 272-0921
Westlake Skate Center, 311 Gross Rd., Mesquite (972) 285-9058
Southern Skates, 2939 E. Ledbetter, Oak Cliff (214) 670-8156
Interskate Roller Rink, 1408 South Business Hwy. 121, Lewisville (972) 221-4666
Slapshot Inline Hockey Leagues, Richardson Sports Complex, 1000 Hampshire Lane, Richardson (972) 644-2777. Mites to adults. Website: www.slapshothockey.com
The Edge at Allen Station Park, limited open roller hockey, 201 E. St. Mary, Allen (214) 509-4860. Website: www.cityofallen.org
Faceoff Hockey Center, 222 S. Mahill Rd., Denton (940) 383-8439. Website: www.faceoffhockeycenter.com

RUNNING

See **Nature** in **Chapter 2**: **Tidbits** about the hike/bike/jog trails in the nature areas of the Metroplex. The sports section of the *Dallas Morning News* mentions upcoming runs in "Around the Area," and many of these have a children's division and a one-mile fun run/walk. These runs are often part of festivals or fundraisers, such as Artfest Run for the Arts, Zoo Run, Thanksgiving Turkey Trot, the Symphony Fun Run, and the companion/pet SPCA runs. Most area communities have jogging trails and parcourses. There are parcourses at Richland College, White Rock Lake, and Bachman Lake. Just contact the Parks and Recreation Department for locations. The **Dallas Running Club** (Website: www.dallasrunning-club.com) has a good list of places to run in the D/FW area.

SAILING AND MOTORBOATING

Many area lakes, including White Rock Lake and Lake Ray Hubbard, have sailing clubs that feature regular sailing events and beautiful regattas. The U.S. Coast Guard Auxiliary offers lessons and certification in boating. Look under "Boat Rental" and "Charter" in the Yellow Pages and under **Lakes, State Parks, and Recreation Areas** in this chapter about renting boats of all kinds. Some of the marinas with rentals also offer lessons in boating and waterskiing. Some private yacht clubs offer lessons and camps for nonmembers, and students do not have to have their own boats.

Remember, the Coast Guard Auxiliary requires that all children in a boat wear approved life jackets, and a jacket should be in the boat for each adult on board. For information about the nearest certified safety instructor for Texas Parks and Wildlife's boating safety course, look online. Website: www.tpwd.state.tx.us.

Chandler's Landing Yacht and Tennis Club, Lake Ray Hubbard, Rockwall (972) 771- 2051 Website: www.clytc.com
Corinthian Sailing Club Junior Sailing Program, White Rock Lake (214) 320-0841 Website: www.cscsailing.org
North Texas Sailing School at Rush Creek Yacht Club, Lake Ray Hubbard, Rockwall (972) 771-2002 Website: www.northtexassailing.com
Magellan Sailing Center, Lake Lewisville, (214) 827-8990 Website: www.saildallas.com

SCUBA DIVING

For information about learning to scuba dive, look under "Divers Instruction" in the Yellow Pages. Some of the businesses that sell equipment also offer PADI lessons, and the first Discover Scuba lessons are free. Scuba lessons may also be offered through recreation centers, YMCAs, some of the community colleges' continuing education programs, and the Tom Landry Sports Medicine and Research Center, (214) 820-7800. **Divers Training Center** has an indoor heated pool at its Plano location, 1108 Dobie Drive; website: www.diverstrainingcenter .org. **Dive West** is located at 6336 Greenville Ave., Dallas (214) 750-6900. The **Scuba Ranger** program begins at age 8 for pool certification only. At age 10, juniors may achieve Open Water Certification with a depth limit. **Richardson's Aqua Adventures** stocks kids' equipment and offers PADI scuba courses (972) 422-9400. Popular lakes for scuba diving are Possum Kingdom and Lake Travis.

Athens Texas Scuba offers underwater visibility of up to 70 feet, dive platforms, and camping sites. Owners sank a houseboat, Ray Price's tour bus, an airplane, and much more to interest divers. It operates from March to August at 500 North Murchison St., Athens (903) 675-5762 Website: www.athensscubapark.com.

Clear Springs Scuba Park has a 22-acre spring-fed lake, 63 feet maximum depth. 8131 County Rd., Terrell (972) 524-6820 Website: www.clearspringsscubapark.com

SKATEBOARDING AND ROLLERBLADING

Skateboarders have a good variety of parks to have fun and hone their skills. Some parks ask that you bring your own equipment and some have equipment to rent. A helmet and knee and elbow pads are always recommended.

Lakeland Hills Skatepark, 2801 Rickenbacker Dr., Dallas (free)
Eisenburg's Skatepark, 930 E. 15th, Plano (972) 509-7725 Website:
www.eisenburgs.com
Alliance Skatepark, 1002 Lone Star Pky., Grand Prairie (972) 262-4479
Lively Pointe Skate Park, 909 N. O'Connor Rd., Irving (972) 721-8090
The Edge at Allen Station Park, 201 E. St. Mary, Allen (214) 509-
4860

SKIING, WATER

Waterskiing is usually great on area lakes from June through September. Listen to news reports for wind advisories and lake levels. Marinas with boat rentals may offer skiing lessons, and some summer sports camps offer lessons.

Top Gun Water Ski School, Metro (817) 360-4990, operating on Lake Worth by the former Carswell Field
Dallas-Ft. Worth WaterSki and Wakeboard School and Camp, (903) 527-4692, operating on private lake, www.dfwski.com

SOCCER

Millions of youngsters across the nation are enthusiastically playing a game that their parents knew little about as children. Soccer has become incredibly popular as a sport for both boys and girls and will probably become even more popular as a spectator sport as these young players become adults. Soccer teams are fielded by recreation centers, YMCAs, and private athletic associations. For the name of an association near you, call the North Texas State Soccer Association, (972) 323-1323, which is the regulating group for area soccer. Also, look in the Yellow Pages under "Soccer Clubs" or online at www.ntxsoccer.org. *The Pitch* is an informative monthly publication of NTSSA.

Soccer usually begins with an under-6 league and ends with under-19, and members play on a team determined by where they live or go to school. Avid players may try out for a select team at the under-11 age group and sign yearly contracts. Children also play indoor soccer almost year-round. Some indoor facilities have pro shops, concessions, and video games. Below are listed some indoor parks. For a longer list of indoor arenas, look online at www.ntxsoccer.org.

Soccer Spectrum, 1251 Digital, Richardson (972) 644-8845 Website:
www.soccerspectrum.com
Inwood Soccer Center, 14800 Inwood Rd., Dallas (972) 239-1166
Website: www.inwoodsoccercenter.com (Inwood Fitness Center
within.)

Mesquite Indoor Soccer Center, 1600 E. Highway 80, Mesquite (972) 329-4625
Website: www.miscgoal.com (Batting cages, go-cart track, birthday parties.)
Sole Roll Indoor Soccer Center, 4435 McEwen Rd., Dallas (972) 490-0006
Website: www.solerollsoccer.com. (Soccer Tots, Lil' Sluggers, parties.)

The **Rockwall Indoor Sports Expo** (RISE), a sports facility at 2922 S. Highway 205, Rockwall (972) 772-9061, offers two soccer fields, two basketball courts, and facilities for roller hockey, volleyball, flag football, lacrosse, and virtual reality baseball batting cage area. Website: www.ris-erockwall.com.

An exciting annual international youth tournament is the **Dallas Cup**, held each Easter week at Frisco's Pizza Hut Park. Approximately 180 teams from 30 countries compete for championships in five boys' divisions and two girls' divisions. Close to 150,000 spectators are entertained during the soccer tournaments. The Dallas Cup HomeStay Program helps young athletes find a place to stay to keep costs down. Website: www.dallascup.com

SoccerTots is a program for children ages 18 months to 6 years, which is held at various indoor facilities. Players can develop soccer skills, social behavior, and motor skills. Website: www.soccertotsdallas.com.

Other online sites are www.soccer.org, www.usysa.org, and www.soccerjr.com. Camps and clinics are ubiquitous in North Texas. Two are offered by FC Dallas and Bobby Moffat.

SPECIAL OLYMPICS AND DISABLED SPORTS ASSOCIATION

Each year in May, more than 3,700 athletes and 1,700 coaches participate in the Special Olympics for athletes who are mentally or physically disabled. The Olympics begin with an opening ceremony on a Wednesday night and end with a closing ceremony on Friday afternoon. Cities bid on the right to host the games. For more information, call (214) 943-9981.

Bachman Therapeutic Recreation Center. Programs for children and adults with disabilities are available at Bachman Recreation Center. For youth ages 6 to 22 with disabilities, there is an after-school program from 3 PM to 6 PM. Call (214) 670-6266 for program information. In the summer, Bachman offers "Olympiad" camps in which campers will experience activities such as sports, table games, canoeing, arts and crafts, music, outdoor games, nature, swimming, and other social activities.

Also, the **Garland Therapeutic Recreation Center** (972-205-2619) offers special programs year-round and summer camps for children with disabilities, as well as Special Olympics programs. The following are some nearby cities that offer therapeutic recreation programs: Richardson, (972) 744-7850; Plano, (972) 941-7272; Carrollton, (972) 466-9816; and Irving, (972) 721-8090.

Plano annually hosts the **Very Special Arts Festival** on a Sunday afternoon in January. The **Studio Movie Grill** invites special needs children for designated films. **Camp Summit** is a nearby residential camp for any age child with disabilities. 921 Copper Canyon Rd., Argyle (972) 484-8900. Website: www.campsummittx.org.

See **Playgrounds** and **Horseback Riding** in this chapter for more activities for physically challenged youth.

SWIMMING

Swimming in the Texas summer heat is next to breathing. The Dallas Parks and Recreation Department offers pools at 22 recreation centers. Samuell-Grand and Lake Highlands North have a wading pool. Swimming lessons are offered at many of the recreation centers for a low fee. A responsible person 16 years or older must accompany children ages 6 or under. Parks and Recreation offers a **Junior Lifeguard Program** for ages 12 to 15 and another program for ages 15 and up. Below is a list of Dallas's public pools:

Bachman, 2750 Bachman Blvd., (214) 670-6266 (persons with disabilities only)
Bonnieview, 2124 Huntingdon Ave., (214) 670-6821
Churchill, 7025 Churchill Way, (214) 670-6177
Everglade, 5100 N. Jim Miller, (214) 670-0940
Exline, 2430 Eugene St., (214) 670-0350
Fretz, 14739 Hillcrest, (214) 670-6464
Glendale, 1534 Five Mile Drive, (214) 670-1977
Grauwyler, 2157 Anson Rd., (214) 670-6444
Harry Stone, 2403 Millmar, (214) 670-0950
Hattie R. Moore, 3122 N. Winnetka, (214) 670-1391
Jaycee-Zaragoza, 3125 Tumalo Trail, (214) 670-6465
Juanita Craft, 3125 Lyons St., (214) 670-0343
Kidd Springs, 807 W. Canty, (214) 670-6817
Lake Highlands North, 9940 White Rock Trail, (214) 670-1346
Martin Weiss, 3440 W. Clarendon, (214) 670-1989
McCree, 9016 Plano Rd., (214) 670-0389
Pleasant Oaks, 8701 Greenmound, (214) 670-0941
Samuell-Grand, 3201 Samuell Blvd., (214) 670-1379

Thurgood Marshall, 1808 Ariel, (214) 670-1917
Tietze, 6115 Llano, (214) 670-1380
Tipton, 3607 Magdaline, (214) 670-6466
Tommie M. Allen, 6901 Bonnie View, (214) 670-0982
Walnut Hill, 4141 Walnut Hill Ln., (214) 670-6433

Some of the Dallas parks have **spraygrounds** for young children:

Campbell Green, 6600 Parkhill Dr.
Danieldale, 300 W. Wheatland Rd.
Janie C. Turner, 6424 Elam Rd.
Lake Highlands North, 9940 White Rock Trail at Church Rd.
Mildred Dunn, 3322 Reed Ln.
Ridgewood, 6818 Fisher Rd.
Umphress, 7616 Umphress Rd.

Members of the **YMCA** also enjoy swimming and lessons, and some of the community colleges schedule lessons for youth and adults and public swimming hours. Many public and private pools offer lessons and a summer swim team. Swimming for ages 6 and older and diving classes are taught at SMU, (214) 692-2200.

Private swim lesson businesses include the following:

Dolfin Swim School, 4347 W. Northwest Hwy., Dallas (214) 361-4542
Website: www.dolfinswimschool.com
Mockingbird Swim and Total Fitness, 6465 E. Mockingbird Ln., Dallas (214) 841-1020
Emler Swim School. Two locations: Preston Rd. and Forest, Dallas (972) 851-SWIM. West Park Blvd. at Ohio, Plano (972) 599-SWIM. Website: www.iswimemler.com
Swim Plus, 1108 Dobie Drive, Ste. 103, Plano (214) 227-2398 Website: www.swimplus.com (with Divers Training Center)

Check to see if your local school district has a **natatorium** because it usually has open swim hours. Some may require a membership. A popular indoor swimming pool is **Don Rodenbaugh Natatorium**, located at 110 E. Rivercrest Blvd. in Allen, (972) 747-4150.

Call the **Parks and Recreation Department** or the **school district's athletic director** in your community to see if there are lessons and competitive swim teams for youth.

Dallas's **Loos Natatorium**, 2839 Spring Valley, (972) 888-3191, is the site of many exciting swim meets. The **Dallas Mustangs**, (214) 768-1641, is a swim team for children ages 6 to 18, which ranges from learning to swim to elite swimmers who can compete nationally. Check online for tryouts. There is a fee to join. The teams practice at Loos and various other sites around Dallas. Website: www.dmswim.com.

Plano has two indoor swim centers: **Harry Rowlinson Community Natatorium** and **Plano Aquatic Center**. To find out more about swim teams and lessons in your area, you might try this website: www.clubswim.com. Most of the swimming pools are available for rent outside of scheduled swim times.

Swimming water parks mentioned in chapter 1 include Garland's **Surf and Swim** and **Hawaiian Falls**, as well as Arlington's **Hurricane Harbor** and Carrollton's **Sandy Lake**.

Additional swim fun centers include:

Bahama Beach Water Park and Spraygrounds, operated by the City of Dallas, 1895 Campfire Circle, Oak Cliff (214) 671-0820. Website: www.bahamabeachdallas.com

NRH₂O wave pool with water slides, endless river, and children's area in North Richland Hills on Grapevine Highway across from Tarrant County Jr. College N.E. Campus, (817) 427-6500

Rowlett Wet Zone, 5304 Main St., Rowlett (972) 412-6266

Splash Factory, 601 E. Grand Prairie Rd., Grand Prairie (972) 263-8174

Burger's Lake is a favorite swimming hole near Fort Worth. See **Chapter 6: Day Trips**.

See the sections in this chapter about **Lakes** and **State Parks** and **Chapter 6: Day Trips** for more great swimming holes. Other community pools and facilities include the following in case you would like to try new pools every week:

Carrollton: **Rosemeade Aquatic Center**, 1330 Rosemeade Parkway, (972) 466-6399. Pools: wading with fountain, training, main pool, diving well with three platforms, water volleyball.

DeSoto: **Mosely Park Pool**, 600 E. Wintergreen Rd., (972) 224-7370. Pools: baby, wading, main pool. Across from a **Leathers-designed playground**.

Duncanville: **Armstrong Swimming Pool**, 200 James Collin Blvd., (972) 780-5083. Pools: wading pool, main pool. By a **Leathers-designed playground, Kidsville**.

Farmers Branch: **Don Showman Pool**, 14302 Heartside, (972) 243-0286. Pools: baby pool, main pool with water slides and high dive.

Garland: **Bradfield Pool**, 1150 Castle Drive, (972) 205-2774. Pools: 50-meter pool, wading area, two-story water slide, sprayground.

Mesquite: **Evans Pool**, 1200 Hillcrest, (972) 289-9151. Pools: wading pool, main pool with water slide.

Plano: **Jack Carter Pool**, 2800 Maumelle, (972) 208-8081. Pools: wading pool, main pool with diving board.
Richardson: **Cottonwood Park**, 1321 West Belt Line, (972) 680-8209. Pools: wading, main, and diving pools. **Spray playgrounds** at Arapaho and Glenville pools.

TENNIS

Tennis is a favorite sport year-round in Dallas, especially with some communities and clubs offering indoor courts. The **City of Dallas** operates five tennis centers, which offer lessons, ball machines, tennis merchandise, racket repair, league play, and lighted courts. Court reservations can be made one day in advance. See **Spectator Sports** in this chapter for popular tournaments. A helpful website is www.tennisindallas.net.

Fair Oaks, 7501 Merriman Pkwy., (214) 670-1495
Fretz, 14700 Hillcrest, (214) 670-6622
Kiest, 2324 West Kiest Blvd., (214) 670-7618
Samuell-Grand, 6200 East Grand Ave., (214) 670-1374
L. B. Houston, 11223 Luna Rd., (214) 670-6367

Call (214) 670-8520 for reservations at neighborhood courts. The Parks and Recreation Department works in cooperation with the **National Junior Tennis League** to provide year-round tennis programs for children of all ages, including lessons, clinics, and tournaments. Call the **Dallas Tennis Association** at (972) 387-1538 for more information. Website: www.dallasparks.org.

The **National Junior Tennis League** is an eight-week summer program in which the Park Department in conjunction with several sponsors provides instructors, courts, and equipment for clinics, lessons, and tournaments for youth in more than 30 recreation centers. Call your nearest recreation center for more information. Some of the community colleges and SMU offer summer lessons, and some country club tennis programs include nonmembers in lessons.

TRIATHLON

Swim, run, and ride are the ticket for kids' triathlons, which are held throughout the year mainly for ages 7 to 14. Two organizers of North Texas events are PlayTri and Ironhead Race Productions. Websites: www.playtri.com; www.ironheadrp.com. Participants are required to be members of USA Triathlon. Website: www.usatriathlon.org.

VOLLEYBALL

Most middle and high schools offer girls' volleyball, and the competition for spots is usually pretty fierce. City recreation centers and sports complexes offer team play, clinics, and camps. A pricier route, but particularly good if young athletes hope to play in college, are the select volleyball clubs. **North Texas Region Volleyball**, (972) 247-3002, is the go-to place for tryout information, regulations, teams, camps, clinics, athletic facilities, events, special needs teams, and more for local indoor and outdoor volleyball. Most teams are made up of girls ages 11 through 18, and adult play is also offered. Website: www.ntrvolleyball.org.

A very active volleyball center is the **Volleyball Institute of Plano (VIP)**, (469) 229-0700, where two clubs, Dallas Summit and Dallas Premier, train and play. The Plano VIP center, located at 1909 Tenth St., offers strength and conditioning training, lessons, camps, tournaments, and clinics.

SUMMER SPORTS DAY CAMPS

With schoolwork out of the way, the summer is a great time to sharpen skills in favorite sports. A good place to check for camp listings is the February issue of *dallas child* or at the annual Kid Camp and Sports Expo, also in February. Website: www.dallaschild.com. *North Texas Kids* magazine has a March summer camp issue. Annually, in April, the *Dallas Morning News* prints its "Parents Guide to Summer." The American Camping Association (ACA), (765) 342-8456 (Websites: www.acacamps.org; www.campparents.org; www.acatexoma.org) provides a database of camps that have ACA approval.

Park and recreation centers, high schools, YMCAs, country clubs, indoor sports arenas, sports-related businesses, churches, professional and minor league sports teams, Boy and Girl Scouts, and Campfire organizations offer day camps in most of the popular sports for youth. For example, look under **Tennis**, **Swimming**, and **Golf** in this chapter for opportunities with the Dallas Parks and Recreation Department. Some private schools, such as St. Mark's, Jesuit, Episcopal School of Dallas, Greenhill, and Hockaday, and other organizations offer sports camps with instruction in more than one sport, in addition to other types of day camps. **Trinity Christian Academy Camps** (972-931-8325) include football, basketball, wrestling, baseball, and tennis for boys and volleyball, basketball, and tennis for girls. **Premier Sports Camps** offers camps for basketball, football, and volleyball at various locations. Call

(972) 353-5100 or look online. Website: www.allstarcamps.com. Listed below are some programs that provide sports instruction and fun. Sometimes only websites are listed because the locations of the camps may change each summer.

RECREATION CENTERS AND PLAYGROUNDS

RECREATION CENTERS

The recreation centers in Dallas literally have something for everyone from tots to seniors. The Parks and Recreation Department operates more than 40 centers, and half of them have swimming pools. Signing up for classes and teams is usually done quarterly, and those for youth include almost all popular sports, arts and crafts, cooking, music, technology, and performing arts. Gymnastics Mom and Me classes begin as early as 2 years old, and swim lessons are offered at many of the pools. Most of these classes are free or inexpensive. Recreation centers often schedule special events, such as father-daughter Valentines dances, Easter egg hunts, and Fourth of July parades.

The Dallas Parks and Recreation Department publishes a guide to their activities called Park and Recreation *Leisure Connection* brochure. While usually available at Dallas Parks and Recreation facilities, it may also be accessed online, and patrons may register online, also. Website: www.dallascityhall.com, scroll to "Other Items of Interest," then to "Park and Recreation *Leisure Connection* brochure."

Summer day camps are annual favorites, with some that are conducted at the recreation center and others that include many field trips. Performing arts groups, such as the Junior Players, and sports facilities, such as bowling lanes and skating rinks, combine resources with the centers to provide excellent instruction. Look online at the **City of Dallas Park and Recreation** website for details. Website: www.dallascityhall.com.

PLAYGROUNDS

One activity of which youngsters never tire is time at the playground, and thankfully, this activity is free. The Metroplex area has seven fantastic playgrounds designed by New York architect **Robert Leathers**, who consults with children about what they would like in a playground before designing it. His castle-like wooden playgrounds are listed below:

Armstrong Park, 200 James Collins, Duncanville
Friendship Park, 525 Polo, Grand Prairie

Grimes Park, 600 East Wintergreen, DeSoto
Kidd Springs, 711 East Canty, Oak Cliff
Prestonwood Elementary, 6625 LaCosa, Dallas
Victoria Park, Northgate and Pleasant Run, Irving
Waggoner Park, 2122 N. Carrier, Irving

Baby swings may be found at Armstrong, Grimes, Victoria, and Waggoner parks. At Armstrong Park's Kidsville and Safety Town, youngsters can ride their bicycles and tricycles down a miniature street that has traffic signs and a railroad crossing. A trip to Kidd Springs might include a walk through the oriental gardens nearby.

Toddlers especially enjoy the small, picturesque playground at **Central Square** on Swiss Avenue by the Wilson Block near downtown. A larger preschool playground is at **Lake Highlands North Recreation Center** at Church Rd. and White Rock Trail. Both have sandy floors, so a pail and shovel would be a plus. Playgrounds for both preschoolers and older children are at **Lakewood Park**, 7100 Williamson; **Ridgewood Park**, Trammel and Fisher; Richardson's **Huffines Park**, 1500 Apollo Road; Richardson's **Cottonwood Park**, Cottonwood and Belt Line; Garland's **Audubon Park**, Oates and O'Banion (site of Surf and Swim); and Highland Park's **Prather Park**, Lexington and Drexel. Toddlers enjoy **Bob Woodruff Park** at 2601 San Gabriel Park in Plano, while older kids circle the lake and ride on the bike trail.

The following are some more highly rated parks: **Caruth Park**, Hillcrest and Greenbriar; **Cherrywood Park**, Cedar Springs at Hedgerow; **University Park** at Lovers Lane and Dickens; **City Lake Park**, Lakeside and Parkview, Mesquite (allows catch-and-release fishing in the city lake); **Gussie Waterworth Park** next to City Hall in Farmers Branch; **Martha Pointer Park** on Scott Mill Road and **Kid's Corral** in **Mary Heads Carter Park** on Kelly Blvd. in Carrollton; **Willowdell Park**, 12225 Willowdell, east of Central and north of Forest; and **Kid's Country** across from Coppell City Hall. Another large wooden castle-like playground is **KidsQuest** at **DeBusk Park**, 1625 Gross Rd. at LBJ in Mesquite.

Special needs playgrounds include the **Scottish Rite Hospital Playground**, 2222 Welborn, which is primarily for hospital use; **ChildsPlay** at Bachman Lake; Oak Cliff's **Fantasy Landing** (wheelchair accessible) in **Kiest Park** at 3080 S. Hampton; Farmers Branch's **Oran Good All Children's Playground** (Lion's Playground), 2600 Valley View; Grand Prairie's **C. P. Waggoner Park** on North Carrier Parkway near N.W. 19th; **Friendship Park** on Polo Road; **Nance James Park** at 2000 Spikes Street, which is used by Dalworth Elementary School; and Plano's **Enfield Park** at Legacy Drive and Alma. **Casey's Clubhouse** at **Dove Park** in Grapevine has ramps and surfaces wide enough for wheelchairs. It is a completely handicapped accessible play structure. Near Scottish Rite Hospital, at 3505 Maple, is a playground at **Reverchon Park** for kids with special needs. It has wheelchair access and signs in Braille. Call the Parks and Recreation Department of the city in which the park is located for particular information about suitability.

YOUTH ORGANIZATIONS

Boy Scouts of America, (214) 902-6700. Website: www.circle10.org. The **Circle 10 Council** and national headquarters are located in Irving. In addition to traditional favorite activities such as hiking and camping, the Boy Scouts have added atomic energy and computers to their merit badge activities. In the last 10 years, the number of Scouts in the Dallas Council has risen from 29,000 to more than 50,000, and more than 6,000 have physical disabilities. Boys may begin in the first grade as a Tiger cub and move up. The Boy Scouts sponsor both day camps and resident camps in the summer. "Family Camping" is a guide offered by the Scouts at their stores to encourage families to camp anywhere from the backyard to state parks. The **National Scouting Museum** in Irving is fun for all, Scout or not. See **Historic Irving** in **Chapter 2: Tidbits** for more information about fun things to do there. If you have a special needs child and have questions about provisions for specific disabilities, call (214) 902-6700.

Big Brothers Big Sisters, (214) 871-0876. This organization pairs disadvantaged youth with individuals or couples for two to four hours per week of one-on-one companionship for a period of at least one year. Often, the children come from single-parent homes where there is no father. After applying, there is a screening process, and a caseworker makes the assignment.

Boys and Girls Clubs of Greater Dallas, Inc. (214) 821-2950. Website: www.bgcdallas.org. Boys and Girls Clubs have 14 branches in the metro area. Youngsters ages 6 to 18 pay for a yearly membership, and there are no other fees so disadvantaged youth can participate. They meet after school Tuesday to Friday and on Saturday during the school year, and Monday to Friday in the summer. Activities are related to these five areas: character and leadership development; education and career development; the arts; health and life skills; and sports, fitness, and recreation.

Camp Fire USA, (214) 824-1122. Website: www.campfireusadallas.org. The **Lone Star Council** of Camp Fire now accepts both boys and girls in the program. The club tries to meet the emotional, social, and physical needs of today's kids through camping, community service, and self-care programs. Boys and girls who are between the ages of 5 and 21 years old may join. Summer day camp at Camp Ellowi is offered for youth ages 6 to 15. Campers will spend their days canoeing, learning archery, cooking outdoors, swimming, hiking, and doing nature crafts. They also learn safety and survival skills.

Girls Incorporated of Metropolitan Dallas, (214) 654-4530. Website: www.girlsincdallas.org. Girls Inc. operates four centers for girls ages 6 to 18. Girls are encouraged to be "strong, smart, and bold" and to take charge of their lives. The purpose is to provide after-school care and build self-esteem to help prevent pregnancy and substance abuse and help girls learn how to deal with other challenges. Programs include Operation Smart to help girls excel in science, technology, and math, and Discovery Leadership, which partners girls with women in community action projects. In conjunction with the Parks and Recreation Department, summer day camp is offered for both boys and girls, with the weekly fee based on family income.

Girl Scouts of America, (972) 349-2400. Website: www.tejasgsc.org. **Girl Scouts of Northeast Texas** headquarters is located in Dallas. With an emphasis on community service, the Girl Scouts are actively involved in projects to help the community, in outdoor activities, and in wellness education. Girls may begin the program at age 5 as Daisies. Troops are available for girls with special needs, and some literature is printed in Spanish. Scouts attend day camps, weekend camps, and week-long camps. Successful completion of activities usually earns the girls badges that are displayed on their uniforms. Many Dallasites eagerly await their annual cookie sale. Their motto is "Be prepared."

YMCA, (214) 880-9622. Website: www.ymcadallas.org. The YMCA has around 15 branches in the Metroplex area, and participants in the programs may buy memberships. There are additional fees for classes, camps, and other programs, but fees are reduced for members. Some of the activities and services include full-day and after-school onsite child care, programs for preschoolers, sports lessons and teams, babysitting while parents participate in classes, summer day and resident camps, Christmas and spring break camps, and Adventure Guides.

YMCA Adventure Guides (formerly Indian Guides and Indian Princesses). A YMCA program originally designed to bring boys and girls and their fathers closer together, this group sometimes involves moms, too. Guides usually meet once or twice a month in members' homes and participate in two or three campouts, which are often held at Camp Grady Spruce at Possum Kingdom Lake. These groups may form in kindergarten, and most continue through the second or third grade. Even fathers who are very reluctant campers look forward to the campouts and the friendship of the other dads and the time with their children. The general YMCA number is (214) 880-9622.

Young Life, (214) 265-1505. Website: www.younglifenorthtexas.org. Young Life is a nondenominational Christian organization offered to youth in grades 7 to 12. The main group meeting is held for students at junior high and high schools by grade levels twice each month at a designated location. Some groups have Campaigners, which is a smaller group that meets in members' homes during the weeks that there is not a general meeting. The purpose is to strengthen Christian values and provide good, clean fun and fellowship for teenagers. Some groups go on day trips and campouts. Their leadership is usually young adults who are positive role models. Frontier Camp is a popular summer camp in Colorado.

Junior Achievement, (972) 690-8484. Website: www.jadallas.org. Since its beginning in 1919, Junior Achievement has become the "world's oldest, largest, and fastest-growing nonprofit economic education organization." JA seeks to "educate and inspire young people to value free enterprise, business, and economics to improve the quality of their lives." A club consists of a volunteer from the business community who leads a group of students from kindergarteners to twelfth graders in meetings usually held at a school or community center and shares with members his or her expertise in business as well as the JA curriculum. Members learn about budgets, investments, products, marketing, resumes, the economics of education, insurance, and careers.

RANCHES AND HORSEBACK RIDING

The barn door is open at local ranches to help young cowpokes learn the skills needed not only to ride a horse but also to take care of one. The following are a variety of things offered at stables and ranches: lessons, camps, trail rides, pony rides, boarding, birthday parties, Scout badges, and special needs therapeutic riding. At some riding camps, bonus activities may include crafts, games, and a dip in a swimming pool. Hardhats are required, but the riding academy may provide them. Instructors want riders to wear boots with heels. Packing water and sunscreen might be a good idea.

Rocking M Stables, 7807 Fair Oaks, Dallas (214) 348-5933, ages 5 up. Website: www.rockingmstables.net.

Capricorn Equestrian Center, 6101 Ben Rd., Sachse (972) 530-1124. Website: www.capricornhorse.com.

Merriwood Ranch, 2541 W. Campbell Rd., Garland (972) 495-4646, ages 6 up. Website: www.merriwoodranch.com.
Rockin' River Ranch at Frisco Horse Park, 13100 East Hwy. 121, Frisco (972) 335-8000. Website: www.friscohorsepark.org.
Windmill Stables, 2029 North Cliffe Dr., Richardson (972) 238-9820, ages 5 up. Website: www.windmillstables.com.

Day party ranches for groups include the following:

Double D Ranch, 12809 Eastgate Drive, Mesquite (972) 289-2341. Website: www.ddranchdallas.com.
Park Lane Ranch, 8787 Park Lane, Dallas (972) 340-9593. Website: www.parklaneranch.com.
The Barnyard at Park Lane (214) 349-2002.

Guest ranch:

Rocking L Ranch, (903) 560-0246; toll free, (866) 841-1137. Website: www.rockinglranch.com. Horseback riding at the Rocking L Western guest ranch is great, but for an additional grounds fee, families and groups may fish, swim (catch and release), picnic, play volleyball and basketball, and play games in the recreation room. Hayrides are also offered. Rooms and a bunkhouse that sleeps a large group are available for use except during the summer, when a resident horsemanship camp is held for ages 8 to 15. Birthday parties and Scout troops are also welcome. This ranch is east of Dallas, near Terrell.

Television series ranch:

Southfork Ranch, made famous by the television series *Dallas*, is open for tours, shopping, and special events. Call (972) 442-7800.

THERAPEUTIC HORSEBACK RIDING

Equest, 3800 Troy Rd., Wylie (972) 412-5040. Website: www.equest.org
TROT Therapeutic Riding of Texas, 1724 Old Hickory Trail, DeSoto (972) 293-3388; (972) 293-0722. Website: www.trottx.org
SpiritHorse Therapeutic Riding Center 1960 Post Oak Dr., Corinth (near Denton) (940) 497-2946. Website: www.spirithorsetherapy.com

LAKES, STATE PARKS, AND RECREATION AREAS

Texans gravitate to the area lakes and state parks year-round for fishing, camping, hiking, and water sports. Various agencies provide public boat ramps, fishing piers, picnic areas, campsites, and marinas that rent boats and sell bait. Beautiful wooded areas inspire hikers and other nature lovers, and spotting wildlife is pure delight for all ages. See **Chapter 1: Places to Go** for information on **White Rock Lake** and **Bachman Lake**.

For information about the facilities at the lakes and state parks, write **Texas Parks and Wildlife Department**, 4200 Smith School Road, Austin 78744; look online www.tpwd.state.tx.us; or call (800) 792-1112 for their brochure *Information: Texas State Parks*. TPWD sells a $60 **Texas State Parks Pass** that is good for one year and offers unlimited entrance to state parks and historic sites, fishing at all state parks without a license, and a discount on overnight facility fees.

Some Texas lakes and parks are overseen by the **Fort Worth District of the U.S. Army Corps of Engineers**. Website: www.swf-wc.usace.army.mil. Select "Recreation Info."

Generally, these lakes were formed to be reservoirs, but other organizations, such as adjoining cities, counties, state parks, federal lands, etc., may also be in the mix. Private businesses may lease a park. On the federal government website, visitors may purchase an America the Beautiful **Federal Recreations Lands Annual Pass**, which offers discounts. Website: www.recreation.gov. This site was designed to be a customer-friendly recreation portal with information to help plan visits to federal recreation sites and to make campground and tour reservations. Visitors can also call (877) 444-6777 to make reservations. Agencies like the Corps of Engineers mentioned earlier are federal, so they are on this site. Another locally very helpful site that has lake information, a rating system, an outline of a day there, and photos is www.texasoutside.com. Individual city and county websites have park and recreation information for their turf.

State park entrance fees range from $2 to $7 per person, and children 12 and under are admitted free. Overnight camping ranges from $7 to $36, higher for screened shelters and cabins. Facilities, which range from primitive campsites to rustic cabins, may be reserved 11 months in advance by calling a central reservation number, (512) 389-8900. TP&W schedules **Texas Outdoor Family Workshops** to help families learn basic outdoor skills. Call (512) 389-8903. A calendar of events is provided by TP&W's website. For information about other Texas campsites, call the **Texas Association of Campground Owners**, (800) 657-6555, for a booklet called *RV and Camping Guide to Texas*, or you may contact the Corps of Engineers or Park Superintendent at the lake you wish to visit. *Important:* Be sure to contact the lake during rainy seasons to see if flooding or drought has closed facilities such as boat ramps, and check the wind advisories.

Many park areas have a day use and overnight camping fee, and campers pay both each day. Some parks operated by the Corps of Engineers and those privately owned also charge an additional fee for use of boat ramps and beaches. Look online at www.swf-wc.usace.army.mil/index.htm for the **Fort Worth District U.S. Army Corps of Engineers** under "Recreation and General Information" for Texas reservoirs. Some entrance fees are per carload and some per person. Call (800) 460-9698 for a home boater course or look online at the TP&W site. On public lakes, fishermen 17 and older must have a fishing license.

Two popular fishing programs for youth are KIDFISH and "Get Hooked on Fishing, Not Drugs," (800) 792-1112. **National Fishing Week** is the first week of June.

At the following local fishing ponds, no license is necessary:

Catfish Corner, (972) 222-2823. Catfish are raised here, and fishing is year-round. Call for hours. Admission is $2, with $2 per pound for fish caught. Bait is available. It is located east of Mesquite at 120 Lawson between I-20 and I-30.

Texas Freshwater Fisheries Center, 5550 FM 2495, Athens 75752 (903) 676-BASS. Website: www.tpwd.state.tx.us/fishboat. This super fish hatchery and aquatic nature complex has 300,000 gallons of aquaria and is the home of the ShareLunker Program. Fish are stocked in a two-acre casting pond, and here children can learn the fundamentals of fishing. Rods, reels, and bait are included in the entrance fee. Special programs and special events for junior anglers are scheduled regularly. No license is required for catch-and-release. The center is open Tuesday to Saturday and Sunday afternoon. Located four miles east of Athens, near Cedar Creek Lake.

BONHAM STATE PARK

1363 SP 24, Bonham (903) 583-5022 Website: www.tpwd.state.tx.us

A 261-acre park with 65-acre lake. Picnic and campsites, overnight group facility and day-use group facility, a group tent camping area (enjoyed by Scouts), playgrounds, 11-mile hiking and mountain biking trail, and boating—5 mph no-wake, boat ramp, boat dock, lighted fishing pier, swimming allowed. Nearby in Bonham are the house and library/museum of former Speaker of the House Sam Rayburn and Fort McInnish Park. Details are on the website: www.bonhamchamber.com. To reach the state park, take Texas Hwy. 78 So. one mile to FM 271. Then go east about two miles.

CEDAR CREEK LAKE

Chamber of Commerce, (903) 887-3152 Website: www.cclake.net

The 33,750-acre reservoir is overseen by the Tarrant Regional Water District. Website: www.trwd.com. Commercial campsites, public boat ramps, marinas with boat rental, fishing, skiing, sailing, swimming, has golf courses. **Chamber Isle** is a small public park with boat ramps, picnic tables, and swimming located between Seven Points and Gun Barrel City on the south side of 334 (small fee). **R. H. Lee Park** is located on FM 3062 (fee). **Finley Park,** located on SH-334 at Seven Points, has a public beach.

Don's Port Marina, 1937 Island Circle, Tool 75143 (903) 432-2268. Website: www.donsportmarina.com. Tiki Hut family restaurant (open mid-April to October). Boat launch. Rentals: ski and pontoon boats, jetskis, water skis for kids and adults, life jackets, kneeboards, wakeboards, tubes.

Sunny Glenn Marina Fishing Pier is on Highway 198, (903) 489-0715.

To reach Cedar Creek, take 175 south. Exit SH 274 south. Go nine miles to Seven Points. From here it depends on where you are going. You can take 334 East toward Gun Barrel City. The lake is about 70 miles southeast of Dallas.

COOPER LAKE AND STATE PARK

Corps of Engineers, (903) 945-2108 Website: www.tpwd.state.tx.us/cooperlake (see also Corps of Engineers website)

This is a relatively new lake of 22,740 acres. It features facilities for handicapped visitors. To visit the state park, call about **Doctor's Creek Unit** (903-395-3100) and **South Sulphur Unit** (903-945-5256). Doctor's Creek (1664 FR 1529 South) has cottages, a boat ramp, and a jetty. South Sulphur (1690 FM 3505) has a fishing pier, boat ramp, campsites, screened shelters, and 15 cabins for rent as well as an equestrian area and hiking trail. Located 75 miles east of Dallas between Commerce and Cooper.

DAINGERFIELD LAKE AND STATE PARK

455 Park Rd. 17, Daingerfield (903) 645-2921 Website: www.tpwd.state.tx.us/daingerfield.

Eighty-acre lake surrounded by 502 pine-covered acres. A lighted pier, swimming area, boat ramp (5 mph—no wake), canoe/paddleboat/rowboat rental, three cabins, 52 campsites, and a group facility for 20 people. Take I-30 to Mt. Pleasant, exit at Ferguson Rd., and take Hwy. 49 East for about 18 miles.

GRAPEVINE LAKE

110 Fairway, Grapevine 76051, (817) 865-2600. Website: www.swf-wc.usace.army.mil/grapevine

A 7,380-acre reservoir. Seven public parks with boat ramps and camping facilities, fishing, swimming, picnicking.

Silverlake Park offers a visitor center, boat rentals, fishing supplies, and swimming. Call Silverlake Marina, 2500 Fairway Drive, #1. Metro (817) 481-1918. Website: www.silverlakemarina.com. Just For Fun at Silverlake Marina rents ski boats and pontoon boats, (817) 310-3000 Website: www.jff.net.

Oak Grove Park includes Scott's Landing Marina, 2500 Oak Grove Loop. (817) 481-4549. Website: www.scottslanding.com. Take I-635 to Hwy. 121 and go west to 121 and Fairway Drive. A lake map will help with park sites. Ask about summer boating lessons for children by the **U.S. Coast Guard Auxiliary.**

JOE POOL LAKE

6399 FM 1382, Cedar Hill (972) 299-2227. **U.S. Army Corps of Engineers.** Website: www.swf-wc.usace.army.mil/joepool/

A 7,470-acre reservoir with 1,800-acre state park (354 campsites) and 1,700 acres of other parkland (over 200 campsites) maintained by Trinity River Authority.

Loyd Park, 3401 Ragland, Grand Prairie. Website: www.loydpark .com. Eight cabins, swim area, 221 campsites, group campsites, showers, fishing piers, two playgrounds, four-lane boat ramp with dock, softball field, volleyball court, biking/hiking trails, and October hayride and haunted trail.

Lynn Creek Park, 5700 Lake Ridge Pky., Grand Prairie. Two four-lane boat ramps, beach, 81 picnic sites, three group sites, playground, restrooms, amphitheater on shore with lawn seating for more than 1,000. Lynn Creek Marina, Metro (817) 640-4200, rents ski boats, fishing boats, pontoon boats, and a 25-foot pontoon boat that seats 14 people at 5700 Lake Ridge Pkwy. Take I-10 west to Great Southwest exit. Go south. Southwest becomes Lake Ridge. The **Oasis** is a floating restaurant located at Lynn Creek. You might see some ducks to feed. Website: www.lakeparks.net/lynncreek.htm.

Cedar Hill State Park,1570 FM 1382, Cedar Hill (972) 291-3900. Website: www.cedarhillstatepark.com. $5 per person, 12 and under, free; 10 boat-launching lanes and two fishing jetties; 355 wooded campsites;

two group pavilions; four playgrounds; swimming beach; picnic sites; 12 comfort stations; perch pond for kids; 4.5-mile hiking trail; 10.3-miles mountain bike trails; and **Penn Farm Historic Agricultural Center**. John Penn came to Texas in 1894 and built up his family farm. Buildings preserved here will show visitors how a Texas farm operated at the turn of the 20th century.

Joe Pool Marina and Park Store: rentals—ski boats, wave runners, paddle boats, pontoon boat, and houseboat with a slide, (972) 299-9010. Website: www.marinequest.net/joepool. Located 10 miles southwest of Dallas.

LAKE ARLINGTON

Green Oaks Blvd., south off Loop 303, Arlington

A 2,275-acre lake. Boating, fishing, picnics. **Arkansas Lane Park**, 6300 W. Arkansas. **Bowman Springs Park**, 7001 Poly Webb Road.

LAKE LAVON

3375 Skyview, Wylie. U.S. Army Corps of Engineers, (972) 442-3141. Website: www.ci.wylie.tx.us/Parks/Lavon.htm

A 21,000-acre reservoir northeast of Dallas, 20 public parks. **Collin Park**: swimming, picnic tables, boat ramps, camping (972) 442-5711. Ron's Harbor House Restaurant. Lavon Boat Rental, (972) 429-7500, at **Collin Park Marina**, (972) 442-3567, rents ski boats, fishing boats, jet-skis, pontoon boats, and a large party barge; lessons in skiing and wakeboarding. To reach **Collin Park Marina and Campgrounds**, take US 75 to Parker Rd. (2514) and turn right. Turn right onto 1378 south and then take County Rd. 727 to Collin Park. **Sister Grove Park**, County Rd. 562, between Princeton and Farmersville. Off-road biking trail.

LAKE RAY HUBBARD

Dallas, Rockwall, Heath, and Garland. Website: http://www.texasoutside.com/txorails/public/reviews/show_lake/18.

A 21,671-acre lake. Fishing, sailing, skiing (no swimming beaches or camping). **Elgin Robertson Park** located at I-30 and Dalrock Rd. (on right) near Bayview Marina.

North Texas Sailing School at Rush Creek Yacht Club: 320 Rush Creek Dr., Heath (972) 771-2002). Website: www.northtexassailing .com. Lessons for all ages. Juniors, ages 7 to 17. Summer, three two-week sessions. Great story on website about Ollie the sailboat that helps with terminology.

Harbor Bay Marina (exit Ridge Rd. from I-30): Fishing barge; $8 per person, one pole for 12 hours; ages 9 and under free with paid adult; bait for sale. (972) 771-0095.

Marina Del Ray (2413 Rowlett, exit Belt Line off I-30) rents small fishing boats, jet-skis, pontoon barge; fishing on the bank; fishing dock, fee. (972) 240-2020.

Public boat ramps. Exit Ridge Rd. from I-30 for public boat ramps next to the highway. Near **Captain's Cove Marina** (5965 Marina Dr.) (972) 226-7100.

NorTex WaterSports. 716 E I-30 at Bobtown Rd., Garland (214) 389-3178. Boat and water sports dealership. Rental boats.

LAKE RAY ROBERTS

U.S. Army Corps of Engineers, (469) 645-9100, Lewisville. Website: www.swf-wc.usace.army.mil/rayroberts

A 29,350-acre reservoir. State park website: www.tpwd.state.tx.us.

Isle Du Bois State Park Unit, 100 PW 4137, Pilot Point (817) 686-2148. 1,397 acres off FM 455 east of the dam. Has 115 multi-use campsites with water and electricity, 14 equestrian campsites, lighted boat ramp, beach area, picnic sites, group picnic pavilions, lighted fishing pier, greenbelt, 12 miles of dirt trail, 4.5 miles of paved trail (part is handicapped accessible) along banks of the Elm Fork of the Trinity River, and playgrounds.

Johnson Unit, 100 PW 4153, Valley View (940) 637-2294, north shore, 1,514 acres. Camping, swimming, boating, hiking/biking, interpretive programs, kidfish pond, boat ramp, jetty.

Sanger Unit, Lake Ray Roberts Marina (940) 458-7343. Website: www.rayrobertsmarina.com. Rental boats.

LAKE TEXOMA

U.S. Army Corps of Engineers, Denison Dam, Denison 75020 (903) 465-4990 Website: www.laketexoma.com.

An 89,000-acre lake in Texas and Oklahoma. Fifty-four parks, 100 picnic areas, marinas, fishing, boating, skiing, **Cross Timbers Hiking Trail** (14 miles), **Hagerman Wildlife Refuge**, (903) 786-2826. Refuge Center, bird and wildlife observation, auto tour, hiking trail, fishing, boating, paddling. Don't go after a recent rain. For more about sites and activities in Denison, look in **Chapter 6: Day Trips**.

Eisenhower State Park, 50 Park Rd. 20, Denison (903) 465-1956. Website: www.tpwd.state.tx.us/eisenhower. Named for the 34th U.S. president, Dwight D. Eisenhower, whose Denison home is now a historic site. On 423 acres. Fishing piers, 4.2-mile hiking trail, 35 screened shelters, 48 campsites with water, 50 trailer campsites, 45 campsites with water and electricity, small beach, picnic areas, group recreation hall, pavilion. **Eisenhower Yacht Club Marina** rents pontoon boats, canoes, and kayaks. Take US 75 to 1310. Go west to Park Road 20 and park entrance.

Texoma marinas/resorts:

Grandpappy Point Marina, 132 Grandpappy Dr. (888) 855-1972; (903) 465-6330. Website: www.grandpappy.com. Sailboat charters and lessons, cabins, RV hookups.

Texoma Rental, (903) 327-8286; Website: www.texomarentals.net. Ski boats, wave runners, pontoon boats.

Highport Marina, 120 Texoma Harbor Dr., Pottsboro (903) 786-7000. Website: www.highport.com. Yachts, volleyball and basketball courts, no beach, Island Bar and Grill. Texoma Rentals: Pontoon and ski boats, jet-skis (see above).

Cedar Bayou Marina, 513 Cedar Mills Blvd., Gordonville (903) 523-4248. Website: www.cedarbayou.com. Boat ramp and pontoon boat rental, store.

Cedar Mills Marina and Resort, Gordonville, (903) 523-4222. Website: www.cedarmills.com. Beautiful view of lake and sailboats; campground, boat charters, cabins, RV and trailer hookups, sailing school, store, and restaurant (open Wednesday to Sunday).

Tanglewood Resort Hotel and Conference Center, 290 Tanglewood Circle, Pottsboro (800) 833-6569. Golf, pools, tennis, ski boat and bike rental, dining room, playground, volleyball court, boat slips, no beach.

LAKE WHITNEY

285 CR 3602, Clifton (254) 622-3332
Website: www.swf-wc.usace.army.mil/whitney

A 23,560-acre reservoir with 14 federal parks as well as marinas, fishing, swimming, boating, and scuba diving.

Lake Whitney State Park. FM 1244, Whitney (254) 694-3793. Website: www.tpwd.state.tx.us. A 1,315-acre park, two-hour drive southwest. Seventy-eight campsites, recreation hall, boat ramps, lighted airstrip, hiking and mountain bike trails, ask about swimming beach and screened shelters (problems with flooding).

Lake Whitney Marina at Juniper Cove, (254) 694-3129 or (866) 600-1206. Air-conditioned cabins, RV campgrounds, campsites, boat rentals, lighted indoor fishing barge. From I-35, exit Hillsboro and take Hwy. 22 west to Whitney. Follow signs west three miles on FM 1244 by state park.

LAKE LEWISVILLE

1801 N. Mill St., Lewisville (469) 645-9100
Website: www.swf-wc.usace.army.mil/Lewisville

A 23,280-acre lake. Fourteen parks. Fishing, skiing, swimming, sailing, camping.

Lake Park, operated by the City of Lewisville, (972) 219-3550. Swimming beach, boat ramps, camping, and playground. Lighted, air-conditioned fishing barge to the northwest, fee: (972) 436-9341. Campground: (972) 219-3742. Take I-35 north. Exit Justin Rd. (407) and take a right to Lake Park Rd. Fee.

East Hill Park, operated by the U.S. Army Corps of Engineers, (469) 645-9100. Swimming, fishing (no pier), ramps.

Pier 121 Marina: (972) 625-2233. Just for Fun rents a variety of boats: (972) 370-7700.

Hidden Cove Park (privately leased). 20400 Hackberry Creek, The Colony (972) 294-1443 Website: www.marinequest.net. Marina being built. 721 acres. Fifty campsites, 38 screened shelters, three pavilions, enclosed dining hall that seats 100 at water's edge, playground, picnicking, ramps, swimming in day-use area. Daily entrance fee. Take Hwy. 423 to Stonebrook Rd. Park is at the end of the road.

In **Chapter 2: Tidbits** under **Nature**, you will find a description of the Lake Lewisville **Environmental Learning Area**, which offers many outdoor activities south of the Lake Lewisville dam.

POSSUM KINGDOM LAKE

Overseen by the Brazos River Authority (888) 779-8330 Website: www.brazos.org/pkHome.asp

Helpful PK website: www.possumkingdomlake.com. A 17,700-acre lake. Campsites, marinas, scuba diving to 150 feet, swimming, boating. Canoeing on the Brazos River is very scenic on a 20-mile section between Texas Highway 16 and Highway 4 in Palo Pinto County.

Possum Kingdom State Park. 3911 Park Rd. 33, Caddo (940) 549-1803 Website: www.tpwd.state.tx.us. Go to "Find a Park" and then to "Region One." 1,528 acres, 116 campsites, six small air-conditioned and heated cabins, lighted fishing pier, boat ramp, playgrounds, swimming area, two-mile trail, park store, restrooms, showers, wildlife. Take US Hwy. 180 to Caddo. Drive 17 miles north on Park Road 33. Park fee and water use fee.

Camp Grady Spruce, YMCA camp at Possum Kingdom Lake, 3000 Park Rd., Graford (866) 391-7343. Website: www.campgradyspruce.org. Camp is 120 miles west of Dallas.

Naylor by the Water. 461 North FM 2353, Graford (940) 779-3142. Rentals: pontoon and ski boats, jet-skis, towables.

PURTIS CREEK STATE PARK

Rt. 1, Box 506, Eustace 75124 (903) 425-2332

A 355-acre lake. Fifty-nine campsites with water and electricity, 13 primitive campsites with water nearby, one-lane boat ramp, two docks, 50-boat limit with idle-speed, no-wake restriction, picnic sites, playground, hiking trail, fishing for bass on catch-and-release basis but may keep catfish and crappie, two lighted fishing piers, swimming area. Park store with canoe and paddleboat rentals. No waterskiing or sailing. Near Cedar Creek Lake. From Dallas, go east on Hwy. 175 to Eustace. Turn left (north) on FM 316 for 3.5 miles to park. Fee.

5. FESTIVALS AND
SPECIAL EVENTS

Around Dallas there is always something to celebrate. The theme for the festival might be related to cultural heritage, history, physical fitness, the arts, nature, sports, or technology and products. Whatever the reason for the gathering, appreciative crowds show up for the fun, and very often, worthy service and health organizations benefit from the proceeds. Call or watch for newspaper announcements about the festivals because all may not be held annually, or they may change months and/or locations. Keeping current telephone numbers for information is also difficult. Please look in **Chapter 3: Performing Arts** for festivals and in **Chapter 4: Sports and Recreation** for sporting events. The Dallas Convention and Visitors Bureau maintains a calendar of major events on its website: www.visitdallas.com. Also, try www.2chambers.com for suburban cities.

JANUARY

SBC Cotton Bowl Classic. Moved from Fair Park to the new Cowboys football stadium. This annual college football game is a clash between two of the nation's best teams.

Kidfilm. Angelica Theater. Kidfilm, an international children's film festival sponsored by the USA Film Festival, takes place on a Saturday and a Sunday afternoon.

Martin Luther King Jr. Birthday Events. Martin Luther King Day **Parade** passes by the South Dallas Cultural Center and ends at Fair Park. Look for special events and parades announced in the newspaper at places such as SMU, Martin Luther King Jr. Recreation Center, South Dallas Cultural Center, and other area colleges and community centers, as well as the African American Museum.

Annual Very Special Arts Festival. Plano Convention Centre. Colorful, creative crafts booths will entice children of all ages and abilities.

Dallas International Boat Show. Dallas Market Hall, 2200 Stemmons. Motorboats and sailboats, exhibits, water sports products and services, and the trout fishing tank fill Market Hall during this show. It's family fun even if a boat is not in your budget.

Dallas Area Train Show. Plano Convention Centre. Trains running and for sale, clinics, videos, and home layout tours entertain all who love trains.

Texas Fishing and Hunting Outdoor Show. Arlington Convention Center. Exhibits of rods, reels, lures, and boats turn the heads of avid fishermen at this exhibition. Youngsters like the fish tank and raptors.

Chinese New Year Events. Celebration of the new year usually takes place at the Crow Collection of Asian Art and at Chinese restaurants in the area.

Dino Dash and Discovery Fest. Annual run to benefit the Dallas Museum of Nature and Science, which also features activities for children.

Second Saturday on the Square. Old Downtown Lancaster. Crafts and unique items for sale. Music and entertainment each second Saturday of the month.

Canton First Monday Trade Days. Canton, Highway 19. Thursday through Sunday before the first Monday of each month.

Third Monday Trade Days. 4550 University, McKinney. Friday to Sunday preceding the third Monday of each month.

FEBRUARY

Harlem Globetrotters. American Airlines Center. Basketball at its best and funniest is the forte of this traveling troupe.

African American History Month Activities. Check online and the newspapers throughout this month for special activities at museums, bookstores, galleries, recreation centers, colleges, and performing arts centers.

Texas Rangers Midwinter Banquet and Carnival. Arlington Convention Center, 1200 Stadium Drive, Arlington. Outstanding players are honored at this annual banquet and carnival.

Valentine's Day Events. Many of the public libraries plan special activities for Valentine's Day, and the Arboretum sometimes offers free admission for sweethearts. Look for the special Hearts and Flowers market at Farmers Market, downtown. Some recreation centers and churches have father-daughter banquets and dances.

Dallas Spring Home and Garden Show. Dallas Market Hall. This large show features must-have items for the home and garden and includes demonstrations and entertainment.

Mystiqal Mardi Gras Parade. The parade floats down Main St. to the West End. It promises live music, spicy food, and beaucoup beads. This is probably not an event for young children.

Krewe of Barkus Parade. McKinney Mitchell Park. Pooches in costume are a hit at this mardi gras fundraiser. Food, music, and contests follow.

Taste of Collin County. Downtown McKinney. Restaurants set up booths of delectables, a concert steps up the fun, and kids bounce and get their faces painted at this culinary festival.

Golden Gloves Tournament. Fair Park Coliseum. For more than 70 years, this annual boxing tournament has been in Dallas.

Stars on Ice. American Airlines Center. Olympic world and national champions entertain the crowd with their skill and showmanship.

Trout Fish Out. Armstrong Pool, Duncanville. Two days of fishing for all age groups.

MARCH

North Texas Irish Festival. Fair Park. Forty musical groups on eight stages, Irish food and drink, performance workshops, jugglers, magicians, and Urchin Street Children's Faire highlight this celebration of the Irish, held on an early March weekend.

Dallas Blooms. Dallas Arboretum and Botanical Garden, 8617 Garland Rd. The opening of Dallas Blooms signals that springtime has arrived in Dallas. The event lasts about one month, and the beautiful flowers are breathtaking every year. Call (214) 327-4901.

Arts and Letters Live Jr. Dallas Museum of Art. A pint-size version of the adult series, which includes lectures, readings, discussion groups, and maybe even food and movies.

Downtown Dallas St. Patrick's Day Parade. Intersection of Commerce and Griffin to Ervay, west on Pacific to West End. This mid-afternoon celebration features marching bands, floats, clowns, and more. About 4 PM, the West End Festival on the Plaza begins, with more family entertainment, live music, and food.

Hoop-It-Up Spring Warmup. Lone Star Park, Grand Prairie. Three-on-three outdoor basketball tournament on weekend.

Big 12 Women's and Big 12 Men's Basketball Games. American Airline Center. These college basketball games are played by the best of the season.

Greenville Avenue St. Patrick's Day Parade. On Greenville from Blackwell to Yale. A very informal, enthusiastic parade of inventive floats and bands is planned annually for Greenville Avenue.

Tejas Storytelling Festival. Denton. Civic Center Park on the weekend.

Dallas New Car Auto Show. Dallas Convention Center. Here's a chance to see the newest and shiniest from automakers.

Dino Day. Museum of Nature and Science, Fair Park. In celebration of dinosaurs, a parade and costume contest, films, scavenger hunt, and art work are featured each year.

Spring Breakout. Six Flags. Look for special events in addition to regular Six Flags fare.

Shrine Circus. Resistol Arena, Mesquite Rodeo Grounds.

Annual Dallas Video Festival. Angelica Theater and Dallas Museum of Art. A film festival that is primarily for adults features screenings of local, regional, and internationally produced programs.

Special Olympics Uptown Run and Trolley Walk. Uptown. This event, which has been held for more than 17 years, includes a kid's K and a special Olympian run.

Disney on Ice. American Airlines Center. Skaters portray favorite Disney characters.

Out of the Loop Festival. Water Tower Theatre, Addison Theatre Centre. Family performances and entertainment.

Kite Weekend Celebration. Heard Museum, McKinney. This high-flying event includes stunt kite demonstrations, kite-making workshops, nature walks, and more festivities.

Village Egg Roll. Dallas Heritage Village. Annual egg roll. May bring a picnic.

Texas . . . History Alive! Farmers Branch Historical Park. 2540 Farmers Branch Lane. The Texana Living History Association promotes this annual fest with historical costumes, prairie campsites, crafts, and Wild West–era games.

APRIL

Earthfest. Pegasus Plaza, Downtown. Environmental presentations, live entertainment, food, activities for youngsters.

Ennis Bluebonnet Trails. Pierce Park, 112 N.W. Main, Ennis. Follow a map guiding you to brilliant fields of bluebonnets during mid- to late April. Arts and crafts, food, antique show, and more adds to the festival. Call (800) 452-9292, the Texas Department of Transportation hotline, for information on where to spot beautiful wildflowers.

Dallas Cup Youth Soccer. Pizza Hut Park, Frisco. Young people from around the world compete at this annual event held at various fields and stadiums.

Hot Dogs and Hoops Fest. American Airlines Center, Dallas. A basketball hotdogging competition for kids 14 and under and family entertainment highlight this festival. Six winners get to compete at a Mavericks home game. Free admission and parking.

USA Film Festival. Magnolia, Inwood, Angelica, and various theaters. For more than 30 years, filmmakers and fans have gathered for films and discussions.

Scarborough Faire. FM 66 and I-35E, Waxahachie. At Scarborough Faire, an English Renaissance village, families watch knights in armor competing, feast on hearty foods, marvel at the falconer and his birds of prey, watch jugglers and sorcerers, enjoy a variety of performing artists, and browse in village shops. The festival takes place on weekends and Memorial Day from latter April to mid-June.

North Texas Jazz Festival. Crowne Plaza Hotel, Dallas. For more than four years this festival has brought both nationally and locally recognized jazz musicians to perform incredible music.

Folklorico Festival. Arts District, downtown. Multi-ethnic artists share their music, food, customs, and dance at this two-day festival.

The Learning Fair. Northpark Center. Sponsored by the Brain/Behavior Center, the fair brings together both public and private agencies to provide services for the learning disabled. Counselors, educators, and parents are at 35 booths, and entertainment is scheduled. Free.

Galleria Primavera. Galleria, LBJ and Dallas Parkway. Garden exhibits, music, and ice skating events are scheduled in the shopping mall during one week in April.

Metroplex Annual Doll Show. Plano Convention Centre, Plano. Large annual doll show. Sometimes changes locations.

Easter Egg Hunts: Farmers Branch Historical Park, Garland Easter Eggstravaganza, Las Colinas, recreation centers, West End Marketplace, selected Grand Prairie parks, Grapevine parks, Plano parks, Rockwall parks. Easter Bunny: Valley View Center, downtown Carrollton, Highland Park Village. Parties: recreation centers and libraries. Zoo parade and scavenger hunt. Sunrise service: Check with local churches.

Easter Brunches with Special Celebration: Check with the Adolphus, Blue Mesa, Harvey Hotel-Plano, Lawry's The Prime Rib, Maggiano's Little Italy, Embassy Suites Park Central Area, The Old Warsaw, Westin Stonebriar Resort, Arboretum, Fairmont Hotel, Gaylord Texan Resort, Great Wolf Lodge.

Easter Concert. Lee Park. The Dallas Symphony celebrates Easter with a free performance.

Arbor Day/Earth Day Celebrations: Dallas Museum of Nature and Science, Grapevine Treefest, Heard Museum, state parks, White Rock

Lake, Dallas Arboretum, Farmers Branch Mallon Park, downtown festivals in Annette Strauss Artist Square and Pegasus Plaza.

KSCS Country Fair. Concerts and rodeo.

Art Fiesta. Old Downtown Carrollton. Arts and crafts, food, children's activities, and music entertain visitors at this annual festival.

Prairie Dog Chili Cook-off and World Championship of Pickled Quail Egg Eating. Traders Village, Grand Prairie. In addition to the chili cookoff, enjoy music, more food, and the flea market.

Mesquite Rodeo Parade and Celebration. Mesquite. This annual parade kicks off rodeo season, which runs from April to September. It features horses, floats, bands, stagecoaches, and drill teams on a Saturday afternoon.

Cardboard Boat Regatta. Hurricane Harbor, Arlington.

Sports: Seasons begin for the Mesquite Rodeo, Lone Star Park Thoroughbred Horse Racing, and the Texas Rangers.

MAY

Richardson Wildflower and Music Festival. Galatyn Park, US 75 at Campbell, Richardson. On a weekend, visitors get a taste of Richardson, music, food, and spring wildflowers to admire.

Memorial Day Concert. Flag Pole Hill. The Dallas Symphony performs outdoors for families. Bring a blanket or lawn chair.

Cinco de Mayo Celebrations: Greenville Avenue, Fair Park (midway, music, food), Latino Cultural Center, Traders Village, Samuell-Grand Recreation Center, Pike Park.

Artfest. Fair Park. Artfest is a lively, colorful weekend celebration of the arts, which includes the work of 300 jury-selected artists, Artfest for Kids, outdoor concert stages with a variety of musical entertainment, and food. Artfest Week includes a variety of activities around town.

Boy Scouts Annual Scout Show. Dallas Market Center. The largest Scout event in Texas, the Circle 10 Council Show is highlighted by more than 400 booths with demonstrations, games, and exhibits. Other activities include outdoor cooking, climbing tower, music, and crafts. Website: www.circle10.org.

PetPallooza. River Legacy Parks West, 701 N.W. Green Oaks Blvd., Arlington. Pets and their people enjoy exhibits, one-mile pet and people walk, entertainment from pet associations, adoption center, and more.

KidFish. City Lake Park, S. Galloway and Parkview, Mesquite. Fishing for 16 and under at stocked lake. Equipment provided if the child does not have his own. Free. Call (972) 290-2108.

Main Street Days. Main Street, Grapevine. Main Street Days celebrates Grapevine's railroad and agricultural heritage with musical entertainment, food, re-enactments, and children's activities.

McKinney Art and Jazz Festival. Downtown McKinney, one mile east of US 75, on Louisiana. Jazz and blues, art, food, car show, and art for children liven up this annual festival.

Safari Days. Dallas Zoo. Annual family day includes zoo animals, live music, bounce house, and crafts.

Texas Black Invitational Rodeo. Fair Park Coliseum. The best of America's black cowboys and cowgirls participate in rodeo events.

Taste of Addison. Addison Conference Center and Theatre Center. Food, music, entertainment, and activities for kids spell fun at this festival.

Mother's Day Weekend and Brunch. Dallas Arboretum and Botanical Garden. The arboretum plans a special weekend for Mom and the family each year. Reservations are required for brunch.

Spring Flower Festival. Farmers Market, 1010 S. Pearl, Downtown. Farmers Market celebrates spring with flowers, music, arts and crafts, games, and more. Call (214) 939-2808.

Cottonwood Art Festival. Cottonwood Park, Belt Line at Cottonwood Dr. in Richardson. Visitors may browse and purchase artwork by local artists. Includes food, entertainment, and ArtStop for Kids. Call (972) 638-9116.

Asian Festival. Downtown. Music, dance, food, arts and crafts, martial arts, activities for children.

Chestnut Square Art Festival. McDonald and Anthony St., McKinney. Art work is displayed on the porches and lawns of historic homes in this two-day event.

White Rock Prairie Fest. Bath House Cultural Center, 521 E. Lawther, White Rock Lake. This annual festival celebrates the prairie on which we live with prairie-related demonstrations, Indian dances, wildflower walks, and more.

JUNE

Pepsi Kid Around. Annette Strauss Artist Square. For more than 11 years, this event has provided a variety of activities to promote creativity, safety, and education. Sometimes the location changes.

Saturday in Fair Park. A special day is planned in Fair Park so families can enjoy its museums and entertainment.

Juneteenth Festivals: City Hall Plaza, Fair Park African American Museum, and South Dallas Cultural Center are usually sites of celebration.

Texas Scottish Festival and Highland Games. Maverick Stadium, UTA. The weekend festival includes bagpipe and drumming competition, Scottish food, Scottish and Celtic athletic events, children's games, and a dog show.

Hoop-It-Up. Downtown. This three-on-three basketball tournament is for children and adults, and wheelchair teams are included. Each team plays at least three games.

Toad Holler Creekfest. DeSoto Towne Center. Games, arts and crafts, food, children's activities, and music add to the fun in DeSoto on the first Saturday in June.

Irving Heritage Festival. Heritage Park, Second and Main, Irving. Demonstrations of historic crafts, food, arts and crafts, and music take place on a Saturday. Call (972) 259-1249.

Fritz Park Petting Farm. Fritz Park, 312 E. Vilbig, Irving. Open June and July. Senter Park (900 S. Senter).

Cool Thursdays. Thursdays at 7:30 PM during May to July, Dallas Arboretum. Relax and listen to live music outdoors. Bring blankets or lawn chairs.

Friday Night Films. Nasher Sculpture Garden. Arrive after 7 PM with a blanket and enjoy movies outdoors in June and July.

CityArts Celebration. Arts District. A three-day celebration featuring Dallas's cultural, artistic, and culinary talents with children's activities and free admission to DMA.

··

JULY

··

July Fourth Celebrations: Dallas and almost all surrounding cities plan festivities and fireworks to celebrate America's independence. Contact your chamber of commerce for their celebration plans if they are not listed here. Fireworks are illegal within the city limits without a permit because they are a fire hazard. Please check in **Chapter 3: Performing Arts** for festivals on the Fourth. Venues such as the Ballpark, Lone Star Park, Pizza Hut Park, Fair Park, Farmers Branch Historical Park, Las Colinas, and more celebrate independence in grand style.

Trinity Fest. Downtown. Trinity Fest includes food, entertainment, kids' activities, arts and crafts, and fireworks.

Old-Fashioned Fourth at Dallas Heritage Village (old City Park). 1717 Gano. This old-fashioned celebration includes an all-join-in parade, contests, dance, music, games, and tours.

Park Cities Fourth of July Parade. Highland Park Town Hall, 4700 Drexel, to University Park Town Hall, 3800 University. For more than

30 years, this Fourth of July Parade has delighted residents because they join in the parade. They ride on floats, bicycles, antique cars, and go-carts and march in bands. Snow cones and hot dogs await them at the end of the line at Goar Park.

Star-Spangled Fourth of July. Downtown Garland. This colorful celebration includes food, crafts, C&W entertainment, children's activities, and fireworks. May be suspended due to economic downturn.

Star-Spangled Spectacular. Clark Recreation Center, Plano. Patriotic festivities, food, music, and fireworks finish the day.

Kaboom Town. Addison. An incredible display of fireworks at the corner of Arapaho and Quorum is simulcast with patriotic music on a radio station on July third. It's a good idea to get to the area by 8 PM to find a good spot. Bring chairs and beverages.

Arlington Fourth of July Parade. Downtown Arlington. The parade, which has more than 150 entries, begins at 9:00 AM.

Las Colinas. Williams Square, Irving. Concerts and fireworks. Parade.

Richardson Fourth of July. Breckinridge Park, Richardson. Richardson's celebration usually begins in the early evening with demonstrations by groups such as kite flyers and remote-controlled car clubs. Adding to the fun are performing arts entertainment, clowns, and face painters. Fireworks end the evening with a bang.

Recreation Centers' July Fourth Celebrations: Check with local recreation centers for special events. Lake Highlands North Recreation Center holds an annual neighborhood parade for all family members on Church Rd., Dallas.

Ringling Brothers Barnum & Bailey Circus. American Airlines Center. This favorite three-ring extravaganza is anticipated each July. There is usually a designated Family Night when the admission is less expensive.

Taste of Dallas. West End Historical District. During this delicious event, restaurants present samples of their best fare. Outdoor entertainment and a children's area are included in the well-attended festivities.

Dallas Zoo Dollar Day. Dallas Zoo. The zoo says thanks through a $1 admission price all day.

AUGUST

Dallas Cowboys Pre-Season Games. Cowboy Stadium, Arlington. For those who miss the Cowboys and can endure the summer heat, the pre-season games begin in August.

Dallas Morning News Dance Festival. Annette Strauss Artist Square. This festival showcases new and seasoned professional dance companies. Sometimes it is held around the first of September.

SEPTEMBER

Labor Day Parade and Jaycee Jubilee. Central Park, Garland. In honor of Labor Day, the Jaycees plan a downtown parade, a festival with crafts, a carnival, and the Junior Miss Garland Program over a four-day period.

Grapefest. Main Street, Grapevine. Grapevine honors its namesake in this festival, which includes wine tasting and judging, vintage cars, GrapeFair, and children's GrapeGames.

TACA Family Festival. Meyerson Symphony Center. Hands-on art for ages 2 to 10 as well as special guests and entertainment.

Japanese Fall Festival. Fujitsu Bldg., 2811 Telecom Parkway, Richardson. Japanese food, dancers, demonstrations, music.

National Championship Indian Pow-Wow. Traders Village, Grand Prairie. Tribes and spectators gather annually for the weekend pow-wow, which features Indian dancing and competition, food, arts and crafts, exhibits of teepees, and more entertainment.

International Air Show. Alliance Airport. A variety of aircraft perform for families.

Oktoberfest. Arapaho and Quorum, Addison. German food, carnival, and children's entertainment are featured in this fall celebration.

Greek Food Festival. Holy Trinity Greek Orthodox Church. Weekend festival offering Greek food, cookbooks, music, and crafts draws appreciative crowds annually. Buy ticket ahead if you can.

Family Fun Festival. Heard Museum and Wildlife Sanctuary, McKinney. Nature activities, crafts, games, wagon rides, nature trails, animals, and food entertain families at this annual festival.

Great Fountain Plaza Festival. Richardson Civic Center, Central and Arapaho. Family games and entertainment.

Oak Cliff's Tour of Homes and Arts Festival. Kidd Springs Park, 711 W. Canty. A tour of six homes and a family festival, which usually includes a parade, arts and crafts show, entertainment, and children's events, is fun for all on a September weekend.

Plano Hot-Air Balloon Festival. Oak Point Park, Plano. Hot-air balloon races, arts and crafts, and music are featured during this colorful weekend event.

Texas Heritage Crafts Festival. Six Flags Over Texas, Arlington. More than 200 crafts folk set up shop at Six Flags on two weekends in September. Live music and food as well as demonstrations of almost-forgotten pioneer crafts add to the entertainment.

OCTOBER

State Fair of Texas. Fair Park. See Chapter 1: Places to Go for highlights of Texas's three-week fair, including concerts, midway, exhibits, food, contests, game booths, parades, Pan American Livestock Exposition, rodeo competition, and much more. The state fair is Dallas's second most popular attraction.

Fishing Derby. Harry Myers Park, Rockwall. Anglers ages 14 and under participate in this annual fishing tournament.

Smith's Pumpkin Patch. This three-acre pumpkin patch, located in Aubrey near Denton, is open for pick-your-own pumpkins right out of the patch. This field trip is great fun for groups such as Scouts.

American Indian Art Festival and Market. Annette Strauss Artist Square. More than 150 documented American Indian visual and performing artists from the Southwest shine at this downtown fest. Sometimes held in November.

West End Cattle Drive. West End Historic District. An Old West–style cattle drive is held through the streets of the West End.

Women's Swimming and Diving Classic. SMU Perkins Natatorium. The competition is among the best women's NCAA swimming programs.

Dallas Blooms Autumn. Dallas Arboretum and Botanical Garden. The Arboretum, coated in many brilliantly colored flowers, lures native Dallasites and visitors alike to the month-long celebration of plants and gardening. Demonstrations, plant sales, special exhibits, and entertainment are scheduled for the entire family.

Texas-OU Cotton Bowl Football Game. Fair Park. This annual football clash is held on Saturday afternoon during the state fair. Fans gather for all sorts of celebrations on Friday night, and the winners continue to celebrate throughout the weekend.

Harvest Fest. Armstrong Park, Duncanville. This shindig is held on the third Saturday in October, with more than 120 art and crafts vendors, exhibits and demonstrations, auto show, and children's area.

Country Day on the Hill. Cedar Hill. Food, games, entertainment, and Children's Corner add up to a down-home good time.

Vineyard Fair. Howell Street between McKinney and the Crescent on Cedar Springs. A benefit for the Creative Learning Center, the Vineyard Fair draws thousands of shoppers to browse at booths stocked by artisans, sample food and wine, and listen to live musical entertainment.

Fall Harvest Festival. Dallas Farmers Market, 1010 S. Pearl, Downtown. This celebration of fall's bounty includes music, Pumpkin Junction, fresh produce, and exhibits on Saturday and Sunday.

Harambee Festival. Martin Luther King Community Center, 2922 MLK Blvd. This all-day festival showcases African American culture.

Plano International Festival. Haggard Park, 901 E. 15th in Plano. More than 60 countries are represented, and visitors soak up the culture through music, food, and performances.

Fright Nights. Six Flags Over Texas, Arlington. A variety of creepy creatures gather for a Halloween celebration at Six Flags.

Haunted House at the Palace of Wax. Ripley's Believe It or Not!/Palace of Wax, 601 E. Safari, Grand Prairie. What is alive and what is not is difficult to ascertain in this annual walk of terror.

Boo at the Zoo. Dallas Zoo. Games, prizes, music, and costumed characters are planned for Halloween fun.

Halloween in the Park. Farmers Branch Historical Park, Farmers Branch Lane at Ford Rd. A haunted house, hayrides, carnival, and more treats are presented for the entertainment of spooks of all ages.

Batty at the Ballpark. South side of the Ballpark in Arlington. Legends of the Game Museum sponsors this annual event with pumpkin decorating, face painting, games, and stories.

Haunted Houses: Begin checking the Friday Guide section in the *Dallas Morning News* from mid-October through Halloween for listings of organizations that offer haunted houses, carnivals, and other Halloween events. *Dallas Family* and *dallas child* magazines also list Halloween activities that are appropriate for children in their October issues. The March of Dimes presents haunted houses at multiple locations. Some events are too frightening for young children. Call first if you have questions about suitability.

NOVEMBER

Dallas YMCA Turkey Trot. Dallas City Hall Plaza. This annual 3.5-mile run showcases the downtown area and benefits a shelter for homeless and abused teenagers. A family tent has activities for children.

Texas Stampede. American Airlines Center. This is an exciting combination of country music and championship rodeo. Call (214) 520-8874.

Annual Dallas Cowboys NFL Four-on-Four Flag Football. Competition with 100 different divisions and special youth teams.

Senior Citizens Craft Fair. Automobile Building, Fair Park. Family members of all ages will appreciate the talents behind the handmade items at this benefit craft fair sponsored by the Junior League of Dallas.

Chi Omega Christmas Market. Dallas Convention Center. This is a favorite annual bazaar featuring over 130 merchants.

Dallas Video Festival. Dallas Museum of Art. Presented by the Video Association and the Dallas Museum of Art, this video festival is an exhibition of more than 250 screenings produced by independent media artists for adults and children. It is scheduled from Thursday to Sunday on either the first or second weekend in November. Parents and children enjoy the kid-video programs and hands-on workshops offered on Saturday and Sunday. Some of the videos are made for children, and some are made by children.

Christmas Activities: Check the newspapers toward the end of November because some tree lightings and special events begin the last weekend of November: Dallas City Hall, West End, Uptown, Galleria, Highland Park Village.

DECEMBER

Tree Lightings, Parades, and Carriage Rides: Most of the city halls and some of the shopping, entertainment, and community centers, such as the Galleria, Crescent, and West End, have breathtaking tree lightings to celebrate the Christmas season. Some, like Dallas, Carrollton, Allen, Richardson, and Grapevine, include parades. Call your chamber of commerce for specific dates and times. The **Dallas Holiday Tree Lighting and Parade** takes place at City Hall Plaza and includes a visit from Santa, Santa's Village, choirs, dancers, Christmas critters, and refreshments. Carriage tours of lights are usually offered at Highland Park Village, Dallas Heritage Village, Old Downtown Plano, and the West End.

Although Dallas rarely has a white Christmas, it truly is a wintery wonderland of holiday entertainment for families, as the following festivities will attest. Also, look for special musical and theatrical events and festivals in **Chapter 3: Performing Arts.**

Adolphus/Children's Christmas Parade. Commerce and Griffith, Downtown Dallas. More than 160,000 people come out to cheer on the annual parade featuring floats, bands, antique cars, horses and riders, clowns, favorite characters, and celebrities. Check the newspapers or call for the route. Reserved bleacher seating.

Holiday at Shops of West End Marketplace. West End Historical District. Be there for the tree lighting, entertainment, kids' activities, and food.

Holiday at the Arboretum. Dallas Arboretum. The December celebration at the Arboretum offers a tour of the DeGolyer mansion decorated for Christmas, workshops for children, an outdoor market, and entertainment provided by handbell choirs, chorale singers, and more. It may have Family Fun Sundays that include Santa, reindeer, and carolers. Tea for moms and daughters is festive and delicious in the DeGolyer house.

Christmas in the Branch. Farmers Branch Historical Park, Ford Rd. at Farmers Branch Lane. Christmas in the Branch begins early in December with Dickens in the Park, which features horse-drawn carriage rides, tours of historical buildings, bells, and choirs. A Christmas Lighting Display Driving Route leads visitors from City Hall into the park. Authentic English teas and demonstrations of Christmas Past are also part of the celebration. Call (800) BRANCH9 for a calendar.

Kwanzaa. This celebration of African culture includes the principles of unity, creativity, faith, collective work, responsibility, cooperative economics, and self-determination. The Kwanzaa seasonal events are usually held at many locations around town, including Fair Park, African American Museum, Paul Quinn College, St. Phillip's School and Community Center, Martin Luther King Jr. Recreation Center, Lincoln High School, and the South Dallas Cultural Center.

Trains at Northpark. Northpark Center. Take a trip through a magical collection of 12 O-gauge trains with 350 cars and 2,500 feet of track that travel through miniature scenes created realistically in minute detail.

Candlelight Tour at Dallas Heritage Village. 1717 Gano. The beauty of this annual event never dims. Special activities include tours of decorated historic buildings, musical entertainment, children's tent, surrey rides, refreshments, and holiday shopping on a weekend in mid-December.

Jingle Bell Run. Meyerson, 2301 Flora. Festive costumes of all descriptions for individuals, groups, and their pets are in vogue for the annual Jingle Bell Run benefiting the Blood Care Center. A 5K run, one-mile fun run, pooch parade and costume contest, and treats at Santa Land are planned for all ages.

Holiday in the Park. Six Flags Over Texas, Arlington. Held mainly on weekends from November to January, Holiday in the Park offers exciting holiday shows, an exhibition of beautifully decorated trees, carolers and other musical groups, rides, and sledding on a hill of snow.

Deck the Hall Holiday Concert. Meyerson Symphony Center. The Greater Dallas Youth Orchestra, dancers from Booker T. Washington Arts Magnet School, and choristers combine for a yuletide celebration.

Christmas in Heritage Park. 4th and Austin, Garland. The Junior League of Garland presents an annual craft bazaar, Santa Claus, music, food, and children's entertainment.

A Christmas Carol. Dallas Theater Center, Wyly Theatre. This play is a much anticipated holiday favorite.

Lantern Light Tours. Heritage Farmstead Museum, Plano. Special holiday foods, music, crafts, and decorated two-story Victorian farmhouse capture the holiday spirit for visitors at the Lantern Light Tour.

Dickens Downtown Christmas. Historic Downtown Plano, East 15th. Held in conjunction with the Christmas Tree Lighting in Haggard Park, this holiday celebration includes live music, strolling jugglers and costumed characters, refreshments, caroling, and a visit from the jolly old elf. Call (972) 941-7250.

Christmas Boat Parade and Bonfire. Lynn Creek Park, Grand Prairie. Decorated boats, Santa, carolers, and fireworks celebrate the season.

Star of Bethlehem Planetarium Shows. The re-creation of the Star of Bethlehem and the Christmas story are presented at area planetariums, such as St. Mark's, Museum of History and Science, and UTD Planetarium.

Santa's Appearances: Confusing as it may be to little children, Santa seems to be everywhere they go. Most shopping malls, larger shopping centers, Christmas festivals, recreation center holiday parties, and parades keep Santa very busy in Dallas. Some malls and large department stores offer **Breakfast with Santa** and other special decorations and activities, such as the model trains, puppet shows, and chorale singers at North Park, and the spectacular holiday tree in the center of the ice rink at the Galleria.

6. DAY TRIPS

Sometimes the best way for a family to get to know one another better is to leave home in the family car to a new or favorite destination for the day, where they can play and learn new things together away from the hectic routine at home. Most destinations outlined in this chapter are within a one- to two-hour driving time. If you have time to plan ahead, writing the town's chamber of commerce for tourist information or looking it up on the Internet and talking with friends who have been there for ideas about what to do and what to take adds to the enjoyment of the trip. When using this guide, remember to **call ahead**, because attractions open and close regularly.

The **Texas Historical Commission** is promoting "Heritage Tourism" in which Texas is divided into 10 scenic driving trails. North Texas is in the **Texas Lakes Region**, and the map in the brochure features 30 cities and attractions from the 31-county area. The Commission has developed suggested itineraries, such as the Dinosaur Trail, the North Texas Horse Country Tour, and the DFW Arts Tour. The brochure may be downloaded, or call (817) 573-1114 or look at their website: www.texaslakestrail.com.

When traveling with children, it is helpful to stop by the bookstore or public library for some favorite books and books on CD. Some older kids like to take along a battery-powered book light in case some of the travel time is at night, as well as their own personal CD player with headphones. Sing-along CDs, snacks, drawing kits, and travel-sized games also help to pass the time peacefully. Some moms pack a surprise bag with play items that the children have never seen before. Including an S&S (stop and stretch) time about midway during travel helps to work out the wiggles.

Traveling with teens is a little different. They will bring a backpack full of technology if you allow it. They see it as their lifeline. There won't be conversation because of the earphones connected to the laptop or the iPod. Their hands will likely be busy with text messaging. Perhaps you could strike a deal and limit the use of the devices. Some families agree that only Dad will have a cell phone. Maybe on a portable DVD player, you could play a movie that the whole family will enjoy.

Always take a first-aid kit that has bandages and something for insect bites. If you will be outdoors, insect repellent and sunscreen are good ideas. If the kids wear contacts, they will need sunglasses. Also, remember the camera, because there will very likely be some moments to capture.

DENISON

The MK&T Railroad gave birth to Denison in 1872 as land was purchased and a town was mapped out, and the new town was named after Katy vice president George Denison. Former President Dwight D. Eisenhower's father was a Katy Railroad employee, and Ike was born here on October 14, 1890. Another important event in Denison's history occurred when Denison Dam was constructed across the Red River, creating Lake Texoma, which covers 89,000 acres in Texas and Oklahoma. Brochures for historical driving and walking tours of Denison, an official Texas Main Street City, are available from the Chamber of Commerce, 313 Woodard, Denison 75020. Call (903) 465-1551. Website: www.denisontx.com. City of Denison, P.O. Box 347, Denison 75021. Call (903) 465-2720. Website: www.cityofdenison.com. Grayson County website: www.co.grayson.tx.us, "Loy Park" link to Frontier Village.

EISENHOWER'S BIRTHPLACE HISTORICAL SITE

609 S. Lamar Ave., Denison (903) 465-8908 Website: www.thc.state.tx.us. Select "Historic Properties" and then "Historic Sites."

Dwight David Eisenhower, a five-star general of the army and two-term U.S. president, was born in this house and lived here two years until his family moved to Abilene, Kansas. The furnishings represent the 1890s. Guided tours Tuesday to Saturday from 9 AM to 5 PM and Sunday 1 PM to 5 PM. Closed Christmas and New Year's Day. A pavilion with picnic tables and handicapped accessible restrooms as well as a headquarters that houses the visitor center, gift shop, and office are across the street. Guided tours of the 10-acre park may be scheduled by calling (903) 465-8908. Park admission for adults, $3 and students, $2.

GRAYSON COUNTY FRONTIER VILLAGE

Loy Lake Park, Denison. Website: www.co.grayson.tx.us. Select "Loy Park."

Located in a wooded area that has a lake, pier, and picnic areas, the Frontier Village includes homes and other structures dating back to the 1840s as well as a museum. An arts and crafts show is in April and November, and a Frontier Festival is held in September. Hours: Open daily,

1 PM to 4 PM from April through August. Remainder of the year, open weekends, weather permitting. Closed major holidays. Directions: Loy Lake Park is located southwest of Denison. From south of Denison on US 75, exit at Loy Lake Exit (67). Go left (west). Park is on the right.

RED RIVER RAILROAD AT KATY DEPOT

101 East Main, Denison (903) 463-KATY. Websites: www.redriverrailmuseum.org; www.katyrailroad.org.

Built in 1914, the MK&T Depot was an active part of life in Denison for many years. The restored depot now houses the Red River Railroad Museum. The park in front looks much like it did in 1914. For museum hours and special events, call or check online.

TEXOMA CHILDREN'S MUSEUM

401 Main St., Denison (903) 463-5678 Website: www.texomachildrensmuseum.org

This colorful, lively museum offers hands-on interactive, entertaining, and educational exhibits. Hours: Thursday to Saturday, 10 AM to 5 PM.

HAGERMAN WILDLIFE REFUGE

6465 Refuge Rd., Sherman 75092-5817 (903) 786-2826 Website: www.fws.gov/southwest/refuges. Select "Texas" and then "Hagerman."

The refuge includes 11,319 acres of habitat for 280 species of migratory birds. Visitors bird watch, picnic, take pictures, hike, and look over interpretive panels at the visitors center. The peak time to see migrating waterfowl is from October to March in early morning or at dusk. Shore birds are often most prevalent in mid-summer. Boat fishing is allowed from April to September within the refuge that surrounds the Big Mineral arm of Lake Texoma, but camping, skiing, and swimming are prohibited within refuge boundaries. Remember your binoculars and camera. A leaflet for a self-guided auto tour is in the headquarters.

Refuge hours: Sunrise to sunset, daily. **Office hours**: Call ahead.
Admission: Free.
Directions: From US 75 at Sherman, go west on FM 1417 and turn right into the refuge. Call first during periods of heavy rain.

EISENHOWER STATE PARK AND LAKE TEXOMA

50 Park Road 20, Denison 75020 (903) 465-1956 Website: www.tpwd.state.tx.us.

For information about this 457-acre park on Texas's third-largest reservoir, please look in **Chapter 4: Sports and Recreation** under **Lakes, State Parks, and Recreation Areas**.

EVENTS: **March**: Art and Wine Renaissance; **April**: Texoma Lakefest Regatta; **May**: Memorial Day Parade; **July 4**: Fireworks; **September**: U.S. National Aerobatic Competition; **October**: Main Street Fall Festival; **December**: Tour of Homes and Christmas Parade. Denison is approximately 75 miles north of Dallas on US 75.

Park day use hours: 8 AM to 5 PM, sometimes later in summer. Fees.

FORT WORTH

Will Rogers said that Fort Worth is where the West begins, and Dallas is where the East peters out. Fort Worth's Western heritage is very much alive in Sundance Square, the Stockyards, Western art museums, Log Cabin Village, Will Rogers Memorial Center, and annual celebrations. Fort Worth began as a frontier outpost in 1849 to help protect incoming settlers from renegade Indian raids. Cattle drives ran through Fort Worth on the Chisholm Trail after the Civil War. Cowboys stopped there to load up on provisions on the way to Abilene, Kansas, and stopped to spend their money and have a good time on the way home, which produced a very rowdy area of town called Hell's Half Acre.

Townspeople worked hard, including their own physical labor, to get the railroad tracks to Fort Worth and succeeded, and their town became known as Cowtown. Cattle were shipped to Fort Worth, and the business of meatpacking thrived at the stockyards. The arrival of the military bases, the discovery of oil, and the use of trucking to replace railroads all had their impact on the development of Fort Worth, as well as an increase in interest in the arts influenced by philanthropists Amon Carter and Kay Kimbell.

To receive information about Fort Worth, write, look online, or call these helpful folks: Convention and Visitors Bureau, 415 Throckmorton, Fort Worth 76102 (817) 698-7822 Website: www.fortworth.com.

If you are just driving in, stop at the Visitor Center at the **Stockyards**, 130 East Exchange Ave., and select brochures of places that interest you as well as a map of the Stockyards. You might stay there and enjoy what the Stockyards have to offer or go downtown to the **Historic Sundance Square** to begin your tour at **Fire Station No. 1**. Fort Worth Transportation Authority, **The T**, offers a premium pass that is good for three types of transportation. Visitors can buy an unlimited day pass to travel on the regular city bus and trolley service as well as the Trinity Railway Express that links Dallas and Fort Worth. Call (817) 215-8600 for information or check online: www.the-T.com; www.trinityrailwayexpress.org. The **Venues and Events Hotline** number is (817) 332-2000. Call or look online for details of special events.

SUNDANCE SQUARE

The old and new blend in the historic Sundance Square in Fort Worth's central business district. The Ssquare is defined by West 2nd St., Houston, West 4th, and Commerce. Brick streets and restored turn-of-the-century buildings add to the charm of this area named for outlaw Sundance Kid who, along with Butch Cassidy, often entertained himself at the disreputable Hell's Half Acre. Shops, Bass Performance Hall, restaurants, AMC movie theater, the Sid Richardson Collection of Western Art, Fire Station No. 1, Jubilee Theatre, Circle Theatre, and other points of historical interest make Sundance Square a great place to begin your tour of Fort Worth. As you walk around the square, be sure to notice the 1893 clock outside Haltom's Diamonds at Main and East 3rd, the *trompe l'oeil* ("fool the eye") artwork of Richard Haas in the Chisholm Trail mural on the southwest side of Main and Third, and the suit of armor high above the Knights of Pythias Hall at Main and Third. Historical markers around the square explain important buildings and events. Call (817) 255-5700. Website: www.sundancesquare.com.

FIRE STATION NO. 1

2nd and Commerce (817) 255-9300

Built in 1873, Fire Station No. 1 now houses a free walk-through exhibition called "150 Years of Fort Worth," which chronicles the history of the land and people who lived in Texas and the Fort Worth area. It is a satellite of the Fort Worth Museum of Science and History.

Hours: Daily, 9 AM to 7 PM.
Admission: Free.

SID RICHARDSON COLLECTION OF WESTERN ART

309 Main Street (817) 332-6554 Website: www.sidrmuseum.org

This Western art museum houses the private collection of oilman Sid Richardson (1891–1959). Many of Frederic Remington's paintings, such as *The Buffalo Runners, Ambush*, and *Bear Hunting*, are displayed. Paintings of buffalo hunters and Native Americans as well as bronzes by Charles M. Russell are also showcased. Saddles, vests, and chaps with beautiful leather and silver artistry are on exhibit. The museum has gallery brochures for children that contain visual scavenger hunts, with the difficulty depending on the child's age. Housed in a replica of an 1895 building, the museum also has a store.

Hours: Monday to Thursday, 9 AM to 5 PM; Friday and Saturday, 9 AM to 8 PM; Sunday, 12 PM to 5 PM.
Admission: Free; free gallery group tours with reservations.

BASS PERFORMANCE HALL

Fourth St. and Calhoun St. (817) 212-4325 Website: www.basshall.com

Designed to look like a classic European Opera House, Bass Hall has an 80-foot-diameter Great Dome atop the Founders Concert Theater, and two 48-foot angels made from Texas limestone watch over the Grand Facade. It is the permanent home of the Fort Worth Symphony, the Fort Worth Opera, and the Van Cliburn International Piano Competition and Cliburn Concerts. Bass Hall hosts musicals, concerts, and a variety of other performances. The Children's Education Program serves the first through twelfth grades.

MUSEUMS AND EXHIBITIONS

In Fort Worth's **Cultural District,** within walking distance of one another, are the Amon Carter Museum, the Fort Worth Modern Art Museum, the Kimbell Art Museum, the Fort Worth Museum of Science and History, and the National Cowgirl Hall of Fame. The Visitor Information Center for the Cultural District is located in a building by the Will Rogers Memorial Center, which has the tower. Admission is free at some of these museums, and groups must schedule their visits to the museums in advance. Handicapped access is available at all of the listed museums. Most museums are closed on Mondays, and summer hours may be extended.

AMON CARTER MUSEUM

3501 Camp Bowie at Montgomery (817) 738-1933 Website: www.cartermuseum.org

The collection by artists such as Sanford Robinson Gifford, Thomas Cole, Georgia O'Keefe, Winslow Homer, Frederic Remington, and Charles M. Russell within this museum was assembled by the late publisher and philanthropist Amon G. Carter Sr. and represents 150 years of American art. Tours are held Thursday to Sunday at 2 PM. A museum store features books of the art collections.

Gallery maps are available at the museum and online. The museum website provides links for art collections that both students and teachers would find useful.

Hours: Tuesday, Wednesday, Friday, and Saturday, 10 AM to 5 PM; Sunday, 12 PM to 5 PM. Closed Mondays and major holidays. Weekend hours subject to change.

Admission: Free.

FORT WORTH MUSEUM OF SCIENCE AND HISTORY

1501 Montgomery Street—one mile north of I-30 (817) 255-9300, (888) 255-9300 Website: www.fwmsh.org

This museum is undergoing a huge building project that will add an additional building with 90,000 square feet which will house art galleries, an auditorium, an education wing, library, and underground parking. While under construction, the museum is temporarily housed in the Cowgirl Museum and Hall of Fame. It presents such permanent exhibits as Lone Star Dinosaurs, Comin' through Cowtown, and Hands-On Science, plus interactive traveling exhibits. KIDSPACE is a children's area that features interactive exhibits, such as a fishing dock, kids' market, and build-a-house display. Amateur paleontologists can dig for dinosaur bones and fossils in DinoDig, an outdoor discovery area.

The **Cattle Raisers Museum** will also be located in the museum complex. This museum helps visitors acquaint themselves with the spirit of longhorns, cattle drives, and cowboys in the Old West.

The updated **Noble Planetarium** will feature 30-minute star shows throughout the day and other special celestial programs. The **Omni Theater,** which has been open during the construction of other parts of the complex, uses an 80-foot domed screen and 72 speakers to present 45-minute IMAX films, which change about every three to four months. Some shows may be too intense for those with motion sickness or very small children. Call about suitability.

Call or check online for museum construction progress, times, and admission.

KIMBELL ART MUSEUM

3333 Camp Bowie, west of University (817) 332-8451, Metro (817) 654-1034 Website: www.kimbellart.org

The Kimbell Art Foundation was established in the 1930s by Kay Kimbell, who left his art collection and fortune to the foundation in 1964 to build an art museum. Outstanding collections in the museum span 3,000 years. There are works of Egyptian, Asian, Mesoamerican, and African origin and others from Western Europe. The collection of Asian arts is particularly remarkable, featuring Japanese screens, hanging scrolls, Chinese paintings, and sculptures of various origins. Free tours, the Buffet Restaurant, and a bookstore are available, as well as a non-circulating library by appointment. Admission is free. Free parking is available off Arch Adams Street. The Kimbell offers a *Family Gallery Guide* to help you tour. The Kimbell Museum plans to have a groundbreaking in 2010 for a two-story, 90,000-square-foot building on the west lawn that will have a new art gallery, an auditorium, an education wing, and an underground garage. Hopefully it will open in two and one-half years.

Hours: Tuesday to Thursday, 10 AM to 5 PM; Friday, 12 PM to 8 PM; Saturday, 10 AM to 5 PM; Sunday, 12 PM to 5 PM.

Admission: Free, except for special exhibits. Half-price all day Tuesdays and Fridays from 5 PM to 8 PM.

MODERN ART MUSEUM OF FORT WORTH

3200 Darnell Street (817) 738-9215, Toll free (866) 824-5566 Website: www.themodern.org

Covering more than 53,000 square feet on two floors, the new Modern Art Museum is located in the Cultural District, opposite the Kimbell Art Museum. Designed by Japanese architect Tadao Ando, the museum houses a permanent collection that consists of approximately 150 works by 125 artists. Various movements, themes, and styles are represented, including Abstract Expressionism, Color Field painting, pop art, and Minimalism, as well as New Image Painting from the 1970s and beyond. Also represented are recent developments in abstraction and figurative sculpture and contemporary movements in photography, video, and digital imagery. Sculpture is both indoors and outdoors, and children will especially like the reflecting pools. The Modern offers lunch at a cafe and has a gift shop.

Admission: General (ages 13 to adult), $10; students with ID and seniors (60+), $4; children 12 and under, free. Admission is free on Wednesdays and the first Sunday of each month.

Hours: Tuesday to Saturday, 10 AM to 5 PM; Sunday, 11 AM to 5 PM.

NATIONAL COWGIRL MUSEUM AND HALL OF FAME

1720 Gendy Street, Fort Worth 76107 (817) 336-4475 Website: www.cowgirl.net

The National Cowgirl Museum and Hall of Fame is the only museum in the world dedicated to honoring and documenting the distinguished women of the American West. Located in Fort Worth's Cultural District, it houses artifacts and memorabilia of the Western woman, including the honorees in its Hall of Fame, and it also seeks out those women who continue to blaze trails with the true grit of the American cowgirl, not only as ranchers and rodeo riders but in today's world as writers, artists, teachers, and entertainers.

As visitors approach the museum, they can take a look at the Richard Hall **mural** on the east side of the museum. The mural features three-dimensional imagery of riding cowgirls. Inside, visitors usually begin with the eight-minute presentation that introduces the many faces of the cowgirl and then explore the interactive exhibits depicting a cowgirl's life on the ranch and her influence on our culture. Two exhibits of note include Dale Evans's silver and black leather saddle and Annie Oakley's .12-gauge, double-barrel shotgun. The gift shop invites browsers, and the Cowgirl Café lures them in for a snack. Special summer programs and birthday parties are offered for the young'uns.

While the Museum of Science and History is under construction in 2008–2009, its exhibits are sharing space with the Cowgirl Museum.

Hours: Tuesday-Saturday, 10 AM to 5 PM; Sunday, 12 PM to 5 PM. Closed Monday.

Admission: Adults, $8; seniors (60+) and children 3–12, $7; ages 2 and under, free.

NATIONAL COWBOYS OF COLOR MUSEUM AND HALL OF FAME

3400 Mt. Vernon St., Fort Worth 76103. Museum: (817) 534-8801 Office: (817) 922-9999 Website: www.cowboysofcolor.org

This cowboy museum honors blacks, Hispanics, and American Indians and their role in developing the American West through art, artifacts, historical records, and current events. Located in the **Renaissance Cultural Center**, the museum includes a gift shop that sells the Cowboys of Color Calendar to benefit the museum. Young visitors enjoy museum scavenger hunts and Saturday morning storytelling. The **Cowboys of Color Rodeo** is held in September at Will Rogers Coliseum.

Hours: Wednesday to Saturday, 11 AM to 6 PM.

Admission: Adults, $6; seniors, $4; students with ID, $3; children 5 and under, free.

PATE MUSEUM OF TRANSPORTATION

18501 Hwy. 377 South, Cresson (817) 396-4305 (Mailing address: P.O. Box 711, Fort Worth 76101)

Just outside Fort Worth on the highway that leads to Granbury is the Pate Museum, where the history of transportation is visualized through their collection of classic, antique, and special interest automobiles such as the Pierce Arrow and Packard, as well as a collection of aircraft ranging from helicopters to transports to jet fighters. An unusual item on exhibit is a Minesweeper Boat 5, because few museums display a seagoing vessel inland. The museum also has a mock-up of a nose cone of a space capsule. Picnic tables are available, but groups of more than six must make reservations. The museum is about a 20-minute drive south of Fort Worth, and from the museum it is only about a 15-minute drive on to Granbury.

Hours: 10 AM to 5 PM, Tuesday to Saturday; Sunday, 12 PM to 5 PM. Closed Monday.

Admission: Free. Donations appreciated.

HISTORICAL SITES

Fort Worth dwellers have invested much of their time and money to preserve Texas history. A website devoted to this goal is www.historic-fortworth.org.

LOG CABIN VILLAGE

2100 Log Cabin Village Lane and University (817) 926-5881 Website: www.logcabinvillage.org

Located across from the zoo in a pretty, wooded area, Log Cabin Village consists of authentic log homes, gristmill, and a one-room schoolhouse, most of which were built in the 1840s to 1890s. Staff and volunteers dressed in period costumes are on the grounds and demonstrate pioneer crafts, such as spinning, weaving, and candle dipping.

Hours: Tuesday to Friday, 9 AM to 4 PM; Saturday and Sunday, 1 PM to 5 PM.

Admission: Adults, $3.50; seniors and children ages 4–17, $3; ages 3 and under, free.

TEXAS CIVIL WAR MUSEUM

760 Jim Wright Freeway North (Loop 820), Fort Worth (817) 246-2323 Website: www.texascivilwarmuseum.com

A Union Army general's uniform and boots and a South Carolina secession flag are among the many artifacts at the Texas Civil War Museum. Although separated into a Union wing and a Confederate wing, the museum tries to keep Civil War pieces as balanced as possible. The 15,000-square-foot historical museum , which opened in 2006, has many interactive and hands-on exhibits to further education and an understanding of Civil War history. The tour includes a movie, *Our Homes, Our Rights: Texas in the Civil War*. Magnolia Mercantile gift shop adds to this step back in time.

Hours: Tuesday to Saturday, 9 AM to 5 PM.

Admission: Adults, $6; students 7 to 12, $3; children 6 and under, free with paid adult.

STOCKYARDS NATIONAL HISTORIC DISTRICT

North Main and 130 E. Exchange. Visitor Center, (817) 625-9715 Websites: www.fortworthstockyards.org; www.stockyardsstation.com; www.fortworth.com

Anyone who wishes to recapture the spirit that was the West, if only for a few hours, must visit the 125-acre Stockyards District, especially during a festival, such as the Red Steagall Gathering in September and the Frontier Forts Day in May.

With the arrival of the railroad in 1876, Fort Worth became the shipping destination for cattle, and the Union Stockyards Company was built. The Fort Worth Stockyards Company bought the company out in 1893 and held the first livestock show three years later. Meatpackers (Armour & Co. and Swift & Co.) moved in around 1902, and construction of the present Livestock Exchange Building began. Today the meatpackers are gone, and the 100 acres of stock pens have been reduced to 15 acres. Visitors enjoy the major livestock buildings, shops, museum, sculptures, horse-drawn carriage rides, and restaurants. **Restaurants** are located in Stockyards Station and on Exchange Ave. Joe T. Garcia's and Cattleman's Steakhouse are near the Stockyards. On the website www.stockyardstation.org, choose "Just for Kids" and you'll see suggested sample itineraries for traveling with children.

Stockyards Station is a Western-themed destination near the end of Exchange St. offering more than 25 unique shops, restaurants, and entertainment venues, indoor and outdoor event facilities, historic walking tours, horseback rides, and the **Texas Cowboy Hall of Fame**. It is the depot for the historic Grapevine Heritage Railroad steam-driven train. For horseback riding, wagon rides, riding lessons, boarding horses, trail rides, and birthday parties, call **Stockyards Livery and Stables**, (817) 624-3446.

Directions: From Dallas, take I-30 or I-20 to Fort Worth and go north on I-35 to the Historic Stockyard District exits.

The **Visitor Center**, located toward the end of East Exchange (east of Main Street) in the Stockyards Station building, helps visitors get their bearings in this 10-block historic district. Parking is also here. A map of the Stockyards and brochures covering most major attractions in the Fort Worth area are available there. The Visitor Center also offers walking tours of the Stockyards and Billy Bob's Texas for a fee. Visitors may do the walking tour with a handheld GPS Ranger that has a multimedia presentation of the sites. You will hear about the Stockyards, interesting characters like Butch Cassidy, the longhorn herd, and the background of the buildings.

Texas Trail of Fame: This trail consists of a virtual chronological history of U.S. Western heritage and of the Fort Worth Stockyards. Bronze stars, which resemble an old-fashioned marshal's badge, are placed in the walkways. Inductees include John Wayne, Will Rogers, Zane Grey, Charles Goodnight, and Roy Rogers.

Livestock Exchange Building: This historic building houses businesses and a **museum** that contains memorabilia from the 1986 Sesquicentennial Wagon Train Collection and artifacts related to the development of the Stockyards. It's toward the back of the main hall on the left. Call (817) 625-5087. Satellite video cattle auctions are held every other Friday on the first floor.

Hours: Monday to Saturday, 10 AM to 5 PM.

Admission: Free.

Fort Worth Herd's Cattle Drive: This brief trail drive takes place daily, weather permitting. Longhorn cattle usually depart from the Livestock Exchange Building twice daily at 11:30 AM and 4 PM, head down Exchange Avenue and back to their holding pens behind the Exchange Building. If the trail boss doesn't think the critters are feeling sociable enough for a walk, he can cancel. Two of the best places to see the drive are in front of the Visitors Center and the lawn in front of the Exchange Building. If you miss their grand tour, you can still see them behind the Exchange Building to the east. Call (817) 336-HERD (4373). Website: www.fortworthherd.com.

Cowtown Coliseum: The Coliseum was the site of the world's first indoor rodeo in 1918. It is open Monday to Saturday from 8 AM to 4:30 PM, and Sunday afternoons just to look through. The **Fort Worth Championship Rodeo** is held here every Friday and Saturday night at 8 PM and lasts about two hours. For information about the rodeo or special events, call (817) 654-1148 or toll free 1-888-COWTOWN or look online at www.cowtowncoliseum.com. Tickets may be bought online.

Texas Cowboy Hall of Fame: The Hall of Fame honors the cowboys and cowgirls who achieved greatness in the sports of rodeo and cutting, through displays that contain photographs, memorabilia, and video. Inductees include Neal Gay, Larry Mahan, and George Strait. The **Sterquell Wagon Collection** includes more than 60 horse-drawn vehicles, and the **John Justin Trail of Fame** pays tribute to the owner of the Justin Boot Company and civic leader in Fort Worth with a variety of boots. New inductees to the Hall of Fame are selected by committee each year. The address of what once were mule and horse barns is 128 E. Exchange Ave. Call (817) 626-7131.

Hours: Monday to Thursday, 10 AM to 6 PM; Friday and Saturday, 10 AM to 7 PM; Sunday, 12 PM to 6 PM. Website: www.texascowboyhalloffame.com.

Admission: Adults, $5; seniors, $4; children ages 5–12, $3; ages 4 and under, free.

Stockyards Hotel. This Western hotel was built in 1907 and restored in 1984, and it offers 52 rooms. You might peek in or stay for lunch at the restaurant called **Booger Red's Saloon and Restaurant** next door to see the saddle bar stools, the five ceiling fans that are turned by one belt, and the mounted buffalo head and horns of the longhorn. The story of Booger Red is framed on the wall. A children's menu is offered, but service is not fast. Stockyards Hotel location: 109 E. Exchange. (817) 625-6427, (800) 423-8471. Website: www.stockyardshotel.com.

Billy Bob's Texas: Billy Bob's claims to be the world's largest honky-tonk. Under a 100,000-square-foot roof are top-name entertainment, dance floor, pro bull-riding every Friday and Saturday at 9 PM and 10 PM ($2.50), gift shop, arcade, and restaurants. Tours are available during the day. Call (817) 624-7117 for information or tickets. The address is 2520 Rodeo Plaza. Website: www.billybobstexas.com.

Cowtown Cattlepen Maze, Inc.: The maze covers 5,400 square feet of wooden pathways that look like the cattle pens of the Old West. Visitors can compete against themselves or each other. A second-story observation deck allows the player to see the maze before beginning, or watch others as they wind through it. Call (817) 624-6666. Hours may change seasonally. Website: www.cowtowncattlepenmaze.com.

PARKS, GARDENS, AND WILDLIFE

BOTANIC GARDEN AND JAPANESE GARDEN

3220 Botanic Garden Blvd., Fort Worth (817) 871-7686
Website: www.fwbg.com

Located in Trinity Park, the Botanic Garden consists of several different gardens on 114 acres. **Rose Gardens** contain more than 3,400 roses, which peak in late April and October. Lush tropical plants fill the 10,000-square-foot **Conservatory**. Exotic orchids are housed in the **Exhibition Greenhouse**; flowering plants such as colorful azaleas are the highlights of the **Perennial Garden**; and seasonal flowering plants bloom in the **Trial Garden**. Leaves release their scents in the **Fragrance Garden**.

The beauty and tranquility of the **Japanese Gardens** will be a delight to all family members. This 7.5-acre hilly garden features beautiful pools and waterfalls, tea garden, pagoda, and other structures emphasizing simplicity and harmony. Children enjoy feeding the large *koi* (imperial carp). A gift shop is available. No tripods for cameras are allowed.

Lunch is a treat at the **Gardens Restaurant**, 3220 Rock Springs Rd. Call (817) 731-2547. Closed Monday. The **Children's Vegetable Garden** has an orchard, vegetables, herbs, and berries on a half-acre.

Hours: Grounds open daily, 8 AM to dusk. **Japanese Gardens**: April to October—daily, 9 AM to 7 PM; (Daylight Savings Time); November to March—Tuesday to Sunday, 10 AM to 5 PM. Closed Monday. **Conservatory**: April to October—Monday to Saturday, 10 AM to 6 PM; Sunday, 1 PM to 6 PM (Daylight Savings Time); November to March—Monday to Saturday, 10 AM to 4 PM; Sunday, 1 PM to 4 PM. **Garden Center**: April to October—Monday to Friday, 8 AM to 10 PM; Saturday, 8 AM to 7 PM; Sunday 1 PM to 7 PM (Daylight Savings Time); November to March— 8 AM to 10 PM; Saturday, 8 AM to 5 PM; Sunday 1 PM to 5 PM. **Note**: Garden Center may close at 5 PM if no events are scheduled.

Admission: Admission to the grounds is free. **Japanese Gardens:** Weekdays, adults, $3; weekends, adults, $3.50; children ages 4–12, $2; children under 4, free. **Conservatory:** adults, $1; children ages 4–12, 50 cents.

HERITAGE PARK

East Belknap at Houston, behind the Tarrant County Courthouse

Heritage Park, a small park on a bluff, has refreshing waterfalls and water walls. It is safest to visit this park in the daytime. At the bottom of the bluff is an eight-mile asphalt trail for bicycling, walking, jogging, or skating alongside the Trinity River. The park is in disrepair, and currently city fathers and historical groups are discussing what should be done.

FORT WORTH NATURE CENTER AND REFUGE

Rt. 10, Box 53 or 9601 Fossil Ridge Rd., Fort Worth (817) 237-1111 Website: www.fwnaturecenter.org

Classes, workshops, story hours, festivals, and camps are held in this 3,600-acre protected habitat for buffalo, deer, many varieties of birds, and more wildlife. It is the largest city-owned nature center in the United States. Visitors may stop by the visitor center for information about hiking on more than 20 miles of trails, and guided trailwalks are offered by appointment. A boardwalk over a marshy area allows a closer look at waterfowl. Ask about naturalist-guided hikes on Saturdays and a guided canoe tour along the West Fork of the Trinity. Picnic tables are available for families but not groups. A gift shop has nature-related items.

Hours: Open daily, except Thanksgiving and Christmas. October to April: Monday to Sunday, 8 AM to 5 PM. May to September: Monday to Friday, 8 AM to 7 PM; Saturday and Sunday, 7 AM to 7 PM.

Admission: Adults, $4; children ages 3–17, $3; seniors (65+), $3; under 3, free.

Directions: Take TX Hwy. 199 (Jacksboro Hwy.) two miles past the Lake Worth Bridge.

FORT WORTH WATER GARDEN

1502 Commerce and 15th Street (817) 871-7275

This 4.3-acre water garden was designed by Phillip Johnson. Many pretty trees shade the area, which is across the street from Tarrant County Junior College and near the Convention Center. This is certainly worth a visit, and it is free. Water displays are around 7 AM to 10 PM, daily.

FORT WORTH ZOO

1989 Colonial Parkway at University, south of I-30 (817) 759-7555 Website: www.fortworthzoo.org

The 68-acre Fort Worth Zoo, which opened in 1909, features more than 3,500 animals, including jaguars, lions, African black-footed penguins, and Asian elephants. Two popular habitats are the World of Primates, a 2.5-acre indoor exhibit that simulates a tropical rain forest, and Asian Falls, which features waterfalls, hills, trees, and an elevated boardwalk. Below the boardwalk are Indochinese tigers, sun bears, and a white Bengal tiger. The zoo's latest additions are **Texas Wild!** an eight-acre recreation of the Lone Star State, featuring nearly 300 native Texas animals and interactive displays; Parrot Paradise; and the Great Barrier Reef. Young visitors may ride the *Yellow Rose Express*, which travels between the Safari Depot and Texas Wild!

Visitors may wish to browse in the Safari Shop and General Store, and dine at the zoo's Crocodile Café food court. Other concessions are available throughout the zoo. Strollers are available for rent. Ask about overnight camping for a group of 15 or more. The zoo is across the street from **Log Cabin Village** and not far from the **Botanic Gardens**.

Hours: Subject to change. Best to call or look online. Summer: 10 AM to 5 PM. Winter: 10 AM to 4 PM.

Admission: Adults, $12; children ages 3–12, $8; seniors, $7. Wednesday is half-price day. Parking, $5, cash only. Note: Beautiful spring break days are very crowded; arrive early or parking lot may be full.

Directions: From I-30, exit at University. Go south one mile and turn left on Colonial. Continue about one-half mile.

Forest Park Train is a miniature steam train that carries visitors into Trinity Park on a ride that lasts about 45 minutes. It is by the zoo, but not part of it. **Summer hours**: 11 AM to 5 PM, Tuesday to Sunday; closed Monday. Call (817) 336-3328. **Winter hours**: Saturday and Sunday, 12 PM to 4 PM. **Fare**: Adults (age 13 and up), $3; children ages 1–12), $2.50; seniors (65+), $2.50. All train rides are subject to weather conditions. Call ahead.

MORE ENTERTAINMENT

BURGER'S LAKE

1200 Meandering Rd., Fort Worth (817) 737-3414 Website: www.burgerslake.com

Near the former Carswell Air Force Base, this spring-fed, filtered, one-acre lake provides great summer entertainment for families on the two sandy beaches. Kids can slide into the lake on a water slide, dive from the diving board, or swing in from a trapeze. There is plenty of shallow water for little ones. In this 30-acre park, plenty of room is available for picnicking, and there are picnic tables, charcoal grills, a concession, and a volleyball court. Recommended items to bring are lawn chairs and floats. A discount is available for groups, and no alcohol or pets are allowed.

Hours: Daily, Mother's Day to Labor Day, 9 AM to 7:30 PM.

Admission: Adults, $12; children 6 and under, free.

CASA MANANA

3101 W. Lancaster at University, directly across from Farrington Field (817) 332-2272 Website: www.casamanana.org

Casa Manana is a theater-in-the-round with 1,800 seats, which is covered by a geodesic dome. Families enjoy musicals, concerts, and plays. Children's theater and summer camp is very active as well as a theater school for all ages.

More Theaters

Rose Marine Theater, 1440 Main St., Fort Worth (817) 624-8333

Jubilee Theatre, 506 Main St., Fort Worth (817) 338-4204

Circle Theatre, 230 W. Fourth St., Fort Worth (817) 877-3040

Stage West, 821 W. Vickery, Fort Worth (817) 784-9378

Hip Pocket Theater, 1950 Silver Creek Rd., Fort Worth (817) 246-9775

GRAPEVINE HERITAGE RAILROAD

140 E. Exchange, Stockyards Station, Fort Worth (817) 625-RAIL
Cotton Belt Depot, 705 South Main, Grapevine. **Websites:**
www.grapevinesteamrailroad.com; www.stockyardsstation.com

Once aboard the Grapevine Heritage Railroad train, passengers can easily imagine what passenger train travel was like not that many years ago when great iron horses like the 1896 Steam Engine #2248 (called "Puffy"), which sometimes pulls four beautifully restored passenger cars, crossed the country carrying passengers who had not even dreamed of air travel. The seats in each railcar have backs that move across so you can face others in your party or always be facing forward. Rich mahogany wood, shining brass, and 10 ceiling fans in each car add to the beauty. The cars are heated in winter, and the fans and open windows cool it in summer.

When the whistle blows, passengers at Stockyards Station begin a nine-mile, one-hour round trip called the **Trinity River Run,** which crosses the Trinity and follows the old Chisholm Trail to Eighth Street and then turns back to the Stockyards. At the Stockyards the train pulls in to a 1925 turnstile to get in position for its next journey. The scenery is not terrific along much of the trip, but the atmosphere is not to be missed. Dusk is a beautiful time to ride because the lights come on downtown and are reflected in the Trinity River.

The train also runs round-trip from **Grapevine** to **Stockyards Station** and back, with time allotted for fun in the Stockyards. The **round trip** is 42 miles and takes about one and one-half hours. Special event trains run on special days and holidays.

A small restroom is located in each car, but no food, drink, or gum is allowed. Picking up your tickets early is a good idea. The depots open one hour before departure. Call or look online for days and times.

MORE SITES OF INTEREST

U.S. Bureau of Engraving and Printing (See **Tours** in **Chapter 2: Tidbits**)

Vintage Flying Museum, Hanger 33 South, Meacham Airport, 505 NW 38th St.

American Airlines C. R. Smith Museum, 4601 State Hwy. 360 at FAA Blvd.

Fort Worth Cats Baseball, LaGrave Field, 301 NE Sixth St. (817) 226-2287

Fort Worth Convention Center, 1201 Houston St. (817) 392-6338

Will Rogers Memorial Center, 3401 W. Lancaster (817) 392-7469

Fort Worth Symphony, (817) 665-6000. Website: www.fwsymphony.org

Fort Worth Opera, (817) 731-0726. Website: www.fwopera.org

SPECIAL EVENTS

Southwestern Exposition and Livestock Show & Rodeo—January and February, 17 days

The Last Great Gunfight—February 8

Cowtown Marathon—last Saturday in February

Main St. Arts Festival—Early April Frontier Forts Day—April/May

Mayfest—first weekend in May

Colonial Golf Tournament—mid-May

Juneteenth Celebration—mid-June

Symphony Concerts in the Garden—June/July

Fort Worth Fourth!—July 4

Cowboys of Color Rodeo—August/September

Gran Fiesta de Fort Worth—July

Jazz by the Boulevard—September

Fort Worth Air Show—September

Red Steagall Cowboy Gathering and Western Swing Festival—late October

Parade of Lights—late November, after Thanksgiving

Christmas in the Stockyards—December

GLEN ROSE

Glen Rose Convention and Visitors Bureau, P.O. Box 2037, Glen Rose 76043 (254) 897-3081 or (888) 346-6282 Website: www.glenrose-texas.net. The drive takes about two hours.

To study the relevant history of Glen Rose, you would literally have to return to the age of the dinosaurs. They have fascinated scientists and 3-year-olds alike with the large three-toed footprints they left behind in the bed of the lazy Paluxy River, which flows through the town. In the 1870s settlers moved into the area, known for its wild roses, and the county seat was established here. Glen Rose citizens were also known for their use of petrified wood as a building material, and some examples of its use are still around. Another claim to fame for a while in the 1920s and 1930s was the use of sulfur water for medicinal purposes in the bathhouses.

Today the town is still built around the rock courthouse, and no one seems in much of a hurry, which is one of its many great appeals. From Highway 67, exiting onto Highway 205 will take you past **Oakdale Park** (254-897-2321), which is the site of many wonderful festivals and a large public swimming pool, past a great swimming area on the Paluxy called the Big Rocks, which you will easily recognize, and into the heart of the square. While in town, stop by the **Somervell County Museum**, located at Elm and Vernon, and soak up local history through the varied collections of fossils and pioneer memorabilia (254-898-0640). When we were there, for a small fee visitors could purchase an authentic dinosaur hunting license (just in case).

Holiday Inn Express Hotel and Suites (254-898-9900), Comfort Inn and Suites (254-898-8900), and Best Western Dinosaur Valley Inn and Suites by Expo Center (800-280-2055) offer rooms and a swimming pool, and Oakdale Park (254-897-2321) rents cabins. Campgrounds are at Oakdale Park (website: www.oakdalepark.com), along the Brazos, and in Dinosaur Valley State Park if your family is having too much fun to go home at the end of the day. If visitors would like a Western upscale resort experience, try Rough Creek Lodge (800-864-4705; website: www.roughcreek.com). Hideaway Ranch and Retreat rents cabins on a 150-acre property that also has a swimming pool and horseback riding. It is located 16 miles west of Glen Rose, (254-823-6606; website: thehideawaycabins.com).

Equipment Rentals: Canoes and tubes—Oakdale Park, Rhodes Rentals (254-897-4214), and Low Water Bridge (254-897-3666).

Expo Center: Just as you approach the city limits on Hwy. 67 is the Expo Center, which includes facilities for conventions and reunions as well as a rodeo arena and equestrian center.

COMANCHE PEAK NUCLEAR PLANT

Visitor Information Center, 6322 FM 56, Glen Rose 76043 (254) 897-2976 (Mailing address: P.O. Box 1002, Glen Rose 76043)

As you pass Cleburne and get closer to Glen Rose, the terrain becomes hilly, and you can see for miles. Look to the right for the two white domes of Comanche Peak's nuclear reactors. Please read under **Science** in **Chapter 2: Tidbits** for more details about the plant. Squaw Creek Lake, which is around four miles north of Glen Rose off Hwy. 144, is a 3,300-acre lake that services the power plant; it is not open to the public at this time.

Hours: Monday to Saturday, 9 AM to 4 PM.
Admission: Free.
Directions: To reach the plant from Hwy. 67, exit on FM 201 and go north. The Visitor Center is about one-half mile inside the front gate.

DINOSAUR VALLEY STATE PARK

P.O. Box 396, Park Rd. 59, Glen Rose 76043 (254) 897-4588
Reservations only: (512) 389-8900
Website: www.tpwd.state.tx.us/park/dinosaur

The Paluxy River, a tributary of the Brazos River, runs through this heavily wooded state park, which is best known for the tracks left in the riverbed by dinosaurs about 113 million years ago. The Visitor Center is located just inside the park, and friendly rangers will accept the admission fee and answer questions. They often will be down at the river explaining the history of the region to interested groups. A little farther down the road on the right are the two life-size replicas of the Brontosaurus and the Tyrannosaurus rex that were donated to the park after the New York World's Fair Dinosaur Exhibit in 1964–1965. Very young children who are not too sure the dinosaurs are really extinct might look at this on the way out instead of in. On the left is a shaded picnic area with some playground equipment. The best tracks are on the road to the left, and park signs guide you. Steps lead down to the river, and they are somewhat steep.

Wearing beach shoes (not flip-flops) or old tennis shoes with some tread on the bottom is best. You can walk across the river bottom on large, exposed rocks, but they can be slippery. The river is usually shallow enough to see the tracks, but in times of heavy rainfall, calling ahead would be a good idea. Two necessary tools for youngsters from 2 to 72 are a small plastic bucket with a handle and a small aquarium fish net. The guppies and tadpoles flourish in the nooks and crannies among the rocks, and trying to catch them is great fun. If not already in a swimsuit, remember a change of clothes because a slip into the water is very likely.

Sunscreen is a must. Shaded campgrounds are available here, as well as restrooms with showers. A small amphitheater provides some interesting summer entertainment, and there are both nature and hiking trails.

Hours: Open daily from 8 AM to 10 PM for day use and overnight also for campers.

Admission: State park admission is adults, $5; 12 and under, free. Camping is additional.

Directions: From US Hwy. 67, south of Glen Rose, take FM 205 to Park Road 59.

DINOSAUR WORLD

1058 Park Rd., Glen Rose (just outside Dinosaur Valley State Park) (254) 898-1526 Website: www.dinoworld.net

Dinosaur World awes visitors with a walking tour featuring more than 100 life-size dinosaur replicas. If not accosted by the dinosaurs, visitors also enjoy a museum, fossil dig, gift shop, and picnic area.

Hours: Daily, from 9 AM.

Admission: Adults, $12.75; seniors, $10.75; children ages 3–12, $9.75. Free parking.

FOSSIL RIM

2299 County Rd. 2008, Glen Rose 76043 (254) 897-2960 Website: www.fossilrim.org

Endangered species are always the focus at this 1,800-acre private wildlife reserve. Excited kids can already spot ostriches as parents pay to enter the park. They will get an audio tour CD that will narrate the safari, and they will probably want to buy cups of food to feed the exotic animals while driving through. More food may be purchased at the Nature Store, which is about midway through the 10-mile drive. Parents might want to keep the windows rolled up until they are past the ostriches because the large birds will stick their heads and long necks into the car as they check for food. The terrain is hilly, and there are lots of dense cedar and small shrubbery, so a pair of binoculars and sharp eyes will help in spotting more recalcitrant species. Taking snapshots or videos is also fun.

An interesting nature store, restaurant, restrooms, short hiking trail, picnic tables, and a petting zoo area that all will enjoy are located at the midpoint. The overlook view of the countryside is spectacular here, and spring and fall are particularly beautiful times to visit. For those with a real spirit of adventure, Fossil Rim offers the Foothills Safari Camp, but children 18 and under must attend preplanned family safaris. All proceeds go toward wildlife conservation efforts. A guided tour, behind-the-scenes tour, and conservation tour are offered. Lodging is available at Safari Camp or the Lodge at Fossil Rim.

Hours: Admitting visitors to the park: October 1 to October 31, 8:30 AM to 4:30 PM (time the last car is admitted). November 1 to March 7, 8:30 AM to 3:30 PM. March 8 to September 30, 8:30 AM to 5:30 PM.

Admission: Prices vary according to the season. The range is $10 to $16. Off-season has half-price Wednesdays. Wildlife feed is available for purchase at the entrance and the park store. Group rates are available with reservations.

Directions: On Hwy. 67 south of Glen Rose, drive about three miles. Signs will direct visitors to the preserve.

TEXAS AMPHITHEATER

P.O. Box 8, Glen Rose 76043 (254) 897-4509
Website: www.glenroseexpo.org
The Promise. (800) 687-2661.
Website: www.thepromiseglenrose.com

On Friday and Saturday evenings from September 5 to November 1, the life story of Jesus unfolds in an outdoor contemporary musical drama, *The Promise,* which is produced on a 65×100-foot tri-level stage that has a six-story archway towering above it. Parts of *The Promise* may be a little intense for very young children. Texas Amphitheater also hosts concerts and special events. Just in case some Texas-size mosquitoes decide to attend the festivities, some insect repellent and no perfume or lotions are good ideas. Concessions are available. Ask about backstage tours, pre-shows, and barbecue dinners.

Hours: Friday and Saturday, gates open at 7 PM.

Admission: Adults, $20 to $33; children ages 5–18 and seniors get a $3 discount. Call or look online for reservations.

Directions: Driving in on Hwy. 67, pass Hwy. 144. Turn right onto Bo Gibbs Drive and go .25 mile. At the Texas Amphitheater/*Promise* sign, turn right onto Texas Drive, and go 1.5 miles to the amphitheater.

ADDITIONAL ATTRACTIONS

Somervell County Expo Center, (254) 897-4509 Website:www.glenroseexpo.org

Creation Evidence Museum, (254) 897-3200 Website: www.creationevidence.org

Historic downtown square: Somervell County Museum, (254) 898-0640

LS Ranches Texas Longhorn Museum, 114 E. Barnard (254) 897-7070

SPECIAL EVENTS

March: PRCA Rodeo; **April:** Oakdale Bluegrass Jamboree, Sunrise Services; **May:** Oakdale Splash Weekend, Oakdale Bluegrass Picnic and Crafts Fair, Art on the Square; **July:** Fourth of July Celebration, Oakdale Bluegrass Pickin' Under the Stars/Fiddlers' Carousel; **September:** Oakdale Campers Jamboree, Labor Day Concert; **October:** Oakdale Bluegrass Reunion, Halloween on the Square; **December:** Christmas on the Square.

TEXAS STATE RAILROAD/PALESTINE AND RUSK

TEXAS STATE RAILROAD STATE HISTORICAL PARK

P.O. Box 39, Rusk 75785 (800) 442-8951 in Texas or (903) 683-2561 Website: www.texasstaterr.com

Steam rises and the whistle blows as the 1896 iron horse pulls out from the Palestine Depot carrying its passengers on a 50-mile round-trip excursion through the East Texas Piney Woods. Aboard the train, passengers visit unhurriedly, tour the different cars, and visit the concession for soft drinks and ice cream. If small children are aboard, bringing some small games and toys would be a good idea. Older children might enjoy a game or deck of cards. Bring a camera to take pictures at the depot as children talk to the engineer and fireman and tour the engine cab. At the midpoint the two trains pass each other as one heads toward Rusk and the other to Palestine.

Flowers and blooming dogwoods are beautiful in the spring, and fall is breathtaking as the leaves change colors. Picnicking at the Rusk Depot is lots of fun, and families may bring their own food or pre-order a brown bag lunch at least 72 hours in advance. You might bring a little extra to feed the ducks on the lake at the Rusk Depot. Passengers then board for the return trip. The Palestine park offers water-only campsites, picnic tables, pavilions, and a playground. At Rusk there are full hookups for campers.

Special event rides, such as Polar Express and Snoopy Train, are very entertaining.

Hours: Days and hours change seasonally. The current calendar is online. The train leaves the Palestine Depot at 11 AM and returns at 3:30 PM, and the gates for boarding trains are opened 45 minutes before train departure. Seating is on a first-come-first-served basis, so families need to arrive at least by 10 AM. Reservations are recommended.

Admission: Regular round-trip prices depend on which engine is pulling the train (steam or diesel) and the railcar selected. Range: Adults, $36.40 to $43:50; children, $19 to $25. Prices are higher for the air-conditioned cars.

Directions: Take I-45 south to Corsicana. Go southeast on US Hwy. 287 to Palestine, and then take US Hwy. 84 east about four miles. Palestine is about 120 miles from Dallas, which is approximately a two- to three-hour drive.

MUSEUM FOR EAST TEXAS CULTURE

400 Micheaux Ave., Palestine 75801 (903) 723-1914 Website: www.museumpalestine.org

Located in a former high school built in 1915, this historical museum houses a replica of a classroom in a country school as well as railroad memorabilia. Their latest renovation is an 1856 log dogtrot cabin, which is in the gym area. The museum has a large camera collection. The museum is in John H. Reagan Park, which has picnic tables and a playground.

Hours: Monday to Saturday, 10 AM to 5 PM; Sunday, 1 PM to 4 PM.

Admission: Adults, $2; children ages 3–11, 50 cents; under 3, free.

Directions: The museum is located about three miles from the Texas State Railroad. Take Hwy. 84 through the downtown business district and past the railroad underpass. Go one block.

TEXAS DOGWOOD TRAILS AND DAVEY DOGWOOD PARK

Located just north of Palestine on North Link Street off US Hwy. 155. Palestine Convention and Visitors Bureau, 825 Spring St., Palestine 75801 (903) 723-3014; (800) 659-3484 Website: www.visitpalestine.com

Each year for three weekends in March and April, the dogwood blossoms and Palestine itself open for visitors to enjoy. In the 400-acre **Davey Dogwood Park**, visitors may drive or walk through the beautiful white-blossomed trees. Additional festivities include a parade, a rodeo, arts and crafts, trade days, tours of Victorian homes, trolley rides, fishing tournaments, and more. Special events include the Oktoberfest and a Christmas Parade and Pilgrimage in early December. The Convention and Visitors Bureau offers information about walking and driving tours of Palestine. A stop by **Eilenberger Bakery** at 512 N. John is a treat (903-729-0881). Also, the **Columbia Scientific Balloon Facility** is located five miles west on Highway 287N to FM 3224. Look under **Science** in **Chapter 2: Tidbits** for more information (903-729-0271).

OTHER PLACES OF INTEREST

Gus Engeling Wildlife Refuge, 16149 N. US Hwy. 287, Tennessee Colony 75861 (903) 928-2251 Website: www.tpwd.state.tx.us/wma. This refuge, 10,958 acres located 20 miles west of Palestine, is home to a great variety of animals, including deer, wild hogs, birds, foxes, squirrels, snakes, alligators, and rabbits. A self-guided auto tour takes visitors through 10 stops with nature-related information. No permits are necessary for the driving tour and trails. Bring water. Restrooms are wheelchair accessible. Sunscreen and insecticide are recommended.

Lake Palestine, a 22,500-acre lake located 20 miles north of Palestine and 15 miles southwest of Tyler, offers boating, swimming, and other water sports. Camping areas, cabins, and motels are around the lake. Overseen by the Upper Neches River Authority, (903) 876-2237. Websites: www.tpwd.state.tx.us/fishboat and www.lake-palestine .com.

Grapeland Drive-Thru Safari. 13440 US Hwy. 287 North at Hwy. 19, Grapeland (936) 687-5292. Website: www.grapelanddrivethrusafari.com. Located 20 miles south of Palestine. Also near Tyler.

TYLER

Tyler Convention and Visitors Bureau, 315 N. Broadway, Tyler 75702 (800) 235-5712 Websites: www.visittyler.com; www.easttexasguide.com.

Tyler is called the Rose Capital of America; its Municipal Rose Garden and the annual Texas Rose Festival in mid-October bring thousands of visitors there each year. The sandy soil is particularly adapted to growing azaleas, pine trees, peaches, and blueberries also. See **Farmers Markets and Pick Your Own Food** in **Chapter 2: Tidbits** for those in the Tyler area.

Tyler was named in the mid-1800s for U.S. president John Tyler, who penned his name on the joint resolution that enabled Texas to be admitted as a state. Once the center of the booming oil business in East Texas, Tyler now focuses more on gardening and other types of agriculture and forestry as major industries, since the oil business has declined. One-third of the commercially grown rose bushes in the world originate in Smith County.

Besides the beautiful gardens, this Piney Woods city offers a variety of activities for visitors at lakes, museums, and a zoo. Tyler is about a two-hour drive east on I-20.

BROOKSHIRE'S WORLD OF WILDLIFE MUSEUM AND COUNTRY STORE

1600 W.S.W. Loop 323, Tyler 75710 (903) 534-2169 (Mailing address: P.O. Box 1411, Tyler 75710-1411) Website: www.brookshiresmuseum.com

In honor of Brookshire Grocery Company's founders, Wood and Louise Brookshire, the museum highlights more than 450 mammals, fowl, reptiles, and aquatic species from North America and Africa. The African exhibit also includes artifacts such as handmade jewelry and woodcarvings. A life-size replica of a 1920s grocery store, the Country Store is stocked with old-time goods, antique toys, and antique merchandising equipment. A 1926 Model T Ford and a 1952 big red fire truck are outside on the grounds, as well as a picnic area, covered pavilion, and playground. Groups of 15 or more should call two weeks in advance for reservations for guided tours.

Hours: October 1 to February 28, Tuesday to Saturday, 10 AM to 4 PM. March 1 to September 30, Tuesday to Saturday, 9 AM to 5 PM. The picnic area and playground are open through lunchtime; closed Sunday, Monday, and major holidays.

Admission: Free.

Directions: Take I-20 east and turn south on Hwy. 69. Go southwest on Loop 323 to the Old Jacksonville Highway and turn right. It is located just past the Distribution Center on the left.

CALDWELL ZOO

2203 Martin Luther King Blvd., Tyler 75712 (903) 593-0121 (Mailing address: P.O. Box 4785, Tyler 75712-4785) Website: www.caldwellzoo.org

The openness of the natural habitats with different species of animals grazing on the lush grasses together are most impressive to visitors at the Caldwell Zoo. More than 2,000 animals from around the world as well as native Texas critters and fowl are offered for viewing on 85 beautiful acres. A favorite spot is on the veranda of the snack shop, where visitors can still see much of the zoo. A picnic area is available. Be sure to visit the walk-through aviary and stop by the petting corral area.

Hours: March to Labor Day, 9 AM to 5 PM; after Labor Day to February, 9 AM to 4 PM; open daily except some major holidays.

Admission: Ages 13 and older, $8.50; seniors (55+), $7.25; children ages 3–12, $5; ages 2 and under, free. All facilities are wheelchair accessible. No radios or pets allowed.

Directions: Take I-20 East to Tyler and go southeast on US Hwy. 69. Turn left (east) on MLK Blvd., and the zoo is on the left.

SMITH COUNTY HISTORICAL SOCIETY MUSEUM AND ARCHIVES

125 S. College at Elm, Tyler (903) 592-5993

Housed in the former Carnegie Public Library building, the History Center features exhibits of artifacts of Tyler and Smith County, as well as Civil War artifacts uncovered from the large prisoner-of-war camp that was located in Tyler.

Hours: Tuesday to Sunday, 1 PM to 5 PM.

Admission: Free.

THE DISCOVERY SCIENCE PLACE

308 N. Broadway, Tyler 75702 (903) 533-8011 Website: www.discoveryscienceplace.org

Named as one of the Top 25 Science Centers in the nation by *Parents* magazine, the Discovery Science Place is a hands-on science museum for children. In the tunnels of Discovery Mountain, kids learn about bats, earthquakes, volcanoes, and more. On the ship *Awakening*, they discover the qualities of wind, solar power, magnetism, and navigation. Other fun, hands-on exhibits will be worth the trip.

Hours: Monday to Saturday, 9 AM to 5 PM; Sunday, 1 PM to 5 PM. Closed major holidays. Closes at 2 PM the day before a major holiday.

Admission: $6 per person; ages 2 and under, free. Educational group rates available.

MUNICIPAL ROSE GARDEN

420 Rose Park Drive, Tyler (903) 531-1212 Website: www.texasrosefestival.com

The beauty of 30,000 plants exhibiting more than 500 varieties of roses on 14 acres is indescribable from May to November. In the one-acre **Heritage Rose and Sensory Garden** located in the southwest corner, varieties that date back to 1867 are showcased. Another garden features approximately 168 camellias. The **Rose Museum Complex**, which covers 30,000 square feet and includes a visitor center, is located at Rose Park Drive and West Front. The 14-acre Rose Garden is the site of part of the **Texas Rose Festival**, including the Queen's Tea where the public can meet the Texas Rose Festival Queen and enjoy refreshments. Also included in the four-day festival are a parade, coronation, dance, art show, arts and crafts fair, rose show, and tours of rose fields.

Hours: Rose Museum—Monday to Friday, 9 AM to 4:30 PM; Saturday, 10 AM to 4:30 PM; Sunday, 1:30 PM to 4:30 PM. Closed Mondays from November through February.

Admission: The Municipal Rose Garden is free, and it is open all day every day. The museum admission is adults, $3.50; children ages 3–11, $2.

TYLER MUSEUM OF ART

1300 S. Mahon, Tyler 75706 (903) 595-1001 Website: www.tylermuseum.org

Located on the east side of Tyler Junior College on Mahon at Fifth, the Tyler Museum of Art features changing exhibits of 19th- and 20th-century contemporary art focusing on regional artists. Another highlight is a permanent exhibition of photographs of the East Texas region.

Hours: Tuesday to Saturday, 10 AM to 5 PM; Sunday, 1 PM to 5 PM.

Admission (voluntary): Adults, $3.50; seniors, $1.50; children, $1.50.

TYLER STATE PARK

789 Park Road 16, Tyler 75706 (903) 597-5338 Website: www.tpwd.state.tx.us/park/tyler

Playing on a 400-foot beach, swimming and fishing for channel catfish and black bass in the 64-acre spring-fed lake, mountain biking, and hiking are some of the outdoor entertainment offered at this 994-acre state park in the Piney Woods. A nature trail, concession, restrooms with showers, boat ramp, and rentals of boats, canoes, and paddleboats during the summer season are also available. Boats are limited to 5 mph—no wake. Picnic tables and camping areas that have some screened shelters are accessible from the main road.

Hours: Day use, 8 AM to 10 PM; overnight for camping.

Admission: Adults, $3.00; 12 and under, free. Camping is additional.

Directions: From I-20, go two miles north on FM 14 to Park Rd. 16.

OTHER PLACES OF INTEREST

Tyler Skate Park. 7922 S. Broadway, Tyler (903) 939-3330 Website: www.tylerskateplex.com. Nearly one acre under the roof.

1905 Cotton Belt Depot. 210 E. Oakland, Tyler (903) 533-8057. Exhibit: Bragg Model Train Collection.

Harrold's Model Train Museum. 8103 N. US Hwy. 271, Tyler (903) 531-9404 Website: www.calicomeadows.com/harrold. The museum has 1,200 pieces of rolling stock on 300 feet of track and 1,100 model trains in lighted showcases.

Heritage Aviation Memorial Museum. 150 Airport Dr., North Terminal, Tyler Pounds Regional Airport (903) 526-1945 Website: www.tyler-hamm.com

SPECIAL EVENTS

Azalea and Spring Flower Trail, **late March to mid-April**; Four Winds Renaissance Faire, **March–April**; East Texas State Fair, **late September**; Texas Rose Festival, **October.**

On the way: Two colorful and energetic towns very much worth a visit are just a little past midpoint between Dallas and Tyler. The town of **Canton** on the south side of I-20 is well known for its First Monday Trade Days. See the **Shopping** section of **Chapter 2: Tidbits** for details. A historical park has opened in **Edgewood**, which is just north of I-20. Exit on Hwy. 859, and drive about eight miles to the park at 106 N. Main. The two-block area called **Heritage Park** contains 15 log cabins, cafe, general store, bandstand, blacksmith shop, farm implement museum, log barn, one-room schoolhouse, barbershop and public bath, early Americana museum, caboose, depot and water tower, church house, and gift shop. Call the Edgewood Historical Society for hours, admission, and tour group information, at (903) 896-1940 or (903) 896-4326.

Just about 30 minutes east on US 80 before it joins I-20 is **Terrell**, which also has some sites of historical interest. Please see **Historic Terrell** in **Chapter 2: Tidbits.**

WACO

Native Americans, outlaws, and Texas Rangers were early inhabitants of Waco. The Rangers built an outpost called Fort Fisher where the Texas Ranger Museum is located today. A Spanish explorer first mapped Waco Village in 1542, and a trading post was established in 1844. The **Chisholm Trail** came through Waco at the Suspension Bridge, which is now only open to foot travel. Dedicated in 1870, the 475-foot bridge across the Brazos River is located at University Park Drive near the Convention Center, with Indian Spring Park on the west bank and Martin Luther King Park on the east bank. A riverwalk runs from there at Washington Ave. to the Texas Ranger Museum and beyond, and it is an enjoyable walk unless heavy rains have caused water to close part of it. The railroad came to town in 1871, and Waco has continued to thrive. For more information about Waco, call the **Tourist Information Center**, which is located at 106 Texas Ranger Trail, I-35 and University Parks Drive, Exit 335B, at (800) WACO-FUN or (254) 750-8696. Visitors may look online at www.wacocvb.com. The Convention and Visitors Bureau's mailing address is P.O. Box 2570, Waco 76702. From Dallas, take I-35 South to Waco and go left (east) on University Parks Dr. The Visitor Center can be seen on the east side of I-35, just north of the university.

BAYLOR UNIVERSITY

55 Baylor Ave., Waco 76798. Mailing address: One Bear Place # 97331, Waco 76798-7331. (800) BAYLOR-U. Website: www.baylor.edu

Take Exit 335 B off I-35 to University Parks Drive. The **Wiethorn Information Center** to the right at the main entrance has visitor parking and permits. A map of Baylor may also be obtained at the Waco Visitor Information Center, which is a short distance north of the campus. Call (254) 710-1921. Chartered in 1845, Baylor has become the world's largest Baptist University. One of the first stops should be at Bear Plaza for a look at the **Baylor Bears** in their fancy lair. Hopefully, the North American Black Bears will be awake and know that they have visitors. Bill and Eva Williams Bear Habitat is across Waco Creek from the Baylor Book Store between 1200 S. Fifth and Seventh streets.

The **Armstrong Browning Library** contains the world's largest collection of material related to Robert Browning, one of the greatest British poets of the Victorian Age. The library also contains major manuscript collections of his wife, Elizabeth Barrett Browning, and of John Ruskin, Charles Dickens, and Ralph Waldo Emerson. What children will appreciate is the 56 stained-glass windows that illustrate the poems and themes of the Brownings and the Pied Piper window in the Sturdivant Alcove.

Location: 701 Speight Ave. between Seventh and Eighth Streets. Call (254) 710-3566. Website: www.browninglibrary.org.

Hours: Weekdays, 9 AM to 5 PM; Saturday, 9 AM to noon. Closed Sunday. Closed in August two weeks prior to the fall semester and major holidays.

Admission: Free. Donations appreciated.

Mayborn Natural Science and Cultural History Museum Complex. The Mayborn Museum Complex includes a new 144,000-square-foot museum building and the Daniel Historic Village. Exhibits include both traditional and walk-in dioramas with exploration stations for interactive learning. The walk-ins include a Texas limestone cave, a central Texas forest, and an exhibit on the 23 Columbian mammoths whose skeletal remains were discovered just outside Waco. Other exhibits include a Waco Indian grass hut, a Comanche tipi made of hide, a log cabin, and a Norwegian rock house, all of which existed in the area in the 1850s. Visitors will learn about the cretaceous sea that once covered Texas, complete with sea inhabitants. Exhibits feature plants and animals that have become extinct as well as specific archeological sites, including the original Waco Native American Village.

Children of all ages are encouraged to participate in the Discovery Rooms. Subjects include vertebrates, communication, energy, recycling, and much more. Young children will enjoy Mrs. Moen's Neighborhood, complete with cars, a house, grocery store, gas station, post office, and more.

Daniel Historic Village focuses on the time period of the 1880s to 1910. It is located on 13 acres just east of Fort Fisher Park on the Brazos River. More than 15 wood-framed buildings re-create a farming community in Texas as well as the life of a river town that had no electricity, water that came from wells and creeks, and wood-burning stoves.

Location: 1300 S. University Parks Dr., Waco (254) 710-1110. Website: www.baylor.edu.

Hours: Open daily. Monday to Saturday, 10 AM to 5 PM, with extended hours until 8 PM on Thursday; Sunday, 12 PM to 5 PM. Closed major holidays.

Admission: Fee for Museum and Village.

CAMERON PARK

University Parks Drive and Martin Luther King Jr. Drive (254) 750-8080

Cameron Park features 416 acres with wooded picnic sites and various forms of wildlife. Miss Nellie's Pretty Place is a wildflower preserve, and across the street is a children's playground with access for handicapped children. At Cameron Park visitors enjoy a sprayground, volleyball, hiking and bridle paths, mountain biking trails, disc golf, and pavilions for picnicking. The park fronts on the Bosque and Brazos Rivers.

It is open daily, and there is no admission charge.

CAMERON PARK ZOO

1701 N. Fourth Street and Herring, Waco (254) 750-8400 Website: www.cameronparkzoo.com

The zoo features both exotic and native wildlife. Highlights include Gibbon Island, Treetop Village and African Savanna, bald eagles, reptile house, educational facilities, and the Texas Heritage area, which includes longhorns, buffalo, and javelina. For more information, contact the Cameron Park Zoological and Botanical Society.

Hours: Monday to Saturday, 9 AM to 5 PM; Sunday, 11 AM to 5 PM.

Admission: Adults, $7; seniors, $6; children 4 to 12, $5.

DR PEPPER MUSEUM

300 South Fifth Street, Waco 76701 (254) 757-1025 Website: www.drpeppermuseum.com

Dr Pepper, the oldest major soft drink in America, was first mixed in Morrison's Old Corner Drug Store by Dr. Charles C. Alderton and was served in 1885. The present museum, a tribute to the "Pepper Upper," houses memorabilia in the former Artesian Manufacturing and Bottling Company established in 1906, which manufactured and distributed Dr Pepper as well as several other soft drinks. The museum also features a gift shop and an old-fashioned soda fountain that sells Dr Pepper and Blue Bell Ice Cream.

Bottling equipment, containers, and an interior artesian well, along with film of 25 years of DP commercials, complete the first floor. The second-floor exhibits concentrate on marketing and advertising campaigns as well as a re-creation of a 1930s corner store. The third floor houses the W. W. "Foots" Clements Free Enterprise Institute, which offers educational programs to scheduled groups, and the Bottlers Hall of Fame.

Hours: Monday to Saturday, 10 AM to 4:15 PM; Sunday, 12 PM to 4:15 PM; extended hours during peak periods.

Admission: Adults, $7; students, 3 to 18, $3; preschoolers, free. Advance reservations are required for groups of 10 or more.

LAKE WACO

Lake Waco's Airport Park off Airport Road has drinking water and restrooms, camping (fee), boat ramp, and a marina with bait and fishing barge. The swimming beach and showerhouse are before you get to the camping area, and there is no fee. Day use. Website: www.swf-wc.us-ace.army.mil/waco.

Hours: 6 AM to 11 PM.

LION'S PARK

1716 N. 42nd, Waco (254) 772-3541

Lion's Park offers a variety of family entertainment in its facilities, which include swimming pool, picnic area, tennis, miniature golf, bumper boats, go-carts, playground, small amusement park with eight rides for children, and miniature train. Call for current hours as they change with the season.

TEXAS RANGER HALL OF FAME AND MUSEUM

100 Texas Rangers Trail, Waco 76706 (254) 750-8631 (Mailing address: P.O. Box 2570, Waco 76702-2570) Website: www.texasranger.org

A visit to Waco might begin by exiting 335B off I-35 to visit the Texas Ranger Hall of Fame and Museum. This museum is dedicated to the history and lore of the legendary Texas Rangers, the oldest state law enforcement agency in the nation and an enduring symbol of Texas and the American West.

It houses over 14,000 irreplaceable artifacts with exhibits that are constantly changing. The exhibits have interactives to delight children and parents alike. These include a stage with costumes where one can pretend to be a Texas Ranger and hunt for bandits on the loose in the museum. Young Rangers locate the bad guys by unscrambling a code. Picnic tables are by the scenic Brazos River and the museum. This is also the location of the Visitor Information Center. Baylor University is across the street.

Hours: Daily, 9 AM to 5 PM, except Thanksgiving, Christmas, and New Year's Day.

Admission: Adults, $6; children, $3.

TEXAS SPORTS HALL OF FAME

1108 S. University Parks Dr. at I-35, Exit 335B (254) 756-1633
Website: www.tshof.org

Located near the Texas Ranger Hall of Fame and Museum, the Texas Sports Hall of Fame honors more than 400 favorite sports heroes through a collection of memorabilia and interactive exhibits. Also included in the museum are the Texas High School Football Hall of Fame, the Texas Basketball Hall of Fame, the Texas Tennis Museum, and the Tom Landry Theater.

Hours: Monday to Saturday, 9 AM to 5 PM; Sunday, 12 PM to 5 PM.

Admission: Adults, $6; seniors, $5; students, $3; ages 5 and under, free.

WACO WATER PARK

900 Lake Shore Drive at Steinbeck Bend Drive (254) 750-7900
Website: www.waco-texas.com/city_depts/parks/aquatics.htm

Located in Waco Riverbend Park, Waco Water Park offers cool summer fun with two pools, water-shooting playscapes, 22-foot slide, zero-depth pool, and more. Special features include umbrellas and trees for shade, locker rooms, and a concession stand.

Seasonal hours: Monday to Thursday, 1 PM to 9 PM; Friday, 1 PM to 7 PM; Saturday and Sunday, 12 PM to 7 PM.

Admission: 48 inches or taller, $6; under 48 inches, $4; ages 3 and under, free.

EVENTS

April: Brazos River Festival; **Summer**: Summer Sounds Concerts and Brazos Nights Concerts at Indian Spring Park; **June**: Car Show at Fort Fisher; **July**: Brazos Boat Races; **September**: Labor Day Great Texas Raft Race; **October**: Heart O' Texas Fair and Rodeo; **December**: Christmas on the Brazos.

OTHER PLACES OF INTEREST NEARBY

Summer Fun Water Park. 1410 Waco Rd., Belton (254) 939-0366 Website: www.summerfunwaterpark.com.

Outlets at Hillsboro. 104 I-35 NE, Exit 368A or B, Hillsboro (254) 582-9205 Website: www.outletsathillsboro.com.

Homestead Heritage: Traditional Crafts Village. P.O. Box 869, Elm Mott 76640 (254) 754-9600 Website: www.homesteadheritage.com.

Visitors may take a walking tour of the Crafts Village of Homestead Heritage's 510-acre working farm, which is operated by a church group. The tour includes the barn, which showcases the work of their craftsmen, blacksmith shop, herb garden, **deli and bakery** (homemade bread, sandwiches, and pies, oh my!), heritage furniture, restored 1750 gristmill, and potter's house. See the craftsmen at work and beautiful wildflowers in the spring. Picnic tables are available. **Special event:** Held annually on Thanksgiving weekend, the Homestead Craft and Children's Fair features craft and farming demonstrations, music, hayrides, delicious food, barn raising, and more. Homestead Heritage is located five miles west of I-35, northwest of Waco.

Hours: Monday to Saturday, 10 AM to 6 PM.

Admission: free, except for parking, $5.

7. RESOURCES

SPECIAL EVENTS AND TICKET/RESERVATION HOTLINES

American Airlines Center (214) 665-4200
Dallas Events Hotline (214) 571-1301
Dallas Parks and Recreation
Main number (214) 670-4100
Tennis reservations (214) 670-1498
Golf reservations (214) 670-7615
Field reservations (214) 670-8740
Field conditions after 4:30 PM (214) 559-5701
Fair Park Info Line (214) 421-9600
Irving Art Centre's Artsline (972) 252-ARTS
MovieFone/Movie Information (972) 444-FILM
SPCA Events Line (214) 651-9611, ext. 160
Tennis Reservations/Neighborhood Courts (214) 670-8745
Ticketmaster (214) 373-8000
Star Tickets (888) 597-STAR

CONVENTION AND VISITORS BUREAUS

DALLAS CONVENTION AND VISITORS BUREAU
Old Red Courthouse, Downtown Historic District, 100 S. Houston
St., Dallas 75202 (214) 571-1000. Hours: Monday to Sunday, 9 AM
to 6 PM. Website: www.visitdallas.com

The Visitor Center would like to say a friendly "Hi, y'all!" to visitors
to the Dallas area as well as natives who keep up with the latest entertainment. The most current *Dallas! Official Visitors Guide*, a publication of
the DCVB, is there as well as countless brochures of great places to visit.
The Hotline, (214) 571-1301, and the website www.visitdallas.com list
special events, businesses, and relocation information, and you may request a visitor's packet. The historical Old Red Courthouse is the site of
the Visitors Bureau, which offers Dallas information kiosks as well as In-

ternet and e-mail access and a museum about the history and growth of Dallas county.

The City of Dallas website is www.dallascityhall.org.

To find the **Chamber of Commerce and Visitors Bureau in your city**, look online at the site of the U.S. Directory of Local Chambers of Commerce and Visitors Bureaus. Here you can also request a state visitors guide. Website: www.2chambers.com.

DALLAS/FORT WORTH AREA TOURISM COUNCIL

This council publishes a free, informative guide to Dallas, Fort Worth, and surrounding cities called *Dallas/Fort Worth and Beyond*, which is available at the Dallas Visitors Bureau location, the convention and visitors bureaus of member cities, or by contacting the council at 701 South Main St., Grapevine 76051, (817) 329-2438. Some coupons are located in the back of the magazine. You may wish to look up the council online at www.visitdallas-fortworth.com. This website is a guide for things to do, accommodations, transportation, events, a site to build your own tour, and more.

OFFICIAL SITE OF TEXAS TOURISM

Office of the Governor, Economic Development, and Tourism. (800) 8888-TEX. Website: www.traveltex.com

This Texas state agency publishes a free, helpful guidebook to Texas cities called *Texas State Travel Guide*, which gives general information as well as information about attractions in the area. Toward the end of the book are descriptions of Texas lakes, parks, forests, rocks, flowers, birds, and tourist bureaus.

HELPFUL WEBSITES

Around Town Kids Online Websites:
www.aroundtownkidsallen.com
www.aroundtownkidsfrisco.com
www.aroundtownkidsmckinney.com
www.aroundtownkidsplano.com
The Dallas Morning News: www.guidelive.com
Dallas Park and Recreation: www.dallasparks.org
Downtown Dallas Association: www.downtowndallas.org
Dallas County: www.dallascounty.org
Collin County: www.co.collin.tx.us
Tarrant County: www.co.tarrant.tx.us

DFW International: www.dfwinternational.org
Lakes/Parks of Corps of Engineers: www.swf-wc.usace.army.mil
Texas Parks and Wildlife Department: www.tpwd.state.tx.us
Texas Historical Commission: www.thc.state.tx.us
Texas Department of Transportation: www.dot.state.tx.us
Texas Department of Public Safety: www.txdps.state.tx.us
Texas Education Vacation Planning Resource: www.texaseducationva-
cation.com
Texas Travel Industry Association/Tourism: www.tourtexas.com
Texas Fun: www.texasfun.com
Texas Outside: www.texasoutside.com
Texas Escapes: www.texasescapes.com

PUBLICATIONS

NEWSPAPERS

Dallas Business Journal, 12801 N. Central Expressway, Dallas 75243
(214) 696-5959

Dallas Examiner, 1516 Corinth, Dallas 75215 (214) 428-3446

Dallas Morning News, P.O. Box 655237, Dallas 75265 (214) 745-8383

Downtown Business News, P.O. Box 1522, Dallas 75221 (214) 748-NEWS

Oak Cliff Tribune, 1005 W. Jefferson, Dallas 75208 (214) 943-7755

Park Cities News, 8115 Preston, Dallas 75225 (214) 369-7570

Park Cities People, 6116 N. Central Expressway, Dallas 75206 (214) 739-
2244

Pegasus News Online, www.pegasusnews.com. Local news and information

The White Rocker News, 10809 Garland Road, Dallas 75218 (214) 327-
9335

BOOKS

Backroads and Byways of Texas, by Amy K. Brown, Countryman Publish-
ers, 2008.

City Smart: Dallas/Fort Worth, by Sharry Buckner, Avalon Travel Publishing, 2000.

Dallas: A History of Big D, by Michael V. Hazel, Texas State Historical
Association, 1997.

Dallas Coloring and Activity Book, by Carole Marsh, Gallopade International, 2004.

Dallas/Fort Worth Alive! by Kimberly Young, Hunter Publishing, 2001.

Dallas/Fort Worth Metroplex, by Robert Rafferty, Taylor Trade Publishing, 2003.

Dallas Reconsidered: Essays in Local History, by Michael V. Hazel, Three Forks Press, 2000.

A Guide for Seeing Dallas County History, by the Dallas County Historical Commission, 1987 (trail booklet available at the Hall of State).

A Guide to Dallas Private Schools, by Lynn Magid, privately printed, 1993.

Hiking and Backpacking Trails of Texas, by Mickey Little, fifth edition,Gulf Publishing, 2002.

Marmac Guide to Dallas, by Yves Gerem, Pelican Publishing, 2004.

Moon Texas Handbook, by Andy Rhodes, sixth edition, Avalon Publishing, 2009.

Newcomers Handbook Neighborhood Guide: Dallas-Fort Worth, Houston, and Austin, by Yu Shan Chang, First Books Publishing, 2006.

Outings and Adventures Everywhere: Ages 1 to 6 and Beyond, by Lynda Morley, fourth edition, Brown Books, 2002.

A Parent's Guide to Dallas-Fort Worth, by Kevin J. Shay, Mars Publishing, 2003.

Quick Escapes: Dallas/Fort Worth Getaways, by June Naylor, sixth edition, Globe Pequot Press, 2008.

Roadside Geology of Texas, by Darwin Spearing, Mountain Press, 2003.

Texas Off the Beaten Path, by June Naylor Rodriquez, eighth edition, Globe Pequot Press, 2008.

Texas Parks and Campgrounds, by George Oxford Miller, Taylor Wilson Pub., 2003.

Texas Wildscapes: Gardening for Wildlife, by Damude, Bender, Foss, and Gowen, UT Press. 1999.

Zagat Survey: Dallas-Fort Worth Restaurants, Zagat Survey, 2008.

MAGAZINES

D Magazine, (214) 939-3636. D is a monthly magazine with information about Dallas personalities, events, and restaurants. Website: www.dmagazine.com.

dallas child and *Baby Dallas*, Lauren Publications, (972) 447-9188. This monthly parenting magazine offers helpful articles about child-raising, kid-friendly restaurants, and exciting places to go, and it is offered free at libraries, children's stores, and day cares or by subscription. Website: www.dallaschild.com.

Dallas Cowboys Star Magazine, To subscribe, call (877) NFC-BOYS, Pro Shop/Catalog Deptartment, or subscribe online. Each week this football news magazine highlights games, coaches, plays, and players. Website: www.cowboysonlineproshop.com.

Dallas Observer, (214) 757-9000. Offered free in newsstands or by subscription, this weekly news magazine includes features about controversial personalities, political and other news, a community calendar of events, and live music and concert information. The calendar does include events for children, but it also contains romance ads that are not for children. Website: www.dallasobserver.com.

The Dallas Weekly, (214) 428-8958. This weekly magazine serving the African American community offers news articles, features, sports, community calendar, and more information about health, education, and youth. It is offered free at some locations, or readers may subscribe. Website: www.dallasweekly.com.

North Texas Kids, (972) 516-9070. Monthly *North Texas Kids: Your Family Guide to Raising Happy, Healthy Kids* includes articles about child rearing, places to play and eat, coupons, and kids' activities. Website: www.NorthTexasKids.com.

Texas Highways, State Department of Highways and Public Transportation, (512) 465-7408. Wonderful things about Texas landscape, wildlife, history, and communities are photographed and featured in this colorful monthly magazine. Website: www.texashighways.com.

Texas Monthly, Austin, (512) 320-6900; (800) 759-2000. *Texas Monthly* features interesting people, places, restaurants, and news statewide. Website: www.texasmonthly.com.

Texas Parks and Wildlife, Texas Parks and Wildlife Department, (800) 937-9393. The nature photography is beautiful in this monthly magazine featuring fascinating facts about wildlife and endangered or threatened species and activities, such as where to fish, swim, and hike, in the state parks. Online are subscriptions, books, and other publications, accommodations, reservations for camping, and Texas getaways. Website: www.tpwmagazine.com.

TELEPHONE SERVICES

The introductory pages of the Southwestern Bell's *Greater Dallas Yellow Pages* are a very helpful guide to the Dallas area. They provide telephone numbers of attractions, service organizations, events, and hospitals as well as maps of seating inside major arenas, maps of Dallas, maps of the DART Rail System, and a map of Fair Park. A zip code directory is also included.

Emergency 911; Non-emergency 311
Time of Day Service (214) 844-6611
Road Conditions/Closings/Wildflowers (214) 374-4100

Telephone: to order or change (800) 464-7928; repairs (800) 246-8464; Website: www.att.com
Weather (214) 787-1111
Poison Center (800) 222-1222
Kid Med, Presbyterian Hospital, day care for ill child: (214) 345-7155

TOP 20 PLACES TO GO FOR FAMILIES

African American Museum
The Ballpark in Arlington, Legends of the Game Museum and Learning Center
Children's Theater: Rosewood Center for Family Arts
Dallas Arboretum and Botanical Garden
Dallas Children's Aquarium (undergoing renovation)
Dallas Heritage Village (Old City Park)
Dallas Museum of Art
Dallas Public Library—Downtown
Dallas Women's Museum
Dallas World Aquarium
Dallas Zoo
Museum of Nature and Science/IMAX
Museum of the American Railroad
Nasher Sculpture Garden
Old Red Museum
Six Flags Hurricane Harbor, Hawaiian Falls
Six Flags Over Texas/Music Mill Amphitheatre
Sixth Floor Museum
Trinity River Audubon Center
West End Historic District/Victory Plaza/Arts District

FREE ACTIVITIES FOR FAMILIES

African American Museum at Fair Park
Animal shelters/pet parades/pet parks
Arlington Museum of Art
Art galleries
Arts and crafts malls
A. W. Perry Homestead Museum and Barn
Bachman Lake

Bath House Cultural Center Gallery
Bike trails
Bookstores: story time
Boy Scout National Scouting Museum (Mondays)
Cedar Ridge Preserve/Audubon
Children's Medical Center miniature trains
Christmas Tree Lightings
City Hall and Plaza activities
Club activities: Watch R/C Fliers, Dallas Area Rocket Society, Dallas Area Kite-Flying Association.
College campuses: Many have ponds with ducks, fountains, tennis courts, and walking trails.
Comanche Peak Nuclear Plant
Connemara Conservatory
Convention Center's Pioneer Plaza with trail ride sculpture
Crow Collection of Asian Art and Sculpture Garden
Dallas County Open Spaces: Nature preserves
Dallas Farmers Market
Dallas/Fort Worth Airport: Founder's Plaza Observation Park
Dallas Museum of Art (check website for special evening hours)
Disc golf
Downtown Dallas historical plazas
Downtown Dallas Underground
Downtown historical squares/Main Streets
Fair Park grounds
Farmers Branch Historical Park
Farmers markets
Festivals and art fairs
Fishing
Flag Pole Hill
Flea markets and trade days
Fritz Park Petting Farm in Irving
Grand Prairie Historic Homes
Hall of State
Heard Museum and Wildlife Sanctuary*
Historic, self-guided trails
International Museum of Culture
Interurban Railway Depot in Plano
Katy Trail
Kite flying and Frisbee tossing at the park

*During limited hours these attractions are free to the public, or admission is free with fees for special exhibits or designated activities.

Lakeland Hills Skatepark
Lakes
Landmark Museum of Garland
Las Colinas Mustang Sculpture
Latino Cultural Center*
Libraries
MADI Museum and Gallery
Magic shops
McKinney Avenue Trolley
Meadows Museum (art) (special evening hours: each Thursday after
5 PM)
Mustang exhibit and canal walk at Las Colinas
Nasher Sculpture Center (Target First Saturday, 10 AM to 2 PM)
Nature preserves, parks, greenbelt areas
Nature stores
Nature trails
Nurseries for plants
Parades
Pate Museum of Transportation
Perry Homestead Museum in Carrollton
Pet stores
Playgrounds/public spraygrounds
Recreation centers*
Shakespeare in the Park (donation)
Shopping malls with play centers
Skating outdoors on trails
South Dallas Cultural Center*
Spectator sports: youth and amateur games
Sports for family play: tennis, basketball, softball, badminton, ping
pong, volleyball
Symphony and community bands, outdoor concerts in parks
Tennis on neighborhood courts
Texas Sculpture Garden/Frisco
Thanks-Giving Square
Tours of the working world
Trinity River Audubon Center (third Thursdays free)
Union Station
Victory Plaza summer outdoor movies
West End Historical District
White Rock Lake

*During limited hours these attractions are free to the public, or admission is free with fees for special exhibits or designated activities.

BIRTHDAY PARTY IDEAS

Adventure Landing
Amazing Jake's Amusement Center, Collin Creek Mall
American Girl Boutique and Bistro
Art-a-Rama and other art centers
Backyard carnival
Ballpark at Arlington/Tour and Museum, Legends of the Game
Batting cages, outdoor and indoor
Bike and skate trails
Bounce house stadiums: Bounce U, Boomerangs, Jump Town
Bowling lanes
Braum's
Broomball at ice rink
Build-A-Bear Workshop
Camping/swimming/fishing at state park
Capricorn Riding Academy
Cedar Hill State Park/Joe Pool Lake
Celebration Station
Cheerleading school
Children's theater
Chuck E. Cheese's Pizza
Cinemark's IMAX Theater
Concert: Superpages.com, Nokia Live!, Music Mill Theater at Six
    Flags, American Airlines Center, House of Blues
Cooking school: Kids' Cooking School
Crystal's Pizza
Dallas Children's Theater
Dallas Cowboys Stadium: tours, games
Dallas Summer Musicals
Dallas World Aquarium
DART Rail Line to a destination
Disc golf
Dress-up party/rental trunk
Dr Pepper Youth Ballpark
Eisenberg's Skatepark
Exotic animal park
Festivals
Fire Station No. 1
Fishing: Catfish Corner
Flight museums

Fort Worth activities
Fritz Park Petting Farm in Irving: June and July only
Frontiers of Flight Museum
GameWorks at Grapevine Mills
Go-cart rides, outdoor and indoor
Grapevine Heritage Railroad train in Fort Worth, Grapevine
Great Wolf Lodge
Gymboree, gymnastic centers
Hawaiian Falls
Heard Museum and Wildlife Sanctuary
Horseback riding, ranches
Ice skating
Incredible Pizza Amusement Center, Mesquite
Indoor rock climbing
Indoor soccer centers
Joe's Crab Shack
Lake parks
Laserquest, Plano
Lego Education Center, Southlake
The Little Gym
Lone Star Park Tour
Magic Time Machine Restaurant
Main Event
McDonald's
McKinney Avenue Trolley
Medieval Times dinner and tournament
Mesquite rodeo
Metroplex Gymnastics
Michaels: craft party
Miniature golf
Movies/Studio Movie Grill
Museum of Nature and Science
Museum of the American Railroad
Natalie's Italian Cooking Make-Your-Own-Pizza Party
NRH$_2$O Water Park
Old Tige: Dallas Firefighter's Museum
Paintball—junior high or older
Paint Yer Pottery
Palace of Wax/Ripley's Believe It or Not!
Palmerosa Ranch in Mesquite
Petting zoo
Planetarium show/IMAX Theater
Planet Pizza Amusement Center

Playground/picnic
Pocket Sandwich Theater
Puppet show
Purple Cow Restaurant
Purple Glaze
Quiggley's Clayhouse
Recreation center
Restaurant
Rock-climbing gym: Exposure, Stone Works
Rodeo
Rowlett's Wet Zone
Samuell Farm/fishing
Sandy Lake Amusement Park
Scavenger hunt
Seventeen Spa
Six Flags Hurricane Harbor waterpark
Six Flags Over Texas
Skateparks
Skating rinks, ice and roller
Smashing Times mosaics
Soccer centers
Space Walk of Dallas rentals
Speedzone race cars, miniature golf, arcade
Sports event—Cowboys, Mavericks, Rangers, Stars, Desperados, Rough Riders, Airhogs, FC Dallas
Sportsridge Athletic Club
Sports Spectrum Indoor Soccer
Storytellers
Surf and Swim
Sweet & Sassy Salon and Spa
Swimming pool, outdoor and indoor
Texas Motor Speedway
Theater: Children's play
Theater: Early-morning rental for private showing and breakfast
300 Dallas: Bowling and more
Top Golf
Tours of the working world
Wagon Wheel Ranch
Wet Zone Waterpark, Rowlett
Whirlyball, Laserwhirld
Wild About Harry's
YMCA: Indoor pool
Zoo

RAINY WEATHER IDEAS

African American Museum at Fair Park
Airport/aviation museums
American Girl
Arcade: Celebration Station, Speedzone, GameWorks
Arena Sports
Art centers, such as Paint Yer Pottery
Art galleries
Bookstore: story time
Bounce indoor stadiums
Bowling
Burger King's or McDonald's indoor parks
Cavanaugh Flight Museum in Addison
Children's Medical Center miniature trains
Children's theater
Cinemark IMAX Theater
Crow Collection of Asian Art
Dallas Children's Aquarium (under renovation—check)
Dallas Firefighter's Museum
Dallas Holocaust Museum
Dallas Museum of Art
Dallas World Aquarium
Dave and Buster's
Grapevine Mills Outlet Mall
Hall of State
Hardware store: Elliott's, Home Depot, Lowe's
Heard Museum
Hobby and craft stores: Michael's, Hobby Lobby
Hotel glass elevators, restaurants
Ice cream and yogurt parlor
Ice skating, roller skating
Incredible Pizza Amusement Center, Mesquite
Indoor archery
Indoor playparks: Planet Pizza
Indoor skate parks
Indoor soccer center
Indoor sports complexes
International Museum of Culture
Interurban Railroad Museum
Legends of the Game Museum at the Ballpark

Library/Bookmarks at Northpark Center
Main Event
Meadows Museum at SMU
Museum of Nature and Science
National Scouting Museum
Nickel Mania
Nickelrama
Palace of Wax/Ripley's Believe It or Not!
Perry Homestead Museum
Pet store
Planet Pizza
Planetarium show
Puppet show
Recreation center
Ripley's Believe It or Not!/Palace of Wax
Rock-climbing gym
Shopping mall
Sixth Floor Museum
Top Golf
Tours of the working world
Toy store: Lakeshore Learning Store
Underground Downtown Dallas
Whirlyball, Laserwhirld
Women's Museum at Fair Park

INDEX

Artist Within, The, 112
Artistic Gatherings, 112
Arts District Friends, 132
Audubon Society, Dallas and Dallas
County Centers, 3–5
autos, 101–2; racing, 163; shows, 102
aviation museums, 20–21, 88, 94–97,
234

University of North Texas Sky
  Theater, 59
U.S. Coast Guard Auxiliary, 176
US Toys, 120

....

V

....

Valley View Center, movie theater,
  118
Vanishing Texas River Cruise, 72
Victory Park: American Airlines
  Center, 135; Channel 8/WFAA
  TV, 89; Hard Rock Café, 126
volksmarching, 171
volleyball, 184

....

W

....

Waco, 245; Armstrong Browning
  Library, 246; Baylor University,
  246; Bear Plaza, 246; Cameron
  Park and Zoo, 247; Daniel
  Historic Village, 247; Dr
  Pepper Museum, 247;
  Homestead Heritage:
  Traditional Crafts Village/Farm,
  250; Lake Waco, 248; Lion's
  Park, 248; Mayborn National
  Science and Cultural History
  Museum Complex, 246; Texas
  Ranger Museum, 248; Texas
  Sports Hall of Fame, 249; Waco
  Water Park, 249
Watertower Theatre, Addison, 145

Waxahachie, 154
websites, 253
West End Historical District, 15, 44,
  100, 134; museums, 12, 41
Whirlyball and Laserwhirld, 53
White Rock Lake and Bath House
  Cultural Center, 45–48, 107
Whitney Lake and State Park, 197
Whole Earth Provision Company, 61
Wild About Harry's, 127
wildflowers and spring trails, 61, 207
wildlife, 71–73, 237, 241
Wildscapes, 73
Wilson Block Historic District, 78
Windmill Hill Nature Preserve, 57
Windmill Stables, 190
Winspear Opera House, 8–10, 133,
  137
Women's Museum, The, 48
Woodland Basin Nature Area, 62
Wyly Theatre, 8–10, 133

....

Y

....

YMCA, 188
Young Actors Studio and Performing
  Arts, 152
Young Life, 189
Younger Generation Chorus, 143
youth organizations, 187–89

....

Z

....

zoos, 16–18, 242, 247